Courtney Weaver is a nativ̶̶̶̶̶̶̶̶̶̶̶
also lived in London and ̶̶̶̶̶̶̶̶̶̶̶̶̶̶ ̶̶aving
packed herself off at the tender age of 17 to study
semiotics – don't ask – at Brown University in Rhode
Island, she later received an MA in creative writing
from New York University. Courtney has worked for
the BBC and written for the *New York Times*, the
Washington Post, *Marie Claire*, *Elle* and the *Wall Street
Journal*, inter alia, and for two years she contributed a
weekly column, 'Unzipped', to the on-line magazine,
Salon. She hates Anaïs Nin.

Praise for *Unzipped*:

'*Unzipped*, a new book by America's most controversial
sex columnist, lays bare the love lives of real people'
Sunday Express

'refreshingly unpretentious . . . a welcome relief'
What's On

unzipped

the extraordinary sex lives of ordinary people

COURTNEY WEAVER

HEADLINE

First published in 1999
by HEADLINE BOOK PUBLISHING

This edition published in 2000
by HEADLINE BOOK PUBLISHING

10 9 8 7 6 5 4 3 2

ISBN 0 7472 6246 2

Printed and bound in Great Britain by
Clays Ltd, St Ives plc

HEADLINE BOOK PUBLISHING
A division of the Hodder Headline Group
338 Euston Road
London NW1 3BH

www.headline.co.uk
www.hodderheadline.com

For Dianne and Samantha

My great thanks to Doug Young and the entire gang at Headline who were a true joy to work with, right from the start. Much gratitude also goes to Magda McHugh, Mary Clemmey, Jay Leibold, Ciarán McDunphy, Debbie Cowell, Savvas Eleftheriades and Sallyjo Caddy, for their warmth and support.

Deepest thanks and gratitude goes to Bonnie Nadell, my US agent, who deserves a special acknowledgement for her generosity, loyalty and hard work – all performed with her trademark no-nonsense brand of humour and aplomb.

Most importantly, this book couldn't have been written without the gut-wrenching honesty and participation of my secret-tellers. Much love and thanks to all; you know who you are.

PROLOGUE

March 1997

I put my key in the front door, and stop, listening. No movement inside. I open the door and step into my dark apartment, and close the door behind me, locking it. I stand there for a moment, looking around, making out the familiar shapes in the dark, and waiting for . . . what? I live alone, and unless the cat suddenly got it into her head to start rearranging furniture, things are going to be exactly the way I left them.

Inside the living room, a dozen electronic red and green eyes glow serenely from every corner: the 'READY' lights on the computer, the printer, the phone, the Caller ID, the phone recharger, the TV, the VCR, signifying their willingness to spring into action in a moment's notice.

I can already see that the Caller ID light isn't blinking. No calls. Okay, I say to myself, as I drop my keys on the couch and turn on a lamp. Maybe it'll be nice to have one night to read and relax, where I'm not talking and thinking and dissecting the vicissitudes of love and sex in my own life or, more likely, as it pertains to my chatty friends.

Because I've been recently dumped, the telephone has been red hot. It's become an entirely new entity, a sudden animate creature who has the power to define, intensify, clarify and muddle my day. I wake up and think, *What are you going to bring me today?* I spend a lot of time in this room – the cluttered living room off my messy bedroom in my cramped yet rent-controlled apartment – and as I sit at my desk working, I can

1

feel the heat coming off the telephone as if there were a little campfire burning brightly on my end table.

My best friend from New York had visited me a month ago, right before the dump. We were sitting on the living room floor, surrounded by newspapers and magazines, trying to figure out if we really wanted to go to the Japanese Tea Garden in Golden Gate Park. 'What do you do there, exactly?' Harriet wanted to know. 'Is there something to see?'

'You just walk around,' I said. I hadn't been to the Tea Garden since I was a kid, but I was feeling so infantilized by all my crazy, sense-of-imminent-breakup behavior that, now that I thought about it, the Tea Garden might be an appropriate venue to revisit. 'You drink green tea. And buy that candy that has the edible wrapper. Is it cherry blossom season?' I asked.

'Well, *I* don't know,' Harriet said.

Sean, in a declaration that he was giving me 'lots of space' to 'spend this important time' with my best friend, hadn't called very much or been particularly available that week. This was pretty much par for the course with him, but now he had an excuse and a good one. However, the first night that Harriet arrived in San Francisco, he'd gone out to dinner with us at Flying Saucer, a pretentious, hip restaurant with uncomfortable pews in the gourmet gulch area of the Mission. He was in classic Sean mode – witty, polite, amusing but just this side of icy. For reasons that I typically can't remember now (probably having to do with his lack of availability), he and I had begun sparring in a witty, polite, amusing but just this side of icy manner, when he suddenly turned to Harriet and asked if she'd read the recent article in *Entertainment Weekly* about all the problems they were having on the set of *The Saint* with Val Kilmer.

Now, there really was no reason to bring this up out of the blue. None of us had expressed a particular interest in Val Kilmer, nobody had a subscription to *Entertainment Weekly*, none of us had seen the original *The Saint* on TV – in short, *no reason* other than the fact that, as everyone knows, Val has a notorious reputation for being 'difficult' and 'high maintenance' . . . just like, ahem, a certain other member sitting at the table that night (although Sean was much too smart to actually make that explicit comparison).

Now, the use of the term 'high maintenance' is to me the equivalent of waving a red flag in front of a bull. Moreover, with the exception of Val Kilmer, it is almost always employed by a man when they want a woman to shut up or back off. And while Sean hadn't employed the term directly, throughout the course of our three-month relationship he had occasionally pointed out in a gentle way that I was very 'demanding' of his time. Anyway, I stood up from my hard uncomfortable pew, threw down my napkin and that was the end of the evening.

The Incident at Flying Saucer (as Harriet and I would later call it) was a Defining Moment, although (by definition) I wouldn't see it that way for some time. Defining Moments are events of humiliation and loss of pride: they are the billboards that scream, *Danger . . . Proceed at great damage to pride, optimism and self-respect*; they are the distant bells. Most of the time it will only be your friends who see the Defining Moments as they occur. Later that week, as Harriet sat in my living room and weighed the pros and cons of going to a tourist site which had nothing particular to recommend it, I picked up the phone that was sitting between us and started punching in numbers.

Harriet eyed me. 'I thought you told me you weren't going to do that anymore.'

'Weeell.' I waited for the voice prompt to enter his password. 'Just once a day. That's not so very bad, is it?'

'Nothing good can come of this,' Harriet said darkly. 'What are you going to do if you find something out?'

'I don't know.' My brows were knit with what my mother calls my 'dog-with-a-bone-expression'. All I knew was, calling into Sean's home voice mail had become a compulsive activity, same as plucking my eyebrows or eating peanut butter from the jar with my finger. I *had* to know. I *had* to find out. *What* I had to know or find out was a little unclear – a voice mail message stating his reasons why he wouldn't behave like a normal boyfriend? Why he wouldn't make plans in advance? Why he never gave me flowers or presents? Why he wouldn't kiss me passionately? Or maybe a message from Val Kilmer himself reiterating my own hollow stance: 'High maintenance, high yield!'

I hung up. 'Nothing,' I said. 'No messages.' As always after these compulsive calls, I felt dirty and humiliated, as if I'd just participated in an anonymous pornographic act. 'I don't know why I keep doing this. I just want – I don't know. Some kind of information. I feel like there's something going on that I don't know about.'

'Well.' I could see Harriet was struggling. Generally speaking, Harriet was of the opinion that whenever women had these suspicions, they were probably correct and had carte blanche to find out what it was that was *really* going on. But this case was a little different; for one thing, Harriet had liked Sean, and for another, she knew that I, as a divorced kid, was paranoid and suspicious about most relationships, and not just him. 'You can't keep checking his messages,' she said. 'He isn't seeing someone else. You asked him, right? I don't think he would lie to you about that.'

'No, probably not,' I admitted.

'Barring the other night at Flying Saucer, he seems to really like you,' she said.

'Why do you say that?' I demanded. 'How so?'

Harriet thought for a moment. 'He lent us his car, didn't he? You two talk on the phone almost every day. Maybe he's not the demonstrative type. Anyway, on paper, it seems like a match made in heaven.' The latter was a typically clinical observation by Harriet, who could evaluate relationships as if she were studying nuclear fission. 'Stop obsessing. Let's go to that Asian tea house park, or whatever it is.'

'All right.' I started to pick cat hair off my leggings but didn't move. 'I'm just going to call one more time. I promise this is the *last* time.'

'Courtney!' Harriet cried. 'Don't!'

With Sean, the Defining Moments were more complicated. This may have been because by the time I'd reached my thirties, I had become more adept at shielding my insecurity – refraining from, say, asking my boyfriend every other day if he thought our relationship was sailing along on course. Poor Sean probably thought he was dealing with a normal, if somewhat more neurotic-than-average woman when he met me. We'd only been dating two months when I just happened to glance over one day as he punched in the code to his voice mail while on his cell phone. We were sitting in his sports utility vehicle on a rare hot and airless San Francisco Sunday morning, and honestly, I tried to forget the numbers as soon as I saw them. (It could have been a lot worse: he used the same code for his ATM card too.)

At first, I only listened to his messages occasionally. They were frustratingly bland – a furniture delivery guy here, a squeaky-voiced telephone solicitation there. But as Sean grew more distant from me – and frankly, who could blame him? – and the more I panicked, the more frequent the checking became. Finally I made a bargain with a faceless God that I would only listen to his messages in moments of *extreme* uncertainty, after a strained phone conversation or a canceling of plans, which he tended to do often and at the last minute. What I hadn't factored in was that *every day* with Sean was by its very definition *full* of uncertainty. At best, Sean had been reluctant to be involved with me from the start; at worst, he plain wasn't in love with me and never would be. Naturally, I felt the complete opposite.

Sean was a lawyer, and not the good, Liberty kind either. He was edgy and extremely intelligent – one of those kinds of people that you sense are holding many deep, dark secrets, not because of anything they have said or done but exactly because of what they haven't said or done. He was short and worked all the time and had thinning hair and bad, cheap suits – later, I would call him the Irish George Costanza. And yet I was . . . *entranced.* I had convinced myself that he was *the one,* that all other bad relationships were the coals I'd had to walk through to get to the other side. The other side was: Love. Marriage. Kids. A Partner for Life. (Never mind that I don't really believe in marriage in theory and feel, at least at the moment, ambivalent about the procreating thing.)

Naturally, that morning with Harriet would not be the last time I would check Sean's voice mail. It would be a few weeks before I would finally hear a message from a purring female detailing in very explicit fashion all the sexual gyrations she would have performed had he decided not to go home the previous night after all. It would be a week after that before I could bring myself to confront him and confess my deeds – and this was only after I'd had Harriet hack in and change his password, just so I would stop checking the damn thing every half hour. (It didn't work – after musing to me about this 'weird technological glitch' that prevented him from getting into his voice mail, Sean went and changed it back to his original password.) But Sean was surprisingly sanguine and forgiving when I confessed – even offering in Clintonesque terms that the message in question was from a delusional female from the office who was sexually obsessed with him. And it would be a few more weeks after that before he would break up with me.

Later, Harriet and I would have long, cross-continental talks about how and why you get to the point in a relationship where low and dirty manipulations are the only option

6

available to you. Here was someone who basically didn't care for me, whom my family disliked for that very reason, who was so clearly not on the same emotional path *and yet I would not see it*. Hadn't I learned anything at all in my dating career? *Anything?* Almost worse is the fact that we would have been a terrible couple had I gotten what I wanted – namely, a commitment.

I can't pinpoint exactly when I began to observe couples with awe and strangeness as they sat in the coffeebars or walked down the street hand in hand, but it must have been around this time; they were as foreign to me as a family from Pluto. Just how does anybody *do* any of this love stuff anymore?

One spring evening a few days after Sean dumped me, I went out on a run that took me west through Pacific Heights, past my mother's house, down and around the million dollar homes in Presidio Terrace, and back up the hills toward Nob Hill. I found myself counting the number of sports utility vehicles that looked like Sean's (five points if they were standard issue SUVs, 10 points if they were black, 15 if they were black *and* Jeep Cherokees). By the time I'd gotten to the circular path at the bottom of Washington Street, I was up to 155 and beginning to lose count. This time, the Defining Moment that arrived was less of a warning than a lightbulb. This DM was not an ignored billboard or a cow's skull warning me to turn back or even a distant bell. This one was just a feeling, but it was as clear as if someone had just screamed in my ear – simply, that I'd reached a cumulative point in my dating career where I wouldn't or couldn't go through this kind of thing again.

CHAPTER 1

A year later, I came in from a run on that Jeep Cherokee route and was just gathering up a pile of smelly, dirty clothes to lug, Santa-like, to the corner laundromat when I glanced in the bathroom mirror and nearly screamed. The sight was horrible: frizzy curls sticking out at odd angles, little nascent grey hairs pricking through my cowlick, a red face, last night's mascara in a streak down my left cheek. The face could be washed, and for that matter, the hair – but it was clear that a visit to Marie was in order. Quickly.

I looked at my ugly sportswatch. It was six o'clock in the evening – if I left the apartment right this second, and ran all eleven blocks down to Hayes Valley, I might just catch her at her salon before she left for the day. If I called first, it would be easier for her to postpone the haircut to a later date, by which time the sense of urgency would be gone, as well as the conviction that all I needed was a trim to make my entire life more manageable, interesting and indeed fulfilling. I dumped all the dirty laundry back into the hamper and grabbed my wallet and keys, but not before dabbing on some lipstick – MAC Pecan Tone. One couldn't look completely bedraggled in front of one's hair stylist, if only as a mark of respect.

'Good God,' Marie said when I burst into the salon, some fifteen minutes later. Despite my optimistic canter down the hill, I hadn't really expected that she would take me – more often than not, two or three women in white-towelled turbans sat around the perimeter of the cavernous space poring over

Elle or *In Style*, patiently waiting their turn – but when I came in, breathless and sweating, Marie was alone and leafing through her heavily marked appointment book, writing in names and crossing things out. Even Eve, the violet coiffed shampooist/receptionist, had left for the day.

'I really appreciate this, Marie,' I said, after a few minutes of wheedling and cajoling. I hopped up into the bright purple leatherette chair that was the shape of a hand. 'You know how it is when your hair gets to that point and you just can't take it anymore.' She eyed me in the mirror with some doubt. 'Okay, well, maybe not you,' I allowed.

Marie inspected the ends of my hair as distastefully as possible. 'Hmmm. You girls with long hair. Why wait this long? I hope your life is looking better than your ends.'

'As a matter of fact, I don't mind my split ends, as a concept,' I said. 'They remind me that I get a free therapy session *and* a haircut.' Marie waved that compliment away as if she were shooing away a fruit fly.

Marie and I had known each other a long time, so there was no need for useless preamble. 'Just the usual,' I said happily. 'You know – a quarter-inch trim that still allows it to be long while transforming it into something shiny, swinging, trendy and completely fabulous every hour of the day.' As it happens, I was speaking to her rump at that point – she'd bent down and was rummaging through her little trolley, collecting aluminum clips and sliding them into her thick, red hair, which was tied on top of her head, giving her the appearance of a rather hip pineapple.

'The miracle cut,' she said. 'Always a favorite. But as long as no one asks for the Jennifer Aniston hairdo, I'm happy. Thank God that fad passed. Now, where is that damn clarifier? This is great stuff, by the way – gets out all that goo and products so you can really have a nice clean scalp.' She straightened up and eyed my head. 'You like products, right?'

'Same as the next gal,' I said. 'That last stuff you gave me –

what was it, the orange syrupy gel in the black tube? Well, it seriously changed my life.'

'Potion Number Nine,' she said confidently. 'Yup. They've discontinued it.'

I nodded. 'That figures.'

Marie fingered a lock and let it drop unceremoniously. 'It has been almost three months, according to your card.' She stood behind me and untwisted my hair band, trying to work her fingers through. 'Well, how are you doing anyway, besides trimming your hair with manicure scissors?'

'I'm pretty good,' I said. 'And I don't do that anymore.' A vision of Harriet, counseling frugality, as she snipped her bangs in the credit-card-sized mirror in her closet-sized bathroom popped in my head. Obviously it had been a mistake to tell Marie last time of Harriet's helpful economic tips. Marie never seemed to forget anything.

'I think the last time I saw you, you were dating some guy who made pastry?' she prodded.

'Flowers,' I said. 'He was a florist.'

'Pastry, flowers, I knew it was something girlie.' She hitched up her black jeans and began to secure a towel under the neck of my orange smock. Some atmospheric humming began to waft out of nowhere. 'Is that the pygmy music I've been reading about?' I asked.

Marie ignored me and settled right into business. It was penitent/confessor time, which of course was 99% of the reason why most women enjoyed getting their hair cut. 'Now who was the one who hated Valentine's Day?'

'That would be the florist,' I said.

'That was never going to last,' she said. She stopped fussing with my hair and looked at me. 'You aren't going out with him anymore, I take it?'

'Uh uh,' I said. 'Actually, it ended fairly recently.' She met my eyes in the mirror and I hastily added, 'No, it's okay. It was one of those Duty-Free Relationships, as my friend

Harriet calls them.' I'd had a few of these involvements since Sean but nothing that merited too many tears or self-esteem plummets. I took it as a good sign that I remained friends with most of these men, although it did occur to me that that might be because the relationships never should have been anything *but* friendships in the first place.

'Okay, say no more. One of my clients calls them the Acapulco Relationships. Warm, relatively cheap, a little tacky and then you gotta go home and face reality. Anyway, he didn't understand your needs,' Marie said. 'Also, never trust a straight man who sells flowers.' She began flattening my hair against my scalp, pulling it down on either side of my head in that unflattering way that hair stylists do for no apparent reason. 'I could have saved you a lot of time and heartache.'

'I know,' I said.

'Money, too, probably. It's expensive to date somebody nowadays. I don't know how you single people do it. All those dinners, movies, vacations . . . God.'

'We never went on vacation together. It wasn't that kind of relationship.'

'Well, of course you didn't.'

I sighed. Talking to Marie could be a curiously pleasant yet irritating experience. She could be diplomatic when she wanted to, but I'd known her so long – longer than many of my friends – that tact simply didn't play a role in our inter-actions. It took me years to realize that she got away with her more pointed comments due to her unnaturally high, almost Valley-Girlish voice, which, if you closed your eyes, you would have sworn was coming out of the mouth of a twelve-year-old. Like most stylists, she was frustratingly accurate in her relationship assessments.

Marie prodded some more, and so I tried to tidy up what had been a gradual, tedious, petering-out with Julian into a compact story. Usually these salon soundbites ended up being a lot more truthful than a long, drawn-out complex trajectory.

'Okay, where did it go wrong?' I began. 'First of all, I think there's a new fad that's taking over the West Coast males.' Marie visibly perked up – she liked to hear about perceived trends outside of the sphere of her cutting-edge world. 'Where had I left off the last time I talked to you?'

'You'd gone down on him in an alley behind Coit Tower,' Marie said with authority. 'Come on, let's go get you shampooed.' She stepped on the chrome bar underneath my seat and my chair sagged to the floor.

'No, that wasn't me,' I said. I got out of my comfy hand seat and tagged along behind her down the narrow dark corridor to the sinks. 'I've been thinking. What is it about strong women liking their man to have a little sexual get-up-and-go? A little initiative? And feeling ridiculous if they have to ask for it?'

'Don't ask *me*,' Marie said, adjusting the sprayer nozzle as I lay down and hesitantly placed my head in the sink. 'Remember, I'm a married lady. We don't have sex anymore. At least, that's what all those girl magazines keep telling me. I think I'm going to cancel the subscriptions to some of them. But then my clients would probably stage a riot.' She sprayed some water on my scalp. 'Too hot for you?'

'Ouch.' I adjusted the towel under my smock as water dribbled down into my ears. 'The water's fine. I just feel like I'm in traction.' I looked at her upside down. 'You know what I mean about the initiative thing?'

'Uh, not really,' Marie said, scrubbing extra hard, her silver earring hoops swinging. 'Explain.'

'Well,' I began, 'I'm sort of floundering around the same as the next person. But I'm beginning to think all this love stuff comes down to who's got the perceived upper hand. Here I am, independent woman in her early thirties. Opinionated so some would say. Aggressive, some others would say. But you know, not a shrinking violet.'

'Uh huh,' said Marie.

'Okay, so this guy – the anti-Valentine's Day guy – apart

from that little wrinkle, he really is incredibly nice. Very sweet. Not *the* one, if you know what I mean, but okay for now.'

'Not Mr Right. Mr Right Now.'

'Yes,' I said. 'But what is up with this passive man thing? Why is it that a man who is sweet and kind and adorable in real life also invariably winds up being one of those take-me-I'm-yours in the bedroom?'

Marie scrubbed a little harder. 'People don't change their personalities when they fuck, Courtney. I'd think you'd have figured that one out by now.'

I considered. 'I'm not so sure about that,' I said. 'I'm not the same personality in bed as I am when I'm, say, at the super-market. There, I stand in front of the apples for twenty-five minutes wondering, *Gala or Mackintosh? Crispy or soft? Sour or sweet? Green or red? Fuji or Branbury? Organic or commercial?* I'm the mistress of indecision. But I'm not like that when I have sex.'

'I'd hate to see you in the cereal section,' she said. She turned off the sprayer and lolled my soapy hair through her palms. 'But, you know, women have lots of different sides. Men aren't like that usually. They're really pretty one-size-fits-all. It's weird if you can get a guy to do different stuff to you. So it came down to sex with the Flower Guy?'

'No,' I said distractedly. 'Well, yes. I don't know. Sex *was* kind of odd though.' One thing about Sean – there was no doubt who was in control in the bedroom. He'd tell me to do things, to lay that way, to put my leg over *there*, to not grip him like *that*. Sometimes I wondered if that was another sub-conscious reason why I felt so humiliated by him, although – disturbingly – I rather enjoyed it at the time. 'Julian liked me to take the initiative. He'd lie flat on his back. His arms flopped to the side. Dreamy expression – "Do with me what you will." It was weird – I started to feel like, well, what a *man* must feel like.'

'Ick,' agreed Marie. 'Maybe he *was* gay.'

I chewed on that for a moment. 'Maybe I will be reduced to roaming the frat halls of Stanford, searching for the guy who crushes beer cans on his forehead.' I started counting the little fluorescent stars on the ceiling. 'Maybe that's the trade-off for having a kinder, gentler kind of man. Anyway, I emerged basically unscathed.'

'Always important for a Mr Right Now.'

'Yes,' I said. 'He just wasn't *the* one. Not that there is any such thing, of course.'

'Bitter and Twisted, Table for One,' Marie said, adjusting the water temperature again. 'Anyway, you just said it. You were dating Mickey Mouse, not a man. Sweet, adorable. Long hair too, I'll bet?'

'Well, yes,' I said.

'Goatee. Sandals. Jesus thing. Good with animals. May or may not own a snake. Likes to do neck massage. Yup, I know the type. Not good for girls like you. I'll tell you, Courtney,' she said, pumping some particularly redolent conditioner into her palm, 'shoes make the man. Remember that.'

I considered that. 'I have a friend who won't date any man in Tevas. She calls them the clogs of the Nineties.'

'Smart chick.' She rubbed the conditioner into my hair, fanning her fingers out and unsnarling some major knots. 'Are you brushing your hair? Or at least combing it? You could get dreadlocks if you're not careful. But maybe you want that – dreads'll *really* attract the Jesus-boys, you know.'

'Thanks for the tip,' I said. I tried to rearrange my head, and Marie rubbed my temples. 'Harriet, my helpful-hints friend from New York, says this *is* a West Coast phenomenon, the passive man thing. She says it all has to do with Berkeley in the Sixties, and feminist moms, and even Reagan. I can't quite remember how she ties Reagan into it, but the first two kind of make sense.'

'Oh, God, am I glad that I'm through with that dating stuff,' Marie said, working on my neck. 'Not to be one of those know-it-all married types, mind you, 'cause we have our own little set of problems. Anybody else out there on the horizon?'

'Well, there's Aidan,' I said. 'He and I used to date, right after the Irish George Costanza, as a matter of fact. But now we're just friends.'

'Friends Who Fuck,' Marie said, deadpan. 'I can tell by that look on your face. Not really a good idea. Especially if one of you was more into it than the other. Let me guess: you weren't really into dating him. You were still licking your wounds after that George Costanza, and probably wanted to see lots of guys and not be tied down. Am I right? Or am I right?' She turned the water back on, giving my head a blast of water.

'Good Lord, Marie.' I looked at her upside-down face – her pug nose, her perky black eyes that flashed silver from certain angles. 'It's frightening when someone knows you that well. I guess you're right.'

'Be careful,' she warned, turning off the water. 'Someone could get hurt. Sit up now.'

She squeezed my hair hard into a towel. 'Gavin used to be one of those Jesus boys,' she continued thoughtfully. 'With a dash of Henry Rollins. It was a weirdo combination, but somehow the tattoos and the sandals all kind of came together and canceled each other out. When we had sex, we'd take turns being the aggressor or the submissive. Until of course I got pregnant and had the baby. Now we just don't have sex.'

I followed her back to the purple chair and hopped back on. She unwrapped the towel from my head and brought my hair forward in a Cousin It style. 'That's the second time you've said that. Are you serious?' I asked from underneath. 'You really aren't doing it?'

'Nope,' she said. She began tugging a wide-toothed comb through my hair, and pinned half of it to the top of my head. 'It's been about five months now. Before Davia was born.

Just wait until you get pregnant. Sex will be the last thing on your mind. And all this man being a man, aggressor, submissive – all that will just go right out the window. It won't matter a hoot.'

'I can imagine,' I said, out of politeness. 'How does he feel about it?' I winced as she yanked a comb through a particularly knotty spot.

'Oh, he hates it. And I feel bad, really I do. But in the seventh month, you know, it just wasn't something I wanted to do. I told him, "Hon, I really just don't want you inside me right now. I feel full up as it is." And then in the eighth month, I said, "Hon, I really don't want you to touch me. No, I really don't want you to kiss me." He looked hurt, but what could I do? Just the thought of his hand on me gave me the heebee jeebies. It's all physiological anyway.' She began to snip quickly, starting from the back, making her way toward the front.

'What happened in the ninth month? I'm almost afraid to ask.'

'I said, "Hon, you really should think about sleeping on the sofa. I can't take another body next to me in bed." So he moved to the sofa. And then I had the baby, and we still aren't having sex. I'm just too exhausted, and really I don't miss it.'

'Okay.' I had speculated when this no-sex-during-marriage secret was going to be revealed once and for all. I'd heard leaks from married friends for years, but so far no one would go on record.

'I read in *Marie Claire* that the non-interest in sex by the mom is so she'll pay lots of attention to the kid, and not the father,' Marie went on. 'You know, when the kid is under a year old. It kind of makes sense – sex can be *soooo* distracting. Another thing for you to remember.'

'Okay.' I wondered if I should start making a list of recommendations, a sort of modern woman's hope chest.

'So anyway, I figure evolution is on my side,' she rattled on.

Even though Marie was explaining herself in that trademark simple, matter-of-fact way, transforming what would be a complicated issue in any relationship to the equivalent of changing one's mind about a brand of laundry detergent, I felt a little surprised by her revelation. She'd always been very open and honest over the years about sex – what she liked, what she didn't like, and what was interesting and what was a downright turn-off. In her wilder, pre-Gavin days, she'd tell me about going to the On Broadway and picking up some hapless black-dyed-hair boy, spiriting him home to her heavily decorated apartment (Marie was a heavy-duty Siouxsie fan before most Americans had ever heard the word Gothic) and having sex all night long, only to send him on his way at the first peep of sunlight. I could never figure out if Marie was one of those people who were ten years ahead of their time, or ten years behind.

I'd met Gavin once a few years ago, when he came in to pick up Marie at the salon one night. In those days, both he and Marie sported a proliferation of tattoos, pierces and motorcycle leather, some of which was still evident in Marie today but softened by a few tokens to yuppiedom: a fourth-hand Land Rover, some Pottery Barn lamps in the salon, a recently removed nose pierce. Gavin had been soft-spoken and friendly – one of those gentle, alternative types who permeate San Francisco like some sort of fungus. He worked at a rowdy yet trendy bar in the Haight that was frequented by what I saw as devotees to the dirty life; it routinely hosted fistfights and received telephone bomb threats for no apparent reason. When things would get particularly hairy, Gavin was known to lead the offender off to a dark corner table, reasoning with him, while everyone else was screaming about calling the police. He'd been with Marie for over five loving years, but I had a hard time imagining how even he was handling this.

'But I know he misses it,' she continued, as she measured two ends against one another, 'so the other day, I sat him down and said, "Look, here's the deal. Why don't you have sex with someone? There must be some cocktail waitress or bartender that wants to sleep with you. I want you to be happy, and I know this is making you really unhappy, but I just don't want to do it right now." '

'Jesus, Marie,' I said. 'Well, I guess – whatever works.' Whatever that was supposed to mean. It was one of those explanations like 'it depends' that seemed to be bandied about a lot by couples nowadays. I glanced down at the pile of hair that was forming around the chrome base of the chair. 'You aren't going too short back there, are you?'

'You always ask me that,' said Marie.

I watched as she picked up a bright blue crystal bottle and started to spritz a eucalyptus-smelling liquid on my scalp. 'That feels good. Well, what did he say?'

Marie giggled. 'At first he was shocked,' she said, pulling the comb through again. 'That's what he said, even: "Marie, I'm shocked – *shocked*." Then when he got used to the idea, I think he thought it might be a good option. So the other day, we started to go through a list of all the possible women. Karen, the one with the white hair? Or Raven, the Goth girl with the tongue pierce? We couldn't make up our minds. There were a lot of good possibilities.'

'Wow,' I said, impressed. 'You always were so cutting-edge. No pun intended.'

'He was funny about it,' she said. 'He seemed to really consider it, like he was trying to decide between a money market or an individual retirement account. I'd notice him frowning, looking at me with this expression, and so I'd throw out another name. "How about Ivy, the chick who works at the vet? Or what about that girl who works at Cala, the one who always runs over to bag our groceries?" Flip your head over,' she commanded me.

'The only thing I insisted on,' she continued, as she ran her hands through my hair, shaking it out, 'was that he tell me who it was and that he use a condom. I just didn't want him sneaking around, you know? But I love him. I want him to be happy, and I know he likes sex, so – okay, come back up now.' She combed a piece in front and snipped a smidgen off. 'You'll see. You might encourage the same thing when you're pregnant.'

'But you're not pregnant anymore,' I pointed out. Marie rolled her eyes as if that were a small matter. 'I don't think so, Marie. I don't think I could do it. I'm not that secure.' If I'd had the same arrangement with Sean, it would have killed me. But then again, if I had some similar arrangement with Aidan, it would have been fine. Did it all come down to how much you loved a person? Or how insecure you were? This story of Marie's was odd and obviously dangerous, but if anyone could deal with it – and indeed, make it work – she could.

'Oh, he won't actually *do* it,' she assured me. 'I knew he wouldn't. I just wanted him to feel that he could. It was all a kind of big joke, anyway. Just to put it out there, you know?'

'Well, how do you know that?' I'd lost all interest in my haircut. I spun my chair around to look at her. She was gathering a broom and dustpan from a tiny closet near the phone and had her back to me.

'Because I know Gavin. I know how his mind works. I mean, the whole point of having sex outside the partnership is how dirty it makes you feel. And that's the turn-on. So I guess, once we talked about the whole thing, it kind of took the wind out of his sail. Maybe if I hadn't told him he could, he would have. Or if I told him he couldn't, he would. Who knows?'

'What if he did have an affair? If he actually took you up on your offer?'

'Oh, I'd probably kill him,' she said cheerfully, sweeping around my feet, gathering all my shorn bits into a mini-haystack. 'Knowing me. This is all hypothetical. I'm sure we're going to be having sex again soon. It's just a matter of time.'

She looked at me as if she remembered something and dropped the broom to the floor with a loud *clack*. She spun my chair around and offered a hand mirror in the shape of a foot so I could see the back. 'Just wait till you have a baby. Everything changes, but sex changes the most. You'll see.' She hummed a little bit.

I mulled over all this as I walked along Hayes Street, peeking into the windows of the ubiquitous shoe stores, tea houses and restaurants in this area which, like all of San Francisco, was clipping along at breakneck speed toward a gentrified land of Oz. I passed by a flower store where I stopped and bought a gardenia, for no other reason but that I had a lone dollar floating around in my pocket. I considered pinning it to my sweater but decided that would look like I was getting ready for the prom. When I got back to my apartment, I would fill one of my glass cereal bowls with water and drop it in, placing it next to my bed like I'd seen my mother do on occasion.

One would think these tokens of affection – flowers, jewelry, the odd gift – would take on less importance in relationships the older we got. Instead, I was finding the exact opposite. I had a deeper appreciation of the semiotics of flower-giving since I'd dated Julian, who obviously took quite a commercial view of the commodity, explaining to me that women put a great amount of importance on them while men merely saw them as a means to some end – that end being sex, forgiveness, affection. (This wasn't a *bad* thing, he hastened to add.) Meanwhile, on the odd occasions that Aidan, the Mr Right Now before Julian, had given me flowers I had internally cringed because I was afraid he was putting more significance on us than I wanted him to. After Sean, Aidan and Julian, I made a point of buying my own flowers.

Harriet and I had been engaged in a hearty debate about To Flower or Not to Flower in February, right before *that certain day* which, like most holidays now, seems to have gotten bigger

21

and more significant in our culture for no apparent reason. Harriet had been complaining that last year, Just Jerry, her boyfriend of six months, had handed her a card without her name written on the front, and had signed the inside with just 'Jerry'. (Hence his moniker.) This year, she said she wanted flowers and if she didn't get them, well, there would be hell to pay. Once again, the chasm between Harriet's and my relationship ideals loomed. 'What are you going to do to him?' I asked, with interest. My version of 'hell to pay' and Harriet's version would be very different, since she was against confrontation of any kind as a matter of principle.

And again, principle weighed in heavily against Just Jerry. It was the principle of the thing, she maintained, that flowers should be offered. He knew she wanted them – in her book, if he wanted to make her happy, if he *cared* enough, he'd bury his cynicism for the day, take the plunge and buy the damn flowers. I considered that; while I hadn't cared a fig if Aidan had brought me flowers or not, it had vexed me that Sean had never showed up proffering a nice little bouquet – *never once* – so I couldn't be that unsympathetic to Harriet's expectations.

I rounded the corner on Gough Street and began the trudge up the hill. Though it was late March, the early evening air still felt like winter, with a blast of Arctic wind sailing down off the bay. I fingered my gardenia that I'd put in my pocket, remembered that touching the petals turned them brown, and wished I'd called Aidan to plan our weekly movie date that night. Maybe I would give Aidan the gardenia, brown petals and all – that was the kind of thing that would please him – and I stood on the corner at Golden Gate Avenue, looking around for a pay phone to call him. Unless he was working that night, Aidan was usually a sport about last-minute plans.

Would Gavin have thought to give Marie flowers on Valentine's Day? She could be a surprisingly light touch when it suited her. I could just hear Harriet weighing in: 'A huge, overblown bunch of roses, lillies, freesia and pine boughs will

22

be just the thing to woo her back to the bedroom!' I found a sticky public phone and tried to touch the receiver as little as possible as I punched Aidan's number in with my pinky.

CHAPTER 2

A month later, I awoke from an afternoon nap clutching my computer in what could only be called a desperate embrace. I was in a work crunch, and somehow I had convinced myself that the more physically close I was to my computer, the more ease I would have in meeting deadlines, which of course had yet to be the case. Between the computer and Caller ID technology would be the death of me. That evil little box that I had installed next to my phone in an effort to avoid wrestling with telemarketers had the immediate effect of making me more neurotic than usual, if that were indeed possible. It is all well and good to fantasize that dozens of friends, editors, job offers and suitors have been trying to reach you all day but just not leaving messages. I hadn't counted on Caller ID smashing that hopeful little notion to bits.

An 'Anonymous' number blipped up on the Caller ID as I dusted around it. My house was never cleaner than when I had a deadline to meet. 'Yes?' I said.

'I'm sure you must know what happened by now,' said Marco immediately. Although we lived in the same city, Marco and I rarely saw one another, preferring the telephone as our mode of friendship since, as he and I both said, 'We can't be bothered to make a plan,' which suited me just fine. Also, he was studying for his PhD and frustratingly arrogant about his time in a way that only professional students can be.

Marco and I had been friends since high school, and by

now were used to our individual quirks and hiccups. If we'd met now, I suspect there might be a fair amount of mutual antipathy – me pigeonholing him as an educated, pretentious slacker, him labeling me a bad-tempered would-be bourgeois hack. The sex issue had been dealt with long ago, when we made out and – I think – fondled one another drunkenly on the front steps of my house when we were sixteen.

'Are you talking about Ms Trouble?' I asked. I could never remember her real name. She had dumped him right before Christmas, probably finding Marco too easy-going and normal, or perhaps having found larger, more limitless check-book balances to plunder (which would not be too difficult, considering Marco's perpetual student status). Marco had had numerous relationships like this since I'd known him – all of them tumultuous, all of them sexually charged – which usually ended with a terrible public row. He was attracted to selfish, beautiful and extremely insane women. Ignoring my advice that he should move to Los Angeles, he'd returned to the shark-infested dating waters recently, despite feeling cynical and listless. 'My sociological clock is ticking,' he'd say, meaning that people were thinking him weird that he was a male in his thirties and still unattached.

I sprayed some Easy-Off on a crusty mass embedded in the slots of the broiler. He was the perfect person to talk to while cleaning, since he didn't really listen to what I said and I only half heard what he said. But I liked hearing his dating stories, since he almost always managed to surprise me with his vulnerability – a quality, he would remind me sternly, that most men shared.

'Ashley? Good God, no. We broke up before Christmas. Didn't you hear? Wait, we *talked* about this.'

'Well, who then?' I asked. 'Oh! Yes. Right, carry on. Your date with Harriet's friend.' Now it was coming back to me. 'Tell me again the series of events,' I said. 'This is the friend of Harriet's who just moved here, right?'

'Uh huh,' he said. 'Your friend Harriet told me to call her. I didn't have to, you know.'

I had already warned Harriet that I thought a set-up with Marco was a bad idea, but Harriet remained optimistic that it was possible to break this Ms Trouble cycle. 'Okay, so you asked her out, you went out, and now she doesn't return your call. Right?'

'Right,' he said. 'I don't get it. We had a good time. I thought we did.'

'Where did you go? What did you do?'

'Uh, some Mexican place. And then, I thought we were going to go to a movie. But suddenly she said she had plans after dinner, so she left.'

'Bad,' I commented. 'Very bad. My advice to you is: just forget it.' I examined an unidentifiable crusty black ball that looked like a charred cherry, imagining this failed date. There this girl sat under the blinking colored lights, looking like a poor man's Christy Turlington (all Marco's dates looked similar – thin, brown hair, garbed in J. Crew, generically pretty), surrounded by serapes and mariachis, sipping a watered-down margarita as her eyes darted around the room. That's how she'd give herself away, the glances at other tables, the close examination of the salt on the rim of her glass. All the signs were there if Marco knew where to look.

I had a feeling I knew what went wrong, but instead, I said 'So you want to know what the word on the street is. Okay, I'll call Harriet.'

'Well, don't do that,' Marco said. 'I mean, no, thanks. I just thought maybe you'd heard something. The way you girls talk. No, actually,' he said quickly, rethinking it, 'no, it's fine. Maybe she's got a boyfriend.'

'She doesn't,' I said. 'I don't mean to be harsh. But wouldn't you like to know the chick's version?'

'What do you mean, "version"? I told you everything. There isn't any version to be had. It was a date, not an Oliver Stone movie.' He sounded embarrassed. 'Besides, it's not worth it. Harriet won't have heard anything, anyway.'

'Okay,' I said. I wondered how, at this point, men couldn't know that women talk about everything, *everything* with their girlfriends. 'If I do find anything out, do you *want* to hear it?'

Marco was clicking a pen between his teeth. 'No, not really,' he sighed. 'I don't have time to get involved with anyone right now anyway – I've got a draft of my thesis due in a few months, and these papers to grade . . .'

I turned my attention back to the oven until Marco piped up something about having dinner soon, and we tried to make a plan. After fifteen minutes of back-and-forthing about nights we were both free, I told him we'd talk later in the week.

'What do you *think* happened?' Harriet asked me later during our nightly session.

'I think I know. It's that quality of Marco's that he calls "easygoing" right?'

'Of course,' Harriet said matter-of-factly. 'I called Christine yesterday, and asked her how her date went. "Horrible!" she said. Right off the bat. She said he'd called her, and they chatted away. On and on, it was a great conversation, she said. After an hour or so of this, he finally said, "So, do you want to go out sometime?" Which, as they both know, was the whole point of the phone call, right? She said "sure", and he said "great!" They talked some more, and he said what was good for her? She said "Friday". On Friday, she gets into his car and says, "So where are we going?" And he does that, "Oh, where do you want to go?" She says, "I don't care. Where do you want to go?" He replies, "I don't care. Where do you want to go?" Back and forth for fifteen minutes. Finally, she picks someplace he'd said he liked a lot. He says, "Sure! I just went there yesterday but that's fine." And at the restaurant, same thing. "What movie do you want to see?" On and on, back and forth. At that point she decided to go home and wash her hair.'

'Marco, Marco.' I'd started on the bathroom and was leaning over the tub, scrubbing. 'I warned you about him. But you'd think after having me as a friend, he'd know by now. Of course, Marco says whatever observation I have can be compressed into a single theory: Women Good, Men Bad. I'm not a sexist, am I?'

'My mother says it's feminism,' Harriet said, and not answering the question, I noticed. We groaned in unison. 'They don't know what to do, so they do nothing. They're scared of being too aggressive, or maybe the woman will get angry and say he's a doltish cad. Instead, he comes off as a congenital weakling.'

'The Contemporary Guy Cripple.' I scrubbed a little harder, thinking of Julian. 'How did work go today?'

'Oh, fine,' she said, off-handedly. Harriet worked at home as a freelance publicist, laboring on her computer over projects on which she spent vast amounts of time and energy, feeling guilty every time she got up to go to the kitchen in search of a cookie, or talked to her friends (of which she had thousands) on the phone during the 9–5 time slot. That was Harriet in a nutshell: diligent, reliable, easily made to feel guilty, still as smoothly gracious as she'd been taught to be, growing up in a tiny town in Texas with her mother and aunt. 'I didn't get very much done. The phone kept ringing. Then the messenger came. Then I was hungry, so I spent an hour staring at my refrigerator trying to think if I could make anything out of pesto sauce, a mango, an egg and a glass of Soave. I ended up ordering Chinese food. What did you do today?'

'I cleaned,' I said. 'I've reached a new low, Harriet. I slept with my computer last night.'

Harriet sighed. 'That *is* bad,' she agreed. 'I want a maid. I think I would get a lot more done if my apartment was cleaner.'

'Probably not,' I said. I shook some Ajax in the toilet. 'In our twenties, we spent so much time moaning about not knowing what we wanted to do,' I said. 'I'm glad in our thirties we know what we want to do with our lives, and can sit around our apartments and complain about not doing it.'

'And I had a lot to do today, too,' she lamented.

'You should try unplugging your phone. That seems to really work for me.'

'My phone doesn't unplug. I still have the old-fashioned kind.' Harriet, between her job and her friends, seemed to spend her lifetime on the telephone. 'You know,' she suddenly began, 'if there's one thing I hear from our girlfriends, time and time again, it's that Contemporary Guy Cripple which is the ultimate turn-off.' She paused as we both considered this.

'Last time we talked about this, you said it was only a West Coast phenomenon,' I said, and Harriet made a tiny *hhhmmph*. 'Well, poor Marco. I'm sure he would just say, "Well, the truth of the matter is I just don't care about where we eat or what movie we see. And you girls seem to really care about those things. So I just make it easier and let you decide."'

Harriet sighed. 'Well, she won't go out with him again.'

'Christine might be a little too normal for him, too,' I pondered. 'He doesn't like those predictable, girl-next-door types. Now if she were a stalker or had multiple personalities, we might be getting somewhere.' I wondered if I should pass along the gist of this conversation to him. The last time I'd veered on this subject, I'd gotten the (admittedly accurate) lecture about how every chick was different nowadays – a Rules Girl here, a free-wheeling crunchy Deadhead there, a semiotics-spewing feminist everywhere – thus making it impossible for guys to know what was expected of them.

'Well, it's his loss. And as for her, she's looking for one thing and one thing only: a Man With a Plan. By the way, how's Julian?'

'Oh,' I said, and swirled the blue, cloudy water around in

the bowl. 'I thought I told you. Valentine's Day shot an arrow in its heart.'

'No, you did not tell me this.'

'I thought I did,' I said. 'Anyway, it doesn't matter. Our . . . "relationship" – or whatever you'd call it – was dwindling and dwindling. Finally it just limped away of its own accord, like a wounded animal.'

'When was this? Never mind him. You weren't that into him, anyway.'

'I know,' I said.

'He was a plaything,' said Harriet.

'Well, it wasn't *that* insignificant.' I turned from the toilet and poured some Clorox in a bucket. I put it under the tap and began filling, swishing it around, talking loudly over the rushing water. 'But you know, it's fine. Back to our regularly scheduled program.'

'What about Aidan?' Harriet asked. 'Have you had sex with him recently?'

'Last Saturday night,' I said. 'It was, well, great. I hate to say this, but it's much better than when we were going out and had the commitment question looming over our heads. Now it just is so much more relaxed.'

'Humph,' she said, shifting the phone around. 'But it sounded like he really cared for you. I don't think Clark ever once came over and brought food or flowers when I had a cold – and we went out for ten years!'

'Yes, well.' I swished the Clorox around.

'It must be hard for him to just sleep with you without a commitment,' Harriet continued.

'I think he'll survive the trauma.'

'Okay,' she said doubtfully. 'How are you going to feel when he starts going out with someone else and ends your arrangement?'

'I'm a big girl,' I said, feeling that little dart of guilt as I said so, because I was fairly certain that Aidan wasn't going to be the one to end the arrangement. 'He and I both know we can't do the monogamous couple thing. It's just not in our nature.'

'You mean, not in *your* nature. What about that guy that you had the affair with when you were going out with Aidan—'

'Fred.' I stared at a little patch of mold that had formed around the bath fixtures. 'It wasn't an "affair", Harriet – Aidan and I weren't married, for God's sake.' I heard Harriet sip something and I looked at my watch – six o'clock in New York. It was the time for her ritual cocktail each evening. 'Oh, I don't know. I don't have any answers, but what am I supposed to do in the meantime? Be a nun?'

'Well, no,' Harriet admitted. 'Free sex can be fun too.' That's what she called my forays and flings: 'free sex', as if it were a new brand of gum being handed out on the streetcorner. 'As long as you don't care about them too much so you don't get hurt.'

'What's the cocktail today?' I asked, shifting gears.

'A Negroni. It's delicious. I wish you lived here – I'd make you one too.'

'Well, that would be delightful.' I turned off the water and began looking around for my scrub brush. 'Besides, someone else is sniffing. That friend of Mary's. We're having coffee next week.'

'Not him!' Harriet exclaimed, after a swallow. 'After this whole discussion about Marco and the Contemporary Man Cripple? Mary wouldn't even give him your phone number! And she's his *friend*.'

'I got an e-mail from him. It's only coffee, Harriet. I'll keep you apprised.' I moved the clothes hamper out of the bathroom and got out the mop.

Scene: We're sitting in a sun-filled café off of Alamo Square, surrounded by slackers and poets and out-of-work musicians and whatever other kind of artistic type that fills the coffee bars of San Francisco on any given afternoon. I'd arrived at the appointed time, ordered a latte and commandeered a clean round table in the corner. He's late. (The mini-Harriet who now sits on my shoulder through every male/female interaction whispers into my ear that this is not a good sign.) I ignore her and flip through the free weekly newspapers, feeling out-of-touch and old as I read about a Bauhaus revival, realizing halfway through the article that they are referring to the band and not the art movement.

Enter Larry, friend of Mary's. He doesn't recognize me and I have to stand up and wave my arms. He walks over to the table looking a tad confused, and says, 'Courtney?' in a faint voice. He asks when I changed my hair color and I tell him weakly I have not – just that when he met me six months ago it was a dark winter red and it has now faded to an early summer brown. I hear my words coming out my mouth and I internally cringe, as mini-Harriet intones something about not giving away too much information, no matter what the topic. Larry goes to the counter to fetch an espresso and there is that uncomfortable little pause while I sit waiting for him, pretending I'm not appraising the shape of his body or his hair, and he's pretending to be intent on this serious action of ordering an espresso. He returns and we begin to talk about the weather, El Niño, the appalling shape of the tennis courts in Golden Gate Park, the amount of human defecation in said park, our useless mayor Willie Brown, our useless Governor Pete Wilson and now, our useless President Bill Clinton – not necessarily in that order. I alternately feel interested, bored and bewildered. I wonder why we are here and is this a just-friends sniffing around (now a mini-Marco pops up on the other shoulder and insists there is no such thing as a just-friends sniff for men) or is this the preamble to the safe date lunch? Larry wants another espresso and I another latte, but then there is the embarrassing dance of the payment issue – if he is to pay for both then is it a date? If I pay for both (Harriet looks outraged) will I feel annoyed? If we are to go dutch, there is all that embarrassing fumbling for change and then who pays the tip? In the end I slap down two dollars and let him do what he will. He looks at it, confused, mumbles something like, 'Are you sure?' then pockets it before heading to the counter. (Harriet shakes her head, Marco nods approvingly.) We talk some more: shifting editorships at the *New Yorker*, the national edition of the *New York Times*, cats vs. dogs, the state of the media, his hatred of TV (not a good sign in my TV-loving opinion) and the semiotics of Larry King's suspenders. After an hour and half, I look at my ugly watch and say I have to go meet some athletically minded women for a track session (Harriet scowls: 'Too much information!') and I gather up my knapsack and there is that little embarrassing minute where we are talking madly, but internally trying to figure out the proper expression of departure. Eventually we gamely shake hands and he says something about e-mail and I smile and wave and off I go into the sunset, wondering what all that was supposed to mean.

I had just opened the computer, closed the computer, and suddenly noticed the amount of dust covering the moldings of the kitchen when the phone rang. Like ninety percent of the calls I receive, this too was helpfully labelled by Caller ID as 'Unavailable.' (The remaining ten percent were 'Anonymous.') So much for the powers of technology.

The sound of breaking glass, followed by gales of laughter, filled my ears when I picked up the phone. Then, the faint hum of the overseas connection. Obviously Mary or Jayne, my extremely loquacious British girlfriends, but it seemed a little late even for them. I looked at my watch: seven in the evening here, three in the morning in East London.

'This is update Central,' Jayne said, not bothering with the falsity of a preamble. 'Mary wants to know how your date went with Larry, but first she has another dirty little secret that we'd like our Yank friend to out for us.'

'Hello to you too,' I said. 'Been drinking, have we?'

'Hello, love.' Now it was Mary purring down the phone. 'We've been meaning and meaning to ring for ages. We do miss you. Have you gone out with Larry yet? Forewarned is forearmed.'

'I liked him,' I said. 'But it wasn't a date.'

'Well, what was it then?'

'I don't know,' I said, my standard response after any initial encounter.

Mary sighed. 'I haven't talked to him so I know not a thing. He's too indecisive and noncommittal for you, I think – that's why I didn't want to give him your telephone number in the first place.' I knew all this but listened politely as Mary continued her drunken ramble. 'Now when are you coming to London? We have loads of things to tell you! When are you coming?'

'Any day now,' I said, another standard response. 'Are you having a party?' I imagined Mary in her strapless black dress and big combat boots, cell phone pressed to her ear. I heard some voices shout jovially in the background and then a door close.

'Now I have Jayne here, sitting alongside me on the settee,' continued Mary. 'I had the most dreadful experience which I'd like to share. And I'm certain this has only happened to me. I'm mortified, I really am.'

'That's rubbish,' Jayne said in the background. 'Ask her.'

Mary cleared her throat as if she were to begin a prepared speech. 'Tonight I had a man actually fake an orgasm on me,' she said primly. 'And I have to know: do all men do this? Has this happened many times before and I just didn't realize? And most importantly, has this happened to you?'

Jayne grabbed the phone. 'I keep telling her he was a wanker anyway and not to worry about it. She got off, which is the only thing that's important anyway.'

'How do you know he was faking?' I asked.

'How does she know?' Jayne cupped her hand over the phone as I heard her say to Mary, 'She's asking the physical evidence question too.'

Mary grabbed the phone back, and continued matter-of-factly, 'Well there's this little biological phenomenon known as ejaculation – perhaps you've heard of it.'

'Oh, no condom then?' This was odd for someone as sexually and politically on the ball as Mary. 'Because, yes, I have heard of men faking it in condoms. It's pretty easy to do, especially if they're getting soft or sore anyway, toward the end. My friend Andrew used to do it with surprising regularity. Or so he said.'

'Now why on earth would he do that?'

'He'd get tired,' I said. 'Same reason why girls do it. Performance anxiety and all the rest. But what happened to you?'

Mary sighed. 'We should have used a Durex, I know. But I'm on the pill to regulate my cycle – and oh, it just seemed too much of a bother.' Jayne and I both murmured a knowing *uh huh*, as Mary continued. 'We'd just returned from seeing The Verve, and I was feeling amorous. And I came, after a while actually, because we'd been drinking all night. Usually I come right away.'

'Always bragging about that, she is,' Jayne put in.

'Shush, you old bag. And I was trying to get him to come, because I was a little sore, employing all my little tricks, and then he came. Or I thought he came. He groaned, arched his back, got softer, rolled off of me immediately. So, fine, I thought. Maybe not the most interesting or creative love-making I'd had but you can't always be at the Albert Hall, right? Sometimes you have to settle with the Mean Fiddler.'

'She doesn't live in London, love,' I heard Jayne whisper. 'Those metaphors aren't useful.'

'Then what?' I asked.

36

'Well, I got up to go to the toilet, like I always do because I can't risk cystitis, now can I?' Mary worked at a woman's health magazine and often peppered her speeches with preventative tips. 'And before I sit down on the loo, I stand there for a moment. And I feel the oddest sensation, like something's missing. You know that funny little internal dripping you get after sex when you stand up, and you know you have maybe two seconds to get to the toilet before his spunk starts running down the inside of your leg? Well, this time – nothing. Not a thing. So I sit down, and think, *Well I'll just push it all out, it's probably caught in some crevice.* Still, nothing. I stand up after having a pee and look down, expecting to see that little frothy, cloudy bit. But no.'

'Now the poor dear is reassessing every lovemaking experience she's ever had,' said Jayne, in the background.

'Yes, I am,' said Mary. 'I'm terribly worried. When did men start doing this? Is it a trend that I don't know about?'

'Maybe he just doesn't come very much,' I offered. 'Sometimes men don't, particularly if they masturbate a lot.' I lay down on the sofa, suddenly tired. 'Did you ask him about it?'

'As a matter of fact, I did.' Mary sounded indignant. 'Jayne thinks I ought not have bothered, but I wanted to know. And when I asked him, as tactfully as I could, he got so wound up and vicious that if I'd had any doubt before, it was immediately obliterated. I sensed he's highly embarrassed, which I find odd.'

Jayne chimed in, 'It's hardly a badge of honor for a bloke, Mary.'

'That's true,' I said, considering. 'I guess guys are expected to come every single time, to always be ready, or there's something wrong or, or, *effeminate* with them.' Mary shifted the phone and I heard their heavy-booted steps return to a noisier part of the flat. 'I'm pretty sure it's happened to most women,' I said.

'Has it happened to *you*?' she said petulantly.

'Well, now, how would I know? But, God . . . I hope not.'

I heard the phone being handed over with Mary saying 'Oh, wonderful,' in the background. Jayne returned on the line. 'She's now downing another gin and tonic, poor thing. Isn't it just like her to blame herself. And you're probably right, it's happened to us lots of times before and we just didn't realize.' We started to say goodbye, as Jayne called to Mary, 'Ignorance is bliss, love. Remember that next time.'

'I was thinking more along the lines of what those Yanks say on their bottles,' Mary responded loudly. 'No Deposit, No Return.' She purred down into the phone, 'Don't be surprised if Larry doesn't phone you again. He's the type that will sit and wait it out until you do something. And you must come over and spend some time with us, because all sorts of sexual secrets and intrigues are happening here between Nigel and Kath. Love you, darling. Must dash.' She beeped off before I had a chance to say anything more.

'I got your e-mails that you forwarded,' said Harriet blandly. From her tone it was clear she was disapproving. 'I thought you were very flirtatious with him. I didn't know you liked him that much.'

'I don't,' I said. 'I mean, I like him, but we just had coffee. I don't know what I think about him, you know, in *that way*, apart from the fact that it's clear he's not gay. I mean, he said it, sort of. He implied he'd just ended a relationship.'

'He's looking for a rebound relationship, then.'

'No, it came up very organically,' I said. 'We were talking about cats. He has two of them, and his ex has the sisters and brothers.' Harriet shifted the phone around which always signified disapproval, impatience, or both. 'I know – a man with cats. Well, see, I started to remember why I thought he was gay.'

'And why did you e-mail him at all? There wasn't really

anything to respond to, judging from what you told me about your date.'

'It wasn't a date,' I said.

'Well, what would you call it then?'

'I don't know.' There was a little silence and I continued brightly, 'You know how e-mail is. There are no hard and fast *rules*. Sometimes you receive it and don't answer but it means nothing. Other times, you answer and it means everything. Besides, it's easy to be flirtatious with e-mail, don't you think? I find now even when I'm writing an e-mail to the phone company, I start to insert the demure lowercase here, the coy semicolon there.' I heard the phone shift again. Harriet and I had had many conversations about the stickiness of e-mail – it was the one area where our opinions converged, but only about the fact that it was a problem. As Harriet and I saw it, e-mail had arrived on the scene just as the dating pool was starting to get the hang of the phone and all its attendant etiquette involving call waiting, cell phones, voice mail, paging, busy signals, and most importantly, the days one allowed between phone tag. Now we were all back at the frontier, trying to make sense out of this new-fangled communication. It was enough to make one long for the days of tin cans and string.

Harriet was silent. 'I'm sorry, I just don't like the sound of this,' she said finally. 'Isn't it enough that Mary wouldn't give him your phone number? She's known him for a long time. She knows what he's really like.'

'Oh, God,' I said. 'You really have been out of the dating loop. When was the last time you got someone's *phone number*? Nobody relies on the phone anymore.' That was a little disingenuous coming from me, since Harriet and I carried on our entire friendship over the phone. A tall, attractive big-boned woman – and the only one I knew who still wore pink sponge curlers to bed on the eve of a special event – she'd sit under her bubble hairdryer in her West Village apartment, either chatting away or screening her calls if she weren't working. When it came right down to it, if anyone still let the phone dictate the parameters of the mating dance, it was Harriet. She made my fifty-seven-year-old mother look down-right avant-garde. 'The phone is almost obsolete,' I said again with a certain forcefulness. 'I mean, come on. This isn't the Fifties.'

'People get each other's phone numbers all the time,' she said. 'The other day, Amanda said she e-mailed a guy she'd met at a party. Do you know what he did? He picked up the phone and said, "I got your e-mail." '

I waited. 'Yes?' I asked. 'And?'

'Well, that's all,' she said.

I sighed. 'Now what is the point of that story?' Sometimes it was as if Harriet spoke Swahili. 'Is it that she made the first move, or that she e-mailed him when she should have called him? Or is it that he bypassed the e-mail and went straight to phone – do not pass Go, do not collect $200?'

'The point is, she shouldn't have done anything,' Harriet said demurely. 'She shouldn't have called him and she shouldn't have e-mailed him.'

'What should they have done to express interest in each other, Harriet? Smoke signals? Carrier pigeons? Hand-written letters?' I heard her give a sniff of approval. 'My God. The human race would all have died out by now if we followed this Byzantine protocol.'

'Well, letters would never work,' Harriet said gravely. 'The mail's too slow now. In the nineteenth century, they'd get two, three deliveries a day. But other than that, it seems like a good idea to me.'

'Ask poor Charlotte Brontë if she approves of courtship through the mail,' I said. 'Remember she spent days, weeks, months, I think *years*, waiting for a letter in reply from that professor she was in love with in France. And when she finally got one, guess what? It was a Dear Jane letter. She ruined her whole life waiting for those letters. Now at least with e-mail, you know instantaneously when you've been given the dump-a-roo.' This was the same sort of argument – in a different format or a different context – that Harriet and I had constantly. It was comforting, in a way, like a familiar *Cheers* re-run. It went along the lines of Harriet counseling patience and pride, and me advocating confrontation and moving on quickly.

Even the light testiness that arose whenever Harriet and I discussed courtship in the abstract was a comfort in its unchanging, choreographed style. Since I'd known her, Harriet held a wary, if extremely old-fashioned view of the opposite sex, seeing them as little more than skittish Dalmations that needed a good dose of training to make them the least bit reliable or worthy of attention.

Then that satanic directive *The Rules* came along, serving to underscore her every point. It was a dark day for us. Now she had a text to which to refer – which she did, although by now she knew not to mention it too often by name. She thought me far too undiplomatic, too direct, too prickly and too extreme. Even if I wasn't interested in nabbing a particular Romeo, á là *Rules*, she felt it didn't do me any good at all to deal with men in a straightforward manner.

'You wait until you get to be in your late thirties, like me,' she would say, as if at age thirty-one I was a mere zygote. 'When I was your age, I let myself get walked all over on like an old shoe. My mother had told me before I moved to New York, "Harriet, honey, eat a banana a day. It'll stave off the blues." When I look back on those years, all I can think of is how many bananas I ate, usually after being dumped by some nobody. Crying and wolfing down a bunch of bananas. I wish I'd known how to protect myself more.' She said all of this cheerfully. A version of this story would pop up every four phone calls or so – something having to do with being chased, the chaser and the method of the hunt. 'All of this is borne out of experience,' she said.

'I don't think e-mailing a man means you've let your guard down entirely,' I now said to her. 'It's not like I've broken into his voice mail. It's not like I'm . . . *obsessed.*'

'Yet.' Harriet fell silent. 'Well, you won't do *that* ever again, will you?' Harriet had not actually been against me checking Sean's voice mail, but she had been *entirely* against me confessing to my actions.

'No, I will not,' I said unconvincingly. I poured some cooking wine into a plastic cup and took a sip. As usual in these discussions with Harriet, I felt like a Martian with my own set of corresponding laws that applied only to my planet. 'You know Harriet, what if I don't want to be chased? What if . . . if I only want free sex?'

'Then you'll practice the Rules without even knowing that you're doing it,' she said flatly, breaking her own moratorium. 'Either way, he'll be at your feet in no time. You may not want that, but it's flattering isn't it?'

'I guess,' I said doubtfully. 'In my experience, the guy who gets turned on by a woman's elusivity is not the kind of guy I want paddling around in my dating pool.' Harriet was quiet, and I could almost see her shaking her head in pity for me, sitting in her tiny, brightly painted studio, surrounded by magazines and newspapers. '*Anyway,*' I said, 'Mary herself says Larry's not a bad guy. Just a little, um, dopey. But he reads a lot. That's a plus, isn't it? We had an interesting conversation.'

I knew 'dopey' wasn't the word she had used. She'd been over here from London at a women's health conference and we'd run into Larry at the museum. He and I ended up having a ribald conversation about orthodonture and cats while Mary went in search of the bathroom. It was only later that I found out he was not in fact gay – and what I'd remembered as the typically friendly interaction that often takes place between a gay man and a straight woman was now revealed to be something else entirely. I mentally flipped through our conversation as if I were going through a Rolodex, trying to remember if I'd inadvertently given him a peek into my female-ness that only women and gay men were privy to. I wasn't a Rules girl, but neither was I completely immune to the intangible laws governing the hetero male/female interaction.

'I think what Mary said was that he was *indecisive*,' said Harriet, enunciating each syllable as if I were a non-native speaker of English, and invoking the ghosts of Marco and Julian in a single word.

'Is that what she said? I guess that's right.'

'You only have to look at his response to *your* e-mail—' Harriet, though she hadn't said so, was against me sending the après-coffee e-mail in the first place but obviously was choos-ing her battles carefully, '—to see how indecisive he is.' I heard her tapping away on her computer. 'See, look at this: "I don't know if you've ever gone swimming in Fallen Leaf Lake, but it's wonderful. So refreshing and clean! You should try it sometime." You should "*try it sometime*"?' I could just see Harriet's round brown eyes getting rounder, like Li'l Orphan Annie. 'What does *that* mean? You say the lake is three hundred miles away from San Francisco. It's not like you're just going to be driving by. The man has a house up there. How about, "I'd love it if you'd come up sometime to Fallen Leaf Lake and go swimming with me." Or, "Maybe some weekend you'd like to visit me for the day and we can go swimming – when would be a good time for you?" ' I didn't say anything. 'What else did Mary say about him?'

'Umm, let me think for moment. Oh, yeah.' Despite my defensiveness, I looked forward to telling Harriet this one. 'She said that when she asked him one time why it was that he was so indecisive and noncommittal about the women he dated, he said, "I guess I'm just waiting for that bolt of lightning to hit me." '

Harriet let out a squawk. 'He did not say that.'

'Mary said he did.'

'My God, where do they learn these things?' she asked incredulously. 'Clark used to say the same thing to me.' Clark had been Harriet's long-term noncommittal boyfriend. He'd been put out to pasture a year ago, but not before a series of tortured make-ups and break-ups, all of which would culminate in Clark's inevitable declaration that Harriet was 'not enough' for him. 'Really, he'd say, "I'm waiting for that bolt of lightning, Harriet. Then maybe I can commit."'

'Of course he did,' I said brightly. 'A certain unmentionable person – he'd say the same thing to me: "I just don't feel that bolt of lightning."'

'Was that before or after he called you Val Kilmer?'

'Um, I think it was after. You know, if I could contribute something to society, it wouldn't be world peace. It would be to permanently remove that phrase from the dating lexicon.' I finished the wine left in the cup and lay down on my brown '70s couch – the one I could never bring myself to pay the exorbitant cost to re-cover. The cat happily jumped up on my chest and settled down for a nap. 'I don't know. I know he sounds like a generic commitaphobe, but maybe he didn't want to be forward. We've only met for coffee, Harriet. Coffee to weekend trip seems a little rushed, even for me.'

'I'm just pointing out the signs right now,' said Harriet lightly. After Sean, Harriet and I had had many talks about the responsibility of best friends to point out Defining Moments. But 'signs' were not Defining Moments. 'As I said, I wish someone had done that for me when I was younger.'

Yes, but you didn't want to get laid for the sake of being laid when you were younger, I felt like saying. That had never been Harriet's style. 'Well, I appreciate that,' I said truthfully. 'But maybe I don't want him to be decisive. Maybe I'm on a fence about him too. In fact, I'm just bored right now. A strange man asks you out for coffee, and whether you admit it or not, it's a little exciting.'

'A Duty-Free?' Harriet asked. 'Well, you never know. I'll

give you that. Sometimes these things have a way of becoming more interesting.' That was what had happened with her and Just Jerry.

I tried to return to the subject of when we were meeting in Los Angeles, the entire reason for my phone call. 'How's work going? When is this trip on?' I asked.

'Should be soon,' she said, as I heard her flipping through the pages of her calendar. 'I'm just waiting for the word from the clients. Work is – oh, you know. Work.'

'How's Just Jerry?' I asked.

'Wonderful,' she said. 'We had a wonderful time last night. Had martinis, then a really romantic dinner at this new restaurant on Avenue B.'

'God, you actually sound enthusiastic about him. That's a switch.'

'He's a very nice man. He's very decent.'

'So you've said.' Over and over, in fact. Despite Valentine's Day, Harriet had high hopes for Just Jerry but he still wasn't showing much initiative, as far as I could tell. They'd been friends for over ten years before jumping into the relationship abyss, and sometimes he still treated her like Good Ole Harriet – which maybe she deserved, given her own moniker for him. 'I guess your little tiff about the flowers has blown over, then.'

'Well, we don't talk about it.' Now it was my turn to shift the phone around. Just Jerry hadn't given her any flowers for Valentine's Day this year either because, as he said, Harriet *expected* him to and that had irked him. She in turn was peeved about his 'little boy stubborness' but for such a skilled tactician, I thought she had been remarkably unstrategic in her own private War of the Roses. 'You know we never talk about problems after a fight. He just clams up if I try to bring it out again. So, I try to let it go, and we had a very lovely time last night.'

'Yeah, you said,' I repeated. Harriet knew my thoughts on this, but I had to throw it out anyway. 'Well, that's good. Just push it all down, right on top of the other issues. I'm sure it will just go away of its own accord. Because whatever you do, don't try to actually resolve or discuss it. That would be just plain silly.'

Harriet giggled. 'What have you got planned tomorrow?'

I sat up. 'Well, right before you called, I called Jemma. We're going to have lunch. I haven't seen her in a long time.'

'Who's Jemma again?'

'Jemma's the one who's married,' I said. 'Actually, she's getting a divorce. I ran into her soon-to-be ex-husband at that Valentine's Day party, and he said I should call her. I hope she's okay.'

'Why are they getting divorced?' Harriet asked lightly, as if these things could be explained in a sentence or two.

'He was vague,' I said vaguely. I wasn't sure I wanted to tell Harriet what I'd heard. 'I'll find out tomorrow.'

'Is she the one who's incredibly in shape? The English one who does all that dance and jogging and stuff? How do you know her again?'

'That's her,' I said. 'I met her about two years ago. Her husband, or her ex, used to play basketball with Michael, my ex. We used to sit on the sidelines, bored out of our minds. I don't know if the team's still together. But now all the couples are broken up.'

'Funny how it tends to work out that way,' Harriet said with an uncharacteristic tinge of tannin – that was more like something I would say. I resolved not to needle her about Just Jerry anymore, and just thank the heavens she wasn't mooning after that dithering Clark.

CHAPTER 3

'How are things going with you and that guy?' Jemma asked me. She met me at Elroy's – a spacious, yuppie hangout in the warehouse district with high ceilings, modern light fixtures and a huge open kitchen. It would normally be the type of place both of us would avoid like the plague but Aidan was working the very slow Saturday lunch shift, which meant free food for us. We sat at the counter and watched as Aidan slipped us barbecued oysters, Caesar salad and fried calamari.

Jemma was looking relaxed but tired, with faint wrinkles that I hadn't noticed before around the edges of her eyes. She'd just come from a karate class and her neck seemed particularly strong: veinous, ropy, almost the width of her head, like a football player. Around it were two thin silver chains, one beaded, one linked, and she had matching silver earrings climbing up the circumference of her right ear.

'Which guy?' I asked. I hadn't seen Jemma in about nine months, and I tried to remember which lifetime I was living the last time we'd talked. 'Not the flower one. That was recent.'

'No, I don't think I know about him,' she said. 'No, this one you weren't sure about. This one, he was really sweet but you were uncertain. You thought you would be better friends.'

That could describe just about every relationship lately, but I finally remembered who she was talking about. 'Oh, well that's *him*,' I said, pointing to Aidan's back. He was shaking a pan, seemingly engrossed, but I could tell from his body language that he was poised to listen in. 'We *are* very good

friends. He's my movie guy. We see lots of movies together.'
Aidan and I had been an odd coupling right from the very
start. On our first date, he gave me a romantic foot massage
and ended up breaking my toe, although I didn't know it at
the time. 'It's just a hairline fracture,' the doctor said, as we
stared at the X-ray two days later. He handed me one of those
very attractive orthopedic sandal shoes and said gravely, 'I
hope the massage was worth it.'

'Why aren't you still dating?' Jemma said, fingering an
earring.

'It just wasn't right,' I said lamely, dropping my voice. 'And
truthfully, I feel bad about it, because I don't think I was very
nice. He was right after that nasty lawyer, and I was smarting
a lot.' The truth was that I had begun treating him the same
way Sean had treated me, even beginning to utter the famous
'bolt-of-lightning' phrase until I caught myself. Aidan, to his
credit, hadn't resorted to hacking into my voice mail (at least
not that I was aware of) – which said a lot about him and not
very much about me. 'Luckily we seem to have segued into a
comfortable place. God! That seems like a really long time
ago.'

'Well, I haven't *seen* you in a long time, have I darling?'
Jemma reached across and put her hand on mine, a surprisingly warm gesture for her. 'I was so glad when I got your
message. I get in these periods where I don't see people, and
then I think, "What is *wrong* with me?" I don't stay in touch –
well, like I should.' She took a giant swig from her water glass
as the waitress clomped up in platform combat boots and
braided pigtails. 'Oh! Let's see. Do I want wine on a Saturday
afternoon? Will you be drinking?'

'God, you really haven't seen me in a long time,' I said.

'I gather that's a yes. Well, all right then. I'll drink if you
are.' She fussed around with the wine list until I finally selected
a bottle and the waitress clomped off again.

'So,' Jemma said, after a pause.

'So,' I repeated.

'I heard you ran into James at a party last month,' she said.

'Yes.' I felt myself lurch into nervous, chattering mode. 'I went with my gay friend Tristan. I'm convinced that gay men are absolutely the only men one should bring to a Valentine's event.' Jemma had put on her sunglasses and was now removing them, wiping the lenses with the corner of her t-shirt.

I continued, 'I, ah – I was happy to hear that you two are still close, even though the divorce is going through. It is going through, right?'

'Yes,' she said, looking out the window at the panhandlers sunning themselves against the parked cars. She squinted and rubbed one of her gray-green eyes, the color of a faded dollar bill. 'If it were up to me, it would not be that way, but there you are.' Jemma had a brisk way of enunciating things, a sunny sort of determinism, which I attributed to her being English. 'What else did James tell you?' she asked softly. 'I sometimes worry with him, since he's so open . . . things come out, people misunderstand.'

I nodded. 'He, um – well. Yes. He told me.'

She looked at me levelly. 'You know about me, then?'

'Yes,' I said. 'I'd like to hear it from you though.'

Jemma had just moved to America with her husband James when I met her three years ago. She had a heavy Manchester accent which was difficult to understand at first, but gradually began to fade away as each month went by. I'd see her at the basketball games and we'd sit on the bleachers, occasionally watching and giving a half-hearted shout here and there, but mostly we'd just chat. She had long, straight hair that she'd wear in a rope-like braid that traveled down the length of her back, and she'd twist it in and around her long delicate fingers with distracted nervousness.

Initially, like most British people I'd observed, she was

friendly but not overly so; conversational but watchful too. I knew she was overwhelmed by all this buoyant Americanism – the talky, immediately intimate tête-à-têtes among the women, and the fun yet competitive spirit among the men. I had enough English friends to know she thought us all a bit strange, and yet – again, like many Britons – she and her husband were avid Americaphiles. Even before they emigrated to America, while living in London, they thrived on American pop culture; they bought *People* magazine for the equivalent of $8 an issue, listened to Bruce Springsteen and Nirvana, watched American football on television, played on intramural softball teams, knew all about *The Brady Bunch* and *The Partridge Family*, *Lost in Space* and more recently, *The X-Files*. Usually these ex-pats were all excruciatingly hip.

'Maybe you know some of my best friends who live in London,' I said, then felt embarrassed at how parochial I sounded.

But Jemma acted as if that were a perfectly reasonable assumption. 'Where do they live?' she said with interest. 'Maybe I do.'

As it turned out, she did in fact know a group of people who knew my friends Mary and Jayne, although she personally had never met them. She was somewhat of a loner, she said, and didn't like to go to parties or large group events. 'That lot has a very active social life,' she told me. 'I wouldn't be able to keep up with them if I wanted to.'

'I know,' I said, thinking of the BritChix friends who, if they lived on this side of the Atlantic, would be known as die-hard party girls. I wanted Jemma to like me – I liked her dreaminess, her self-effacing humor, her way of describing situations with precise language and gestures. She was new blood, and I was curious, particularly about how she could have such a seemingly devoted marriage, with her husband looking at her adoringly, and she laughing at his jokes as if she'd heard them the first time. I didn't have many friends who were married, and Jemma and James were a shock.

Even after ten years of being together, they were nearly inseparable, much to the awe of the women in our clique. Like many finely matched couples they had grown into looking like one another, using the same language and facial expressions, so much so it was hard to define where one individual stopped and the other began. And Jemma on her own was strong and quietly funny, someone that I naturally gravitated toward.

But though she was always friendly, always open to invitations, there was something not quite there – some kind of distance in her eyes, a sense I got that she was forcing herself to socialize. My phone calls would go unreturned, or emergencies would pop up at the last minute if we'd made plans, or conversation would dwindle even though we had more than enough in common – more in fact, than I had with many of my American friends. I put it down to her simply not trusting me yet, and the rare times she did commit to a plan, I was surprised and pleased.

Later I realized that what I'd thought was suspicion was in fact sadness; that evasiveness of hers covered up a certain despair with her situation. Jemma was precisely my age at that time – twenty-nine – and she had no idea what she wanted to do with her life. Her twenty-something drift was exacerbated by the fact that she couldn't work here legally, and James – normally so supportive – was stressed and busy, struggling to get his furniture design business going.

They'd wanted to move to America for such a long time. Now they were here, they had a lovely apartment, two beautiful cats, a potential network of friends and both of them were depressed. 'I can remember lying on the sofa, watching television and him working on the computer, and it was two very separate people, two different relationships going on,' she told me later.

I remember thinking at the time that all Jemma needed was a green card, but if I'd known her better, I'd have seen that her inertia – like most inertia – was based on something more profound. In the meantime, she did volunteer foster-care for newborn kittens for the SPCA – teaching the helpless furry squirming objects to use a litter pan, to eat dry food, to live without a mother. She'd keep the cats for two to four weeks, and just when they started to get little personalities and the cute kitten mannerisms, she brought them back to the shelter so they could be immediately adopted. She was good at babysitting these little cats, taking care of them, seeing that they never went without.

A neighbor told her that a friend needed a nanny. Would Jemma be interested? It wasn't really what Jemma had had in mind when she moved with James to this foreign country, but she was hardly in a position to turn it down. While James had always paid the bills in the five years since their marriage, she felt guilty having no job, with watching kittens and playing around on James' new computer to fill her day.

The family had a newborn and a toddler, and at the interview the toddler immediately took to Jemma, clambering up on her lap as if she were a piece of playground equipment. Jemma liked children – they were not that dissimilar from the kittens at this age – and she took the part-time job gratefully. The pay was $8 an hour, twelve hour shifts for three days a week. The family was pleasant and very nice to her, and they explained that they had very firm rules for the children concerning toilet training, naps, playtime, snacks, and dis-cipline. There was no guesswork involved, which appealed to Jemma's sense of order and balance. In her experience, children and pets thrived under a system of boundaries and limits – it felt safe to them, predictable. Jemma liked rules. And after a few months of nannying, it was as if she had never been meant to do anything else.

It was around this time that a group of us went over to James and Jemma's house after a basketball game. They lived in a spacious apartment in the sleepy and residential Richmond District – because they were technology junkies, it was filled with matt black stereo equipment, speakers, TV, VCR, cameras, as well as a huge computer that took up a corner of their living room. Jemma had told me at the basketball game about all the fun she'd been having playing on this new thing called the Internet – one could go 'on-line,' and meet people over the world in these little 'rooms,' and 'talk' back and forth 'in real time.'

'What do you write about to these people?' I asked.

'Oh, loads of things,' she said lightly. 'I've made lots of friends. You can send pictures to each other, or just talk.'

'Do you and James both do it?' I envisioned this to be like a party game, not unlike Trivial Pursuits or Twister, which one would play and play until they were so sick of it they'd stuff it in a closet and never think about it again.

'Just me. James doesn't like the computer very much.' She looked down at her hands and spread her fingers wide. I'd already heard a rumor to this effect – that she spent all her free time on the computer, completely engrossed, when she wasn't at the nanny job, and that it was starting to drive James a little crazy.

At the computer, a few of us stood in a circle and watched Jemma 'sign on,' then 'enter' a 'room,' and begin to type greetings and how-are-yous to individuals with mysterious monikers such as 'MasterMan,' 'Speed Racer,' 'KittenX' and 'SamIAm.'

'What are you called?' I asked.

'Jex.' She was typing a reply to MasterMan who'd wanted to know who else was with her, telling him that no, there were no saucy maidens that wanted to say hello.

'Weird,' I said, baffled. The others drifted away to inspect James' extensive CD collection, while Jemma typed some more quips and finally said goodbye to her 'friends.' 'Do you want to see something?' she asked me. 'A picture that was sent to me?'

'Sure,' I said.

She turned to the computer again, opening files, clicking away, until she said, 'Okay. This takes a long time to download.' We stood watching, as the blurred screen began to clarify and sharpen, like a photograph floating underwater, creeping up to the surface. It was a picture of a woman on all fours, in a patent leather corset and thigh-high stiletto boots, with a magnum champagne bottle shoved three-quarters of the way up into her ass. 'You know, I've been meaning to find a good use for all those empty bottles lying around my apartment,' I said brightly. Jemma began to laugh, and I did too, as James and my boyfriend looked at us from across the room, unable to see the image on the monitor.

Some time after that, Jemma dropped out of our social circle abruptly and without reason. We all knew she'd been having problems with James, and that they'd agreed to an amicable separation. It was so amicable, in fact, that James and Jemma continued to live together, and carry on various sexual liaisons and relationships with others all under the same roof, with the full knowledge of the other.

But what usually happens in this type of arrangement happened very quickly. In this case it was James who was the reluctant one, who had gone along with the open marriage idea in a last ditch effort to hold on to Jemma. We felt bad for James, that ideal husband, that industry standard of a mate. Jemma, on the other hand, was more restless. She still hadn't figured out what she wanted to do with her life – she wanted to write, to teach, to do something useful. They'd been a couple since she was eighteen.

I'd hear bits and pieces about their dissolution. James had finally moved out, citing Jemma's 'addiction to the Internet' as a source of their unhappiness. She'd been having an affair with a married guy (also in an open marriage) that she'd met in a chat room, and 'the whole thing became too strange, even for me,' James told me at the Valentine's Day party.

Now I said to Jemma as she cautiously sipped her wine, 'I think that night you showed me the picture of the champagne bottle up the woman's butt may have been the last time I saw you.'

'You might be right,' Jemma said thoughtfully. 'That seems like quite a long time ago.' She was picking the cat-food-like pieces of anchovy out of her salad, patiently making a pile on the side of her plate.

'Why don't you ask Aidan to make you another salad?' I asked.

'Oh, no,' she said. 'It's not a bother, not so much.' She finally gave up and started to eat around the anchovy-infected lettuce. She had her sunglasses on top of her head and looked thoughtful – and edgier, older, and more self-confident than I'd remembered. She'd lost that dreaminess, that sleepy expression which had pulled down the outer edges of her eyes.

'So how did James tell you about me?' Jemma asked suddenly.

How to put it? 'Well, he told me that you'd gotten very into being a submissive love slave for this guy,' I said brightly, 'and that he couldn't give you what you wanted now.'

Jemma chewed and swallowed, and carefully placed her knife and fork across one another on her plate. 'Yes,' she said finally. 'Yes, that's true.'

I fidgeted. 'It is? I mean, really?'

She looked at me levelly. 'I'm a submissive. As opposed to what you would call a dominatrix. I don't do it for money, I do it for myself. I have a master. I am his property, his slave, his slut – whatever you want to call it. It's completely consensual, it's absolutely what I want and need in my life. It started out more complicated than that, but that is essentially it. James is not into that world, never has been and never could be. It's not fair to expect him to be something he's not.' She picked up her knife and fork again and began to eat with renewed vigor.

'Well,' I said, feeling like Little Miss Muffet. 'I suppose I could understand that.'

'Is sex important to you?' Jemma asked.

'Well, sure.' I looked over at Aidan again. He was stirring something and I watched as he looked around, then stuck his finger in a sauté pan and tasted it. He threw in a handful of kosher salt and I waved to him, hoping he wouldn't interpret it as an invitation to come over and join in the conversation.

'Sex is very, very important to me,' Jemma said, sounding like she'd memorized a prepared text. 'It's not a matter of preferring a position, or ... or wanting to try something different. This is a whole way of life, and once you go down this road, you can't go back to the vanilla world. I know you don't understand what I'm talking about, so I'll try to be basic for now.'

'Okay,' I said, feeling like I was being advised on how to fill out a knotty tax form. 'I appreciate that.'

'Maybe you could ask me questions and I could answer them. Would that be easier?'

'Sure.' Good Lord. First Marie's arrangement, and now this. That old phrase 'whatever works' drifted in my head, but how could a woman in this day and age possibly choose to be submissive to their mate? Well, at least there wouldn't be any of those pesky issues about who had the upper hand. 'But, Jemma, you don't have to tell me this,' I said, even though I was wildly curious. Jemma, for her part, didn't look a bit embarrassed. 'You don't have to talk about it if you don't want to. You're still the same person to me.'

'But I'm not the same person,' she said patiently. She took her sunglasses off her head and looked at her reflection in the lenses. 'I want to explain it to you. To tell you the truth, it would be somewhat of a relief to talk to somebody about it. It's like living a secret life – no, it *is* living a secret life. It's what I imagine being gay is like, except that being gay is for the most part fairly acceptable. But how do you tell your friends that you're a submissive? That you go to sex clubs and play with your master and that he whips and flogs you, and that you love him for it? How do you tell your mother that you're good at doing this – that it's the first thing in your life that you feel truly good doing? That at the sex club, people who watch come up to you afterward and say it was the most intense thing they'd ever seen?'

I sat back in my stool. 'I don't know. I'm sure I don't have an answer to that.' I thought about how, at age thirty-one, I could barely discuss my method of birth control with my liberal California mom without averting my eyes. 'So – is, is your, um, master – is he like, your boyfriend?'

'Yes. We've been together for a while now.'

'And – well, is it always this situation about being a submissive? Do you wait on him? Or is it only in sex? Or at the sex club?' A vision of Julian popped in my head, lying on his back, waiting for me to ravish him.

'It's all the time,' Jemma said. 'I belong to him. I have a collar with my name on it. He can see whomever he wants, but I belong only to him. That's part of the rules.'

'Oh,' I said. 'You have rules?'

'Well, you have to. Otherwise it screws with your head – with us, there are no mind fucks. He has a certain responsibility to not fuck with the power he has—'

'But isn't it a mind fuck that he can see whomever he wants and you can't?' I interrupted.

Jemma sighed patiently. 'You work up to certain things that both of you agree on. Actually, a lot of things I've offered over to him, so I've said to him that I don't want to fuck any other guys. It would be a mind fuck if he didn't tell me that he had another submissive. But I know, and I've agreed to that arrangement. We give and take on both sides.'

'What does he give?' I said, probably a little more belligerently than I'd intended. There was a long pause, until

Jemma finally said, 'Well, that's a good question. But that's assuming it's an equal relationship in that way, and it's not.'

I pushed my plate to one side. 'And that's okay to you.' Jemma nodded matter-of-factly. I continued, '*Why* is it okay to you?'

'Because he provides me with the lifestyle that I want to live. No one's relationship is absolutely equal on every level. Everyone compromises in one way or another.'

'But he doesn't,' I said.

Jemma gave a tiny shrug. 'Lucky man.' I didn't answer and she said again softly, 'Uh huh. Very lucky man.' Aidan suddenly appeared and handed us over a pizza laid with peachy-colored slices of smoked salmon and we fell silent.

'That looks beautiful,' Jemma said dutifully.

'Yes, it does,' I added. 'Thank you.'

'No problem,' Aidan said, before stealing a glance at Jemma. I'd made the mistake of telling him Jemma's story that morning on the phone and I could see that he was fascinated – albeit a little frightened of her. He waited, standing in his chef's whites, as we each slid a slice onto our bread plates.

'Anything else I can get you right now?' he asked, hanging around.

'No,' I said pointedly.

'That's crème fraîche in the middle,' he said. 'I hope you aren't dairy intolerant.' This was directed toward Jemma, since he knew very well I ate anything and everything.

'No, not at all,' said Jemma, pleased. 'Thank you so much, Aidan.'

I gave him a significant look and he backed away. 'Uh, how do you two have a fight?' I asked lightly as I poured her some more wine. 'Or, I guess you don't fight, since um . . . by definition he's always right?'

'We had a fight just the other day, as a matter of fact.'

'Really.' I sorted through the questions in my head like a pile of dirty laundry, finally settling on, 'What was the fight about?'

'Oh, that one? No idea. I can't remember.'

'But—' I stumbled. 'Uh, those kinds of things – I'm confused. How can you really have a fight with your, um, master?'

'Well, we can,' Jemma said vigorously. 'You have fights in your own little way, whereby—'

'But if the rules are so prescribed—'

'But I don't accept everything per se with a smile on my face and a twinkle in my eye,' she explained. I felt cautiously relieved. 'I mean, certain things happen, and I can get upset. And he knows when I'm upset because I'm very bad at covering it up. He asks me and I tell him, and we start the discussion *again*. The discussion that goes, "I love you, you're number one—" '

This was starting to sound like more familiar couple-territory. 'So, the fights are basically about the same thing.' Other women, clearly.

'They tend to be about the same thing, yes,' Jemma allowed.

'That . . . that he's not paying enough attention to you?'

She hesitated. 'It can be that, yeah. Or if I feel insecure, or . . . I mean, there have been a few occasions where I have actually, *literally* done something wrong. Something against those rules we were talking about.'

What about *him*, I wanted to ask. Doesn't he do wrong things, or was it written in the rules that anything he did was by its very nature okay?

Jemma continued, 'I can occasionally step over the line. I know the line when we play, and we make jokes, and we can make fun of each other to an extent, but there's a line. And sometimes I cross it. Now, let me ask *you* a question: how do you punish a masochist?'

I considered a moment, then said 'Well, I have no idea.' Jemma chuckled and some of my internal ice cubes started to melt. 'That's the same kind of question as, what do you mean you had a fight? Okay, I'll bite – how do you punish a masochist?'

'You ignore them,' she replied. 'Now, things that require a discussion — emotional things, perhaps, like he's done something I haven't understood, or I need reassurance or something like that, we have the discussion and then we get over it. But things that involve some sort of punishment for me, where I've overstepped the line—'

'Like how?' I persisted. The pizza was being completely ignored at this point.

'Like . . .' Jemma thought for a moment. 'Like when I've made a joke at his expense. He hates that. As I said, we can joke to a certain extent but sometimes I get carried away.'

So her master was the sensitive type. Would wonders never cease. 'Go on.'

'Well, most people will punish a masochist by hitting them. Kind of pointless, because I enjoy that. But the way you punish a masochist is you don't hit them. There's only been one time, but he said, "I'm not going to see you for a week, and this is your punishment." He called me on the phone, and we sent e-mail, but he would not come and see me and I wasn't allowed to go and see him.'

It sounded like an adult time out. 'What was that like for you?'

'Pretty horrible,' she admitted. 'But I knew it would end.'

'You did?'

'Absolutely,' she said. 'He also knows that I'm a lot harder on myself than he would ever be. If I do something wrong, I will beat myself up about it, far more than—'

'And love it?'

'No, hate it.'

'I'm just kidding,' I said. 'The opportunity presented itself, and I had to say it.'

'I understand,' she said, and looked amused. 'Okay, along the lines of silly little lines that we say to each other? We'll be joking and joking and joking, and I might go a little too far, and his response will be, "Don't make me not come over there."'

I was silent.

'Hello?' Jemma said after a moment.

'I'm listening,' I said.

'And Courtney falls apart laughing about that,' Jemma said.

'Well, give me time,' I said, 'Jemma, just to play devil's advocate here – someone from the outside would say—'

'Oh, I think everyone from the outside would look at it and say it's wrong,' she interrupted cheerfully, as she cut a piece of pizza with her knife and fork. 'But it's not wrong for me – I *like* the giving over of myself. I *enjoy* it. It makes me feel really good, and it's so much deeper than you, or anyone, I guess, would make it out to be.'

I tried to envision this master, and I couldn't come up with any image at all. 'So he actually sleeps with other women?'

'He has sex with one other woman – Antonia,' Jemma said carefully. 'He can play with other women, but he only has sex with her or me. So Antonia's his other submissive, although their's is a bit more complicated, since she's not collared all the time. I suppose they would have a more, um, equal relationship outside of the sexual realm. I don't really know, to tell you the truth, because it's not my business.'

I said, 'Does it bother you that he has another girlfriend?'

Jemma smiled at me. 'I'm getting better than I used to be.'

I felt simultaneously like Jemma's mother and her little sister in my questions. 'Does he, um, have a name?'

'He does have a name,' said Jemma, smiling again at my discomfiture, 'but I call him Sir.' Seeing the look on my face, she added, 'Feel free to laugh at any time.'

After two hours, the Saturday lunch crowd had now moved on, and the late lunch/early dinner bunch had started to drift in. Some were doing what Marco called the 'Walk of Shame' – slinking in with the same clothes they'd worn Friday night, before they'd gone home with someone. I glanced at Aidan affectionately. Every once in a while, he would drift over, try to talk to us, get embarrassed when he remembered that Jemma was a sex slave, and then flee back to his position by the stove.

Jemma lifted the lid of the teapot and peered in. 'Bloody American tea.'

'Are you still nannying?' I asked. What must her employers think of her? She was so startlingly . . . *normal* from the outside. Jerry Springer, here we come. 'Do they know about you?'

'About all this?' She waved her hand up and down her body, and I wondered if she was perhaps wearing a bondage outfit or some other leather contraption underneath her sweatpants and San Francisco Half Marathon t-shirt. 'No. That wouldn't be appropriate.'

'I guess not. Your mom?'

'No. Although I did send her a picture of me in my leather corset and stilettoes when we were at the Folsom Street Fair last year. I was polishing Sir's bike. What she didn't see was that he was standing above me with a fifteen-foot bull whip in his hand.' She giggled.

I gulped the last of my wine. 'And you don't think she knows?'

'Don't think so,' Jemma mused. 'She wouldn't put it all together.'

'Why did you send her that picture, then?'

'Because I look good,' she said simply. 'I was on the cover of the gay newspaper. It's a great picture.' I imagined a little old lady with white hair living in her council flat in a Manchester suburb, opening a stiff manila envelope marked PHOTOGRAPHS – DO NOT BEND that she'd just received from her daughter in America. She'd be overjoyed, lifting up the flap, sliding the photograph out, expecting a studio portrait of a smiling Jemma with her ropey braid . . .

'That must be odd, being a nanny,' I suddenly said. 'Watching over little ones, telling them what to do all day and then – um—'

'Having a master at night?' She laughed. 'I know. I think about that.' She poured some tea in her cup and touched a fingertip to the honey-colored surface. 'You need to understand that this is something that I absolutely want. That it is completely consensual. That Sir would never do things to me that I didn't want, that we didn't agree on beforehand, that I have free will and could walk away at any time.'

'Are you ever a dominatrix?' I asked. 'That seems a lot more . . . *reasonable* to me, although I can't imagine why.'

'Not interested,' she said, taking a sip of her tea. 'In fact, if someone ever acts submissive to me, I *hate* it. I can't stand it, I have to get away.'

'Now that's interesting,' I said. 'A lot of men, or the ones I meet anyway, seem to really like it when I wear the pants in the family. In fact, I would go so far as to say it's a universal trend – although I have to say it doesn't turn me on in the least.' Jemma shuddered. 'Now, why would I be more comfortable if you were a dominatrix?'

Jemma immediately answered, 'For one thing, it's much more culturally ubiquitous – look around and you see references to being dominated by a woman all the time: in ads, on TV, in movies.'

'Why is that?'

'Because you can laugh at it. It amuses people to think of men being on a leash, to be spanked, or whatever. To think of men being in a mummy/child relationship. It doesn't tend to amuse people to think of women being in that situation.' She was looking at me intently, trying to read my reaction. 'I want to say that it's more scary – not that this is in any way scary to me – because people are much more likely to see a woman in a submissive position being abused.'

'Have you seen that?' I squeaked.

'Well, it happens.' She took another sip of her tea. 'You see women follow men around at a party and get their drinks for them – *do this, do that*, and it's probably not consensual at all.

It's probably that he's emotionally beaten her down into that situation.'

'But that's not you.'

'No, that's not me,' she smiled. 'But think if the positions were reversed – if the man was running around fetching drinks, doing this and that for his mistress. He'd say, "I'm pussywhipped!" and people would think it funny.'

I shifted in my seat. 'Along with finding it pathetic.'

I drank the last drop of wine left in the bottle as I watched the panhandlers outside. Maybe what Jemma was embracing was in some ways revolutionary – albeit in a very retro way. It certainly turned all my ideas of political correctness and male/ female control on its head. As I practically licked the inside of my wine glass, Jemma chattered away, saying as she added more milk to her tea, that 'female submissives are at the top of the pyramid – we represent the smallest numbers, and we're the most sought after. At the bottom of the pyramid are the submissive men; there are lots of those.'

I gulped. 'Maybe it's a Keynesian issue of supply-and-demand. If there are so many males looking for a mommy/ torturer, then I guess dominatrixes saturate the market.' Jemma shrugged and said, 'Don't refer to it as torture, please. That implies no mutual consent.' I hastily apologized, and thus didn't extend the logic of the argument: that if there were so few submissives out there, as she said, maybe that was because they were (thankfully) just not needed. I also didn't add that the whole female dominatrix thing bored me silly – what with all the films, articles, books and appearances on 'Jenny Jones' so rampant.

What I *did* say was, 'Um, believe me when I tell you that I understand about wanting a man to have a little aggression when it comes to sex,' I murmured, thinking of Sean. 'But—' *What kind of man gets off on hurting women?*

Jemma watched me struggle. She nodded, looking at me intently. 'You don't quite get it yet, which is understandable.

It's not really as simple as that. If I weren't enjoying it, he wouldn't enjoy it. And he wouldn't do it. D'you see what I mean?'

'Yes, but—' Jemma was as much of a feminist as any of my other friends, as much as an upper-middle-class, educated liberal white woman would be. She studied English at university. She followed politics. She read newspapers. As a Briton living in America, she wore t-shirts saying 'TAXATION WITHOUT REPRESENTATION – WHAT'S UP WITH THAT?'

I wondered if she had gone off the deep end. She looked like the Jemma that I knew, maybe a little more frayed around the edges. She sipped her tea and wasn't frothing at the mouth or ranting. She still had the same gentleness, that quiet intensity that had attracted me to her in the first place. If anything, she was less wary, which made her even more attractive. She spoke softly, rationally, and – if one were to really analyze it – with more confidence than I'd ever heard. She actually seemed . . . *happy*, if in a resigned sort of way.

'You should come and see us play,' Jemma offered. 'I'll ask Sir, but I think it will be fine. Have you ever been to the Power Exchange?'

'No.' A huge, monolithic building located in that no-man's land underneath where the freeways crossed and diverged. The doorways, of which there were several, were lit with red lightbulbs – I'd seen it driving past, and it was every bit as scary-looking as it intended to be. 'I know where it is, though. Is that place legal?'

'Power Exchange? Oh yes – it's the only straight sex club in California. Everything's pretty tightly controlled. No alcohol. No touching someone unless they want to be touched. Condoms all the time. They don't want any cum anywhere, going anywhere near anyone. Those are the rules.'

'Well, that's good.' Everything was coming out more Miss Muffetty than the last.

'We go most weekend nights. Sometimes to Bondage a Go Go.' She looked at her watch. 'You know, I should go call him. We're going there tonight—'

'To Bondage a Go Go?' I yelped. Bondage a Go Go was a South of Market club that even I knew about. It had a vaguely punk/fetish/Goth theme, and eighteen-year-olds went there to stand around and look outrageous. 'I thought that was for, well, amateurs.'

'Not if you're a player, no,' she said. 'It has a small roped-off area, and you don't have to know what you're doing to go in there, but the audience is going to know that you don't know what you're doing.'

'Oh,' I said, trying to envision this. 'Is, um, Antonia going to be there?'

'I think so,' said Jemma stiffly. 'Probably.'

I peered into the empty wine bottle like it was a spy glass, and then set it down. 'Will that be difficult for you?'

She looked at the bottle, considering. 'It might be. She'll watch him play with me, but I won't— I'm not happy watching him play with anyone. I still find that difficult.' She said this as if she were embarrassed.

'What will you do instead?' I asked.

'I'll wander off. With permission.' She looked in her change purse, fishing around for a quarter and a dime. 'I'm getting better. I didn't used to be – I didn't use to be able to deal with it at all but I'm getting a lot better.'

'A lot better at what?'

'At being around him when he's paying attention to other people. Because I have this fear of being replaced.'

That sounded so California-ish, so pop-psychologyish, coming from Jemma's polite British mouth that even I had to smile, horrified though I was. 'Well, the phone is around the corner, there.' I gestured with my wine glass.

'Is that all right?' Jemma asked.

'Is what all right?' I said. 'Making a phone call?'

'Of course,' she said, jumping down off her stool. 'Sorry. That's the problem with being a submissive. I'm not supposed to be that way with anyone else, but I find myself doing things that I shouldn't be doing.'

'Well, don't worry about it,' I said, wondering where all this guilt was coming from.

She stood there, looking at me. 'Go, go,' I pushed her softly, feeling like a mother hen to a chick.

'Okay. But I think it might be good if you came to watch. Maybe next weekend. I'll ask. Oh, and there's a woman you'll meet on Saturday as well, whom we take to the Power Exchange. I'll have to double-check with her to see if it's okay. I'm sure it will be.'

'Is this Antonia?'

'No,' said Jemma, as a dark cloud passed over her face. 'This is someone that he plays with maybe every two, three weeks. He'll do scenes with her, and uh, she and I will have sex, but he won't have sex with her. Her name is Ellen.'

'Do you like this person?' I asked as Aidan approached and stood across from us with his hands on his hips.

'She's fine. She's just one of his other submissives,' Jemma said matter-of-factly. She smiled at Aidan. 'The one that comes and plays with us occasionally, the one I have sex with. That's not her real name, by the way. That's the name that she goes by in the club. She's a little freaked out that her real identity might get found out.'

I can imagine, I thought – especially with the likes of me hanging around. And 'Ellen' seemed like such a bland, boring name for a pseudonym. Why not Fifi or TrixieBell or Xanadu? 'How did she come up with, um, "Ellen"?'

'I have no idea,' she said, as Aidan pretended to examine a speck of parsley on his lapel. 'Actually, she's a therapist. That's the only thing I really know about her.'

'A therapist,' I repeated. Then to Aidan, I said, 'We'll be leaving right now. I know the waitress wants us to get out.'

Aidan waved his hand. 'Oh, take your time,' he squeaked.

I said to Jemma as she began to walk to the phone, 'What do you mean, *scenes*?'

'S/M scenes,' Jemma said, sotto voce.

'Are you acting in this?' I called.

'No, it's just called a scene,' she called back. 'I wouldn't want you to get freaked out though. Do you think you would?'

'No,' I said, thinking *yes*. I didn't look at Aidan.

'Maybe next Saturday. Next week. I'll ask Sir right now.' Aidan and I both smiled gamely, and watched as she moved away. She had said things like this to me in the past, when I knew her as the old Jemma, and somehow the plans had always fallen apart, or she'd never call. I had a feeling this time it would be different.

'I don't get it,' Aidan was saying as we settled into our seats before *In the Company of Men* began. 'She *seems* to be a nice girl. Why on earth is she doing this?'

It was two hours later and I'd hung around after Jemma had left Elroy's (having been told to go home and prepare for Sir's arrival), waiting for Aidan to get off work. I'd tried to read a day-old *Wall Street Journal* that had been left lying on the bar, but I couldn't concentrate, and sat gazing out of the large plate-glass windows. Now I felt like I could take a nap right in the movie seat.

I yawned and began laughing, in spite of feeling a bit depressed. 'What was it that your granny said when she found out your best friend was a Protestant?'

'Oh,' Aidan said, and downshifted into a strong North Dublin accent. ' "*Is* he now? You'd just never know to look at him." ' I laughed on cue and we fell silent. 'Was she abused?' Aidan asked suddenly. 'Hit as a child? Molested? What?'

'No.' I'd asked Jemma basically the same thing, albeit in more cagey terms. 'She said she'd never been hit as a child. Never even spanked. She said her parents were disgustingly middle-class liberals, and before they got divorced, they'd never had any hang-ups talking about sex or intimacies or relationships.'

'Divorced?' Aidan held a dark view of divorce, despite his protestations to the contrary. He'd resided in America for the last five years, but there were some things he still couldn't get used to – like all the splintered families, and the way American mothers and children fought and were rude to each other. He felt guilty for the kind, happy relationship he had with his Irish mum and dad, thinking it made him look parochial. 'Does her dad know about all this . . . this . . .?' he said, waving his hand in the air.

'She doesn't have any relationship with her father, Dr Freud.' I leaned over and took a handful of popcorn from the giant bucket sitting between his thighs. 'She said, "I try to stay very far away from thinking about Sir as any kind of father figure, because it's not anything I want to find out." ' Aidan nodded gravely. 'She also added,' I continued, warming up, 'that she'd had her first submissive fantasy when she was seven years old—'

'Seven!' Aidan cried.

'And that it didn't have anything to do with a daddy, or a paternal figure in a sexual context. It had something to do about being made to do a dance for pirates – probably based on all those Errol Flynn movies that her mother used to watch on the BBC.'

'I used to watch those too,' said Aidan wistfully. 'But you don't see me wanting to a do a jig for a pirate.'

I picked a few snowy bits of popcorn off his sleeve. 'I'm just telling you what she said. It was a fantasy that made her feel safe. And wanted.' Aidan looked at me as if I'd suddenly started speaking in Urdu.

'Are you okay?' he asked gently. 'You seem a little – funny.'

'Funny . . . how?' I asked. 'Well, I'm hungry. I guess I'm a little creeped out by this. But – whatever works, right?'

Aidan shrugged. '*I* don't know,' he said. He turned to me and added with sincerity, 'Thank you for coming today. It was really nice to see you and meet um, um, what is her name again?'

'Jemma,' I said shortly. I ate another handful of popcorn and felt a stab of guilt. Aidan could be incredibly sweet. It really was too bad that he wasn't *the one*. 'Sorry. Thank you for giving us all that free food. I guess I don't really get it either. It's just – I'm trying to understand it and not be judgmental or harsh on her.'

'Well, that's okay,' he said, settling down in his chair. 'So when they do these things at the S/M club—'

'Scenes,' I interrupted.

'Okay, scenes. When they do this, is she all tied up and he's just flailing away at her?'

'I guess so,' I said. 'I don't know yet.'

'And – she enjoys this.'

'Apparently.'

'And they have a list of rules of what they can and cannot do.'

'Yes, sort of,' I said. 'Well, it's more what *she* can and cannot do. I guess in the beginning they established that neither one of them liked anything to do with pee or shit. And they don't do infantilism – where the submissive is a baby and is diapered and fed and gets spanked for being a bad baby, stuff like that.' Aidan looked horrified. 'I think basically he can do whatever he wants if she agrees beforehand, so there are no mind fucks, as she would say. And from what I can tell, she's going to agree to everything.'

'Why?' he asked weakly.

'Because she's in love with him,' I said simply. There was a little silence between us. 'She wants to do that for him. She says it gives her pleasure to not have responsibility in this area—'

'In which area?' Aidan croaked.

'All areas,' I conceded. 'It's an All-Access pass. Get this – she says, *Sir is not always right but he's never wrong.*'

Aidan was silent again, working that out. 'Now *that* sounds good to me.'

'I thought it might.'

'And does she – well – does she, um—' he hesitated.

I glanced over. 'You're going to ask me if she comes when she gets hit, right?'

'No!' he said defensively. I could see all of this was throwing him for an utter loop. Now he'd really have to reassess these wacky American values. Then again, Jemma was British – and her strange behavior might be viewed by an Irish person like Aidan as par for the course. 'But now that you mention it, does she?'

'She can only come by her own hand,' I said. He reddened a bit, which amused me, and I continued. 'Maybe don't look at it as a linear fucking act, you know, with a beginning, a middle and an end. Try to see it as more of a continuum, on a whole plane of sexuality.' Now I had lost him. I wasn't even sure what I meant by that psychobabble, but it sounded reasonable. He chewed some popcorn thoughtfully, gazing up at the blank screen. He looked at his watch and sighed.

'What?' I said.

'What? Oh, nothing.'

'Go ahead,' I waited. 'What were you thinking?'

'Well, I was just thinking about this time I was a teenager, in Artane,' he said. 'We were all at this disco, you know, like one of those school dances? And these two guys were drinking of course and got in a big fistfight. There was all this commotion with everyone screaming at them to stop, and then this girl got in the middle of the fight. And she ended up getting punched by one of 'em. Well, that was just the end of it. Everyone fell on that guy, absolutely kicking the living shite out of him, because in Ireland what you never, *ever* do is hit a woman. That is really the lowest of the low.' He glanced at his watch again. 'It just made me think of it.'

I slid down in my seat. 'It's not the same thing,' I said unconvincingly, as the lights began to dim.

'How was your lunch with Jemma?' Harriet asked me the next night in our evening check-in.

'It was fine,' I said neutrally. I wasn't sure how much I wanted to tell her. Harriet, though she was open-minded for the most part – she was my only friend who would discuss the trials and tribulations of anal sex in any great detail, for example – would never cotton to Jemma's proclivities. She had some strange Swiss cheese pockets of conservativism, like not abiding any displays of public nudity, and irrationally hating obese people.

'Where did you go?'

'That place where Aidan works. Free food, you know.' Harriet gave a little hiccup of approval.

'And are you feeling bad that you and Aidan aren't going out anymore?' Harriet asked, for the hundredth time. She really didn't understand this let's-just-be-friends thing at all, saying about her ex-lovers, 'I don't *do* friends.' She added, 'You sound kind of low.'

'No, I feel fine about Aidan,' I said sincerely. 'It's – oh, I don't know. Nothing.' I looked outside at the spring night, and the fog gliding down Hyde Street like a sleigh.

'So did she talk about why she's getting a divorce?' Harriet asked.

'Yes, she did.' I wiped a finger along a bookshelf in my living room and stared at the gray residue. 'Did you know that dust is actually human skin? And pet dander?'

'That's gross. Well, why is she?' This was typical of Harriet to be persistent about a subject like a failed marriage. She stored little soured coupling anecdotes and morals like nuts for the winter, little seeds of wisdom that she'd pull out of her sleeve at any given moment. I figured Harriet must have been good at algebra at one time, plugging numbers into formulas and getting a predictable answer, since she did about the same thing with relationships.

'It's complicated.' Not an answer Harriet would like. 'I have to find out more. The short answer is, she's a submissive sex slave and belongs to her master, a man nearly twenty years older than she is, whom she calls Sir. He has lots of sluts but she belongs only to him because that's what the rules are. And her husband James couldn't take it anymore.'

Harriet giggled. 'You are so funny.'

CHAPTER 4

I lurked around the phone that week, wondering if Jemma would call. The phone karma was not good – I noticed a long time ago that one either got many calls on a certain day, or none at all. If the phone had not rung by noon, one could be pretty much assured that it would remain silent for most of the afternoon.

But one person who was leaving regular messages was my mother, who began to sound more panicked as the week wore on. I hadn't exactly avoided talking to her – I just hadn't really gotten around to returning her calls. Plus, we'd had a marathon phone conversation on Sunday, covering all our normal topics: how much money I was spending, how much money she wasn't making, her long distance relationship with Andreas, a generic European, my lack of a significant relationship, US politics, my college-age sister's grades and an episode of *Crossfire*, a show my mother despised but felt compelled to watch.

My mother and I have always been very close but I used to talk to her more regularly when I lived in New York than now, when we live in the same city. Whether this is due to the blazing-hot San Francisco real estate market, of which she is a mover and shaker, or her increasing workaholism as she gets older, or a combination of the two, I'm not certain. But after a period of non-communication for no significant reason, one or the both of us realizes we haven't talked to each other and a series of messages begins to be volleyed back and forth.

Invariably, one (usually me) starts to panic if the messages aren't returned in a timely manner. I start in the morning: 'Just calling to see if you're up for a power walk' – my mother's preferred mode of exercise – 'but I guess I've already missed you. Give me a call.' An hour later: 'Okay, you haven't called back. Everything okay? Call me.' An hour after that: 'I tried your office. They say they haven't seen you since last night at ten, when you were faxing out counter-offers. That was a good twelve hours ago now, and no one's heard from you. Please call me.' Thirty minutes later: 'Call me. Call me. Are you lying dead in a ditch with blood coming out of the side of your mouth?' Fifteen minutes: 'I'm coming over there if you don't call me back within thirty minutes. Now I'm serious.'

Until finally, I get a fuzzy, distracted phone call from her, usually on her car phone, on the way to another real estate appointment: 'For heaven's sake, Courtney. I'm *fine*. Just busy with Pacific Avenue! I told you they found dry rot in the foundation and oh, it's a big mess, lawyers, the whole business—' And she's away on a monologue, at which point I turn off, real estate being about my least favorite subject of conversation, right after dental surgery and whether the Fed will raise interest rates.

My mother lives in a whirlwind of friends and work and chaos – a much busier life than mine, I'm sorry to say. Besides the overseas boyfriend, she has a huge, messy house which she rarely sees, in which resides the family Labrador and the No Name Cat and Conchetta, our housekeeper from San Salvador whom my mother can never bring herself to let go, despite there not being much for Conchetta to do. Papers lie in piles on her desk and in the front hall in her never-ending quest to 'get organized' – newspapers and bills and junk mail and invitations and magazines and receipts and circulars, all waiting for her attention. She lives in a frazzled state and seems to prefer it that way, despite lots of complaining to the contrary.

Now, however, it was her turn to get bitten by the paranoid

bug. 'Are you there?' went the first message from her on Thursday morning. 'Hello? Hello? Hello?' A flicker of irritation passed through me as I listened to her messages – she knew very well I had voice mail and was not standing there, screening her call, but she managed to forget this fact when it suited her. And the second: 'Courtney, pick up. It's your *mother*,' she enunciated in a self-mocking way. 'Hmmm. Where could you be on a Thursday at 10 a.m.? Well, call me. I'm in the car. After that I'll be at 2293 Broadway – the telephone number is um, seven-seven-one-oh-two-nine-two. If it's not seven-seven-one, then it's seven-seven-five. Try the first one first and—' She was cut off, having gone through a tunnel, probably. The third: 'Where are you? I'm getting a little concerned. Did you go out of town? Did you meet somebody? Call my office and leave a message please. I just get these horrible visions of you having slipped and fell, under a bookcase or something. Is your building bolted, by the way? You should tell your landlord . . .' And so on.

I dialled her office. 'Mom, it's me,' I said.

'Oh, good,' she said distractedly. I could hear her shuffling papers, and the fax machine whistling and chortling in the background. 'Where have you been?'

'To eat a toasted bagel at the Nob Hill Grille, if you must know,' I said. 'Where do you think I would be? I wouldn't just take off and not tell you.' Part of my annoyance stemmed from the unpredictable nature of these phone calls. Most of the time my mother would have as much knowledge about my whereabouts as any other mother of a thirtysomething – i.e., not much. And most of the time this seemed to suit her just fine, unless she got something stuck in her maternal, over-protective craw. How and why this occurred I couldn't figure out since it seemed to have no rhyme or reason, nor any history; as a young mom, she was the kind of parent that thought nothing of sending me and my friends down to the playground to run ourselves ragged for a few hours, while she talked on the phone or studied for her real estate exams. I suspected that some client had thrust a gurgling baby into her arms, or gloated about their pedigree border collie – something that had stimulated her maternal gland with a Pavlovian response of paranoia.

'Have you met a man?' she asked.

'What are you talking about?' I asked.

'Nothing,' she said, still rustling. 'I just had a feeling that maybe you'd met someone, which is why you weren't calling me back. That you were otherwise occupied.'

I sighed. 'No, Mrs Bennett. I'm sorry to disappoint you. And I *am* calling you back – you started this campaign of phone calls just this morning.' There was a silence, and I heard her punching some numbers into another phone. 'Mom? I'm going to go now – you sound pretty busy—'

'Courtney!'

'What?' I said, alarmed.

'You are going to get the best present!' She paused. 'But – I can't tell you what it is yet.'

'A present?' I automatically thought, Money? A tenancy-in-common? She sounded serious. 'What kind of present?'

'I can't – that is – I don't. I'm not sure . . .' She trailed off, and called to her secretary, 'Well, just tell him I'll fax over the counter-offer as soon as it comes through. No, wait, tell him to hold, I'll talk to him—'

'Mom!' I barked. This sort of disjointed conversation was all par for the course with my mother but now she'd gotten me piqued. 'Focus your ADD mind over here. What kind of present? Is this why you wanted to talk to me?'

'What? Oh, yes. I was going to maybe drive you over to it.'

Not money then. 'Well, tell me,' I said. 'You can't drop that little landmine and then not say what it is.'

'All right. But nothing's for sure yet. I met the most wonderful—' I started to groan inwardly; another man set-up! '—*bird*.'

I looked at the phone. 'A what?'

'A bird. A cockatiel, in fact.'

I sighed. 'Mom, what would I want with a bird? Besides, don't you remember? I have a cat.'

'This bird is used to cats,' she said. 'He likes them, in fact.'

'How do you know this?'

'I can tell. And he has a special, cat-proof cage. It's a wonderful cage, in fact. It'll look great in your apartment! Really, I can't wait.'

She was totally serious. 'Wait a minute. Why do I need a bird?'

'You like birds,' she said, somewhat accusingly. 'You're good with them. You have a rapport.'

'Mom! I was ten years old! Of course I had a rapport with my parakeet.'

'You had two parakeets, and remember how much they loved you? You'd open the door of the cage, and they'd fly right onto your shoulder. And you used to talk to them, and they'd coo back. Remember?'

'I remember,' I said, and then added suspiciously, 'Is this bird about to become homeless or something?'

'Well, yes,' she said. 'It's the Gilmore's bird.' This was starting to make more sense. My mother had been known to buy paintings, house errant children and purchase unworking kitchen appliances from clients if she thought it would clinch a real-estate deal. But this was the first time I'd been roped into one of her hare-brained little whims. 'He is a great bird, I'm telling you. I wouldn't make this up. And he's used to cats. He meows at them.'

'Great,' I said, not entirely happily. 'But my cat is not used to birds. Did you think about that?'

'They'll get along,' she said airily. 'I know they will.' This was my mother's style with all pets – throw them together and let them fight it out. I had to admit it had worked out with

Buddy the Lab and all our cats over the years, but this seemed a little different.

'What's the bird's name?' I asked curiously.

'His name—' she paused dramatically, '—is Zippy.'

'Zippy.' I felt myself relenting, in spite of myself. 'Well, let me think about it. I don't know how I feel about living in a menagerie.'

'One bird and one cat does not a menagerie make.'

'What if I want to go out of town? I'm already racked with guilt about the cat if I take a trip to the corner store. I can't imagine that, um, Zippy is any more self-sufficient than a cat.'

'Your cat happens to be particularly neurotic,' she pointed out rightly enough, 'and I can take care of Zippy if you go away. Who takes care of the cat now? A neighbor?'

'Aidan,' I said. 'I don't think I could saddle with him a bird too. He doesn't even like pets.'

I heard more bleating from the fax machine and she suddenly exclaimed, 'Oh, damn! I've left Frank hanging on the phone! Courtney, I have to go—'

'Goodbye,' I said quickly.

After I hung up, I immediately remembered that I was due to go to Los Angeles that very weekend. In the midst of all these Power Exchange plans, and now of Zippy, somehow I had conveniently forgotten that I was to meet Harriet in Hollywood on Saturday. She was flying out for work; I was going just to tag along. We'd already planned a few weeks ago to go to the Museum of Jurassic Technology, and to have drinks at Trader Vic's, as well as to tour the grave sites of Natalie Wood and Marilyn Monroe.

'Like a little company this weekend?' I asked Aidan on the phone hopefully.

I heard him turn down the TV which was blaring the Giants game. 'Sure!' he said enthusiastically. 'Are they spraying your apartment?'

'Well, no,' I said. 'It's not me. It's the cat.'

'Oh. Oh, sure. Bring her on over.' I heard the TV click back into action. 'Going somewhere this weekend, are we?'

'Just to L.A.' I said. 'To gang up with Harriet. She's flying there for some work stuff, and I'm going to get away from it all.' I was prying the cardboard cat box out of the closet, which had been shoved, somewhat crumpled now, under an old futon.

'Lucky you,' he said dryly. 'No Power Exchange this weekend then?'

'No. Sorry to disappoint.'

He was back in baseball mode and he said, distracted, 'I'll be home until three today. Then I'm going to work, so you better get her over here soon. Just leave the litter box and stuff. I'll set it up later.'

'Okay, Aidan,' I said. 'Thanks a lot. I know cats aren't your favorite animals.'

'I don't like any animals,' he said. 'We never had pets when I was growing up in Artane —'

'I know, I know.' I'd heard all this before. 'I'm sorry but I gotta go.'

'See you soon,' he said shortly, and hung up.

I dragged the cat out from under the bed by one arm, shoved her in the box before she could figure out exactly what was going on, threw her cat bowls in a plastic bag, dumped her litter box into a garbage bag, grabbed my keys and my wallet, and raced across the city to Aidan's.

'That was fast,' he said as he opened the door, relieving me of the yowling cat box and heavy plastic bag.

'How do you feel about birds?' I asked him hopefully.

Los Angeles in any other season but winter – could Harriet have picked a more uncomfortable destination? 'I always get this sense when I'm in LA that there's several hundred fabulous parties going on and I only see the remnants,' I said. I was driving our rental car, having coordinated our arrival times at LAX, heading westward – or so I thought, since neither one of us had bothered to pick up a map at the rental counter. 'You know how we go to Swingers Hollywood Diner, and see the stragglers in the morning, still looking fabulous in their make-up and dreadlocks and impossibly hip clothes? Listening to Morphine and Rasputina and these other bands on the jukebox at 8 a.m.? And there we are at the counter eating our scrambled eggs, trying to figure out how to get to the museums?'

'You feel that way because there *are* several hundreds of fabulous parties going on, of which we only see the remnants.' She adjusted her seat belt and looked at me. 'You know you say the same thing every time you come to New York, too.'

'Do I?' I glanced in the rear view mirror. A sea of cars was melting in the waves of heat of the freeway. 'Are you sure this is the right way to the Museum of Jurassic Technology?'

'I think so,' Harriet said, following the line of conversation which was by now extremely familiar. She leaned down to adjust the air conditioner, and a blast of heat suddenly exhaled through the Geo Metro. 'Ooops. It's always so funny to see you in person – I can never get used to it. To hear that voice, coming out of that body. It's just weird.'

'I know,' I said, trying to turn and appraise her. 'I think you look the same as before, when I saw you in New York six months ago. Maybe you're blonder now. And you seem – taller, or something.'

'Do I?' Harriet was six feet and she looked down at her long tan legs clad in their khaki Banana Republic shorts as if they were new appendages. 'Maybe I'm standing up straighter.'

'Maybe.' I too was surprised by Harriet's physical presence – it seemed to take us a while, maybe an hour or so, to get used to the other. There were things about her that I managed to always forget: her height for example, and the way she screwed up her eyes at the ceiling when she considered whether to tell a lie, or stretch the truth a little. 'Sometimes I close my eyes when you talk, so I can remember the phone Harriet. Do you ever do that?'

'Well, don't do that now,' she said, tightening her seatbelt, and fearfully eyeing the traffic in front of us as only someone who doesn't drive regularly can do. 'Um, no, I don't close my eyes. You look just the same to me.'

'Good,' I said, and aggressively moved over three lanes in traffic. 'Is this scaring you? Aidan calls it my guerilla driving technique.'

'No, not really,' she said, peering up at the top of the car. 'How is Aidan? Still having sex and pretending you're not a couple?'

'Everything's fine,' I said. 'He's fine. I'm fine. End of story. We're just friends.'

'But have you been seeing him a lot?' Harriet rolled down the window, and I resisted asking her to roll it back up. She fanned her face with the *New York Times*.

'A fair amount. Are you sure you don't want to go to the motel first?'

'I think we should stop and ask for directions,' Harriet said. 'I know you don't do that, but—'

'Oh, I'm sure we'll find it,' I said carelessly.

Three hours later, we looked at an old heavy work boot trimmed with lace that lay forlornly inside a case. 'It says that the bridegroom should leave one of his shoes untied when he gets married so he may deflower the virgin without any problems,' I said. 'What if she's not a virgin to begin with?'

'I know you may find this hard to believe,' responded Harriet in a low voice, 'but some people do wait.'

'I do find that hard to believe,' I said. 'Not that people wait, but that they're foolish enough to think that it's going to be better for the marriage.' That was another rule – something about not sleeping with him until the seventy-eighth date. We moved on to another little room that was filled to bursting with the decrepit memorabilia of a nineteenth-century opera singer neither one of us had ever heard of.

'Is that a pointed comment?' Harriet whispered as a couple moved past us. 'I'm not judging you for having sex with your ex. I don't think it's good, mind you, but whatever turns your crank.' She pretended to read the brochure intently.

'Only sometimes,' I said. 'Not every time.' Harriet nodded knowingly. 'Look at you, Little Miss Oh-Clark-Called-Me-the-Other-Day. It's only a matter of time before he comes slithering back into your life. And I bet I'll be the last to find out.'

'Things are going very well with Just Jerry,' she whispered. 'You know I wouldn't do that to him.'

'Sometimes you can't plan these things,' I said. We both considered a clock inside a case that had no hands. 'Haven't you *ever* had the transitional Sex with the Ex?' I whispered to her.

She studied a display featuring a faded corsage tucked around a pair of long velvet gloves. 'What do you mean transitional?'

'Why are we whispering?' I said loudly into the empty room. 'You know. The time after you decide to stop seeing one another. And you get together as friends but you still sleep together. Everyone I know does this. It helps the transition period.'

'Oh, really?' Harriet shook her head. 'No. I don't know how you can do that. Why don't you just take a knife and stab yourself in the stomach? When I stop seeing someone, I stop. None of this "friends" stuff. None of this Sex with the Ex. Clean breaks are the only way to do it.'

'Well, I like it,' I said firmly. 'While it lasts, it helps. Plus, they already know what you like and you know what they like. The rhythm's all there. You just have to provide the venue and inclination. And afterwards, you can get up and go home or kick them out and there's no bad feelings.'

'Yes, while it lasts,' Harriet said. 'You're talking about human feelings here. Not a cha-cha lesson.' We moved into another dark room. 'How long can this Sex with the Ex last, seriously?' she whispered in my ear.

I considered the empty case in front of me. 'Well, admittedly, it's a short-term arrangement.'

'But you've been going on and off with him for a long time. Months? Before Julian, anyway. That doesn't sound so short to me.'

I stood reading the catalogue in the dim light. 'Alcohol has something to do with it,' I said. 'It's not very often nowadays. Just – sometimes.'

'And you think it helps you get over each other? There never *was* anything to get over, from your point of view.' She shook her head again. 'Is he the one that has the special technique? Is lust driving all this?'

'Lust has a lot to do with it,' I said. 'If you can compartmentalize the sex, and try to leave the emotions out—'

'Like a man,' she interrupted.

'Okay, like a man, if you have to resort to clichés.' *Swirl, swirl, nibble, nibble, suck, suck.* It had been fun teaching Aidan the special technique, although, initially, I felt like a live model in a first-year gynecological exam in med school. I remembered thinking that charts and graphs would have been useful. 'The special technique is, I admit, a plus. By the way, isn't it funny that in this day and age, men still don't really understand what to do with clitorises? They know it's important, they know it should be paid attention to, but I think they're still flummoxed as to the precise directions for usage.' Harriet nodded in agreement. 'Sort of like us females when confronted with a pair of testicles,' I added.

'I'm *still* baffled by testicles,' Harriet said.

'I once read in this book,' I continued as we moved down a dimly lit corridor, 'that a woman tends to greet a man's balls as she would her country cousins if they showed up at her door unannounced. You recognize them, you're happy to see them, but you have no idea what to actually *do* with them.'

We entered a tiny room lit from behind a half wall with a 40-watt bulb. Harriet bent down and put her eye to a microscope. 'Look there,' she said. 'Little figurines inside the eye of a needle. Talk about special technique. So, how did your ex learn his nifty trick?'

'How do you think?' I asked, squinting one eye. 'I taught him. And that's another reason why Sex with the Ex can be preferable. You don't have to re-teach someone all over again.'

'I don't know,' Harriet said darkly. 'From all that you've told me, it seems you're in the wrong business. Maybe you should be an agent. Invest yourself into improving the sex lives of women everywhere – it's good feminism.'

'A pimp for girls,' I said thoughtfully. 'Hmmm. Come on, Harriet, I know you disapprove, but you must admit that transitional Sex with the Ex is no stranger than, say—' I waved my arm around the room, '—this curator's taste. Who's to say what's wrong or right? You do what works for you.'

'God, I knew there was a reason why this place would appeal to you,' she muttered. 'Next time, we're going to the nice conventional Getty Museum.'

Harriet had some clients to meet late in the afternoon, so we left the Museum soon afterwards and headed for Pink's, a semi-famous hot dog stand near our motel. 'Jodie Foster eats here,' Harriet told me importantly. 'I read it in *In Style*.' In the sweltering Geo, over fries and chili dogs and a bottle of warm champagne that she'd thoughtfully transported all the way from New York, she asked me, 'So what are you going to do while I'm at my meeting?'

'I brought some work with me,' I said, and patted my knapsack that was shoved under my legs. I took a swig of champagne out of the bottle – we couldn't persuade Pink's to give us any paper cups gratis, and Harriet had refused to pay as a matter of principle – and coughed a bit as the bubbles zoomed up my nose.

She took a bite of her chili cheese dog. A sizable plop of onions, chili, cheese and mustard landed on her paper napkin covering her lap, and she tried to ladle it back into the bun. 'I was invited to this party,' she said, distracted. 'I think it's a 70s party. We could go, but I'm not sure what it's going to be like.'

'A party!' I exclaimed. I couldn't believe she'd been sitting on this. 'As long as we have a map,' I said. 'Great. Let's go.' Either the champagne had exited my sinuses and traveled up to my brain, or all that talk about Sex with the Ex had gotten to me. I suddenly felt excited. Maybe I would actually attend one of these fabulous shindigs and not be relegated to observe remnants. Maybe I too would stay up all night, and drag myself in a Walk of Shame to Swingers Diner. The world was my oyster.

What is it about Los Angeles that lulls one into the mistaken belief that events that happen here don't 'count' as they would in real life?

That night around eleven, Harriet and I were zooming down Sunset Boulevard. I was starting to feel affection for this little car – its wisp of an air conditioning system, its wheeze as we rolled out of our motel parking lot.

I wiped my brow underneath my baseball cap. 'I love Los Angeles,' I said, and Harriet nodded happily. I gazed up at the billboards featuring a three-storey tall Warren Beatty. 'Nothing seems real. And I am going to say this here and now: I am looking for trouble tonight. Trouble will be my middle name. Just you wait.'

'Oh?' Harriet had heard me say things like this before when

I lived in New York, and usually enjoyed my 'wild hairs,' as she put it, when I made her accompany me to every old man bar in the East Village at 2 and 3 a.m. We'd been game in those days; I was twenty-six – a poor, know-it-all graduate student – and Harriet was usually reeling from some dizziness of Hurricane Clark. 'What kind of trouble?' she asked, looking at me sideways again, but also appearing a little frightened.

'I don't know,' I said airily. 'Danger. Intrigue. Sexual trouble. You know. Nothing serious.' I glanced at her. 'Oh, come on. What happens to you people when you get in these serious relationships? We used to look for trouble all the time in New York, remember?'

'Ye – es,' she said doubtfully. 'But we're older now. Besides, what about Aidan?'

'Will you stop that, please?' I waved at the throngs of rebel teenagers huddled around the street corners with their low-slung trousers and black baseball caps, feeling an affinity. I turned my own hat backwards too. 'Anyway, not really bad, bad trouble. Just mini-trouble. Like – you know, flirting. Maybe kissing. Possibly a grope. That's all. Nothing controversial.'

'Humph.' Harriet had insisted on driving and now braked suddenly at a red light. 'Speaking of which, all these people at this party know Clark. They're actors. So, um, maybe don't bring up Jerry at the party. Just because I don't want information going back to Clark about who I'm dating, and – you know.'

'Ah ha! The plot thickens!' I turned to her. 'Now why would you care what Clark knows?'

She turned left on a red light. 'Can I do that in California? I can never remember. Anyway, um, because I don't think it's any of Clark's business.' She glanced in the rearview mirror and rubbed her lips together. 'I think there's going to be a karaoke machine. Aren't you the one who has that karaoke story?'

She knew very well that a year ago, in New York, I'd gotten hammered at a party thrown by a well-known pop singer and proceeded to make an absolute ass of myself by crooning – with profound feeling – 'Papa Don't Preach.' 'I'd rather you not bring that up,' I said, refusing to have my good mood muddled. 'Karaoke, vodka and me do not mix. The problem is, like most people, I secretly harbor the belief that I'm good singer just waiting to be discovered.'

Harriet snorted. We swung down a hill and careened into a long, heavily wooded driveway. Crowds were spilling out of a low ranchstyle house, and I could hear a woman wailing 'Der Kommissar' already. 'Oh, boy,' I said as we threaded our way toward the cocktail table, brandishing our bottle of wine as if it were a shield.

I poured myself a little dollop of vodka into a plastic cup as Harriet went in search of a bottle opener. 'Hey,' a slightly tanned man said to another man standing on the other side of me, and clinked his bottle against his. 'Hey, didn't we work together last week? On *One Life to Live*?'

The guy squinted. 'Were you the extra in the loud pants? Man, I'm sorry about that wardrobe. What were they thinking?'

'I know,' the guy said cheerfully, but his current wardrobe didn't seem to be much of an improvement. He was wearing a checked orange and brown velvet shirt and big shiny Doc Martens. 'Tim,' he said, extending his hand.

'Gary,' said the guy. I was starting to feel like the Invisible Woman. I backed up so the two wouldn't have to talk across me, when Tim reached out his hand and said, 'And you are?'

'Courtney,' I said, shaking it gamely.

'And you two—' He began pointing back and forth between me and Gary.

'Oh, no,' I said quickly. 'I'm just standing here eaves-dropping. And hiding from the karaoke machine. My friend Harriet – do you know her?' Both men shook their heads.

'Well, that's why I'm here,' I said lamely, not knowing where to go from there.

The Gary guy excused himself then and I stood, feeling a little uncomfortable. I finished my vodka, and said, 'That's a nice, um, costume you're wearing.' He looked somewhat familiar to me, and feeling fortified by the surge of alcohol, I continued. 'Are you an actor?'

He looked at me closely to see if I was joking. 'No, really,' I said, truthfully. 'I mean, I know this is Los Angeles, but you look like someone I've seen before.'

'I was in this soap,' Tim said, pouring me some more vodka, 'and three months ago I was in this off, off, off, off-Broadway play, except it wasn't anywhere near Broadway, it was in West Hollywood, for quite a while that I'm sure you didn't see—'

'Genet's *The Balcony*?' I interrupted. 'In that tiny theater with twenty-five seats?' I surprised even myself. It had been a supremely boring play, and I'd spent the duration watching this Tim because of his huge nostrils that flared in a simian fashion every time he said a line. But there was something alluring about him, then and now.

'My God, you saw that?' Tim was incredulous.

'I did,' I said, somewhat proudly. 'You were the, um, um, The Envoy.'

'The Second Photographer,' he corrected me, but happily. 'I can't believe it. This is wonderful. May I get you another drink? How could you remember me?'

'Well, it's complicated.' The vodka zoomed into my limbs now and I realized I hadn't eaten since the chili dog in the parking lot of Pink's. 'Um, I remember your um – your nose. To be honest. It's very distinctive.' Harriet, successful in her quest for a bottle opener, stood behind Tim and I saw her shaking her head in amusement.

But instead of being piqued that I hadn't mentioned a subtle acting style or a touching inflection, Tim was entirely flattered.

We chatted over the next hour, over 'We Got the Beat' and 'Go Your Own Way' and 'The Immigrant Song,' (excruciatingly enough, it was a '70s/'80s party) moving from room to room, talking with others, then reconnoitering. After two hours, and two more vodka splashes with cranberry, the floor began to dip and sway. The karaoke machine began to look more appealing. And so did Tim.

'They can't play this,' I said with the self-righteousness of a drunk when the Spice Girls came on. No one was listening. I peered at Tim who, along with me, was trying to choose a song from the karaoke list. I looked at his shirt, and admired his shiny shoes. 'Tim?' I asked, and I backed him in a corner. 'Let's kiss.'

And so it was that I suddenly found myself up close and personal with that now notorious nose. Up to that point Tim had seemed like a normal enough kind of guy – true, he did dress oddly, but perhaps that was an expression of his sense of humor. After three drinks, what had been formerly reprehensible now seemed merely representative of that flashy Los Angeles hipness that wouldn't work in any other part of the country.

Ah, vodka. We kissed for another minute. He put his hands on my hips and I reached up around his neck. But there was something tentative to his kissing, something gentle and kind, as if he were waiting, or kissing a stuffed animal. Later, the BritChix and I would discuss all the ramifications of tentative kissing, but for now, I felt a prick of annoyance, amidst all the other thoughts erupting in my sodden mind. A sudden bolt of clarity, like a break in the clouds, beamed through. It didn't matter what this kiss was like, tentative or not, since this event was not real. Besides, the floor was moving at breakneck speed. 'This is very nice,' I said, backing off and stepping away a foot. 'But I'm going to go home now because – well, just because.' I looked around for some water or Diet Coke.

'Okay,' he said. He was looking at me intently. 'Can I see you again?'

'Well, I guess.' Now why did I say that? I knew full well that I was in Los Angeles to see Harriet, not chase after actors. In my foggy little brain, trouble had an expiration date anyway – fresh only for one night, rancid at sunrise. 'I'm only here for the weekend,' I said, as we moved toward a table littered with empty plastic bottles and cups, 'so it's going to be tough.' I poured a cup of orange soda and offered it to him. He was sweet, it was true, in a non-offensive, actor-ish kind of way. I didn't want to hurt his feelings. Besides, he probably felt exactly the same toward me and was just being gentleman-ly with this cute little plead.

'I'll call you tomorrow,' he said, scrounging around for a pen. 'We can have lunch.'

'That sounds fine, maybe.' I'd deal with this later. It was enjoyable kissing him, admittedly, but it wasn't going further than this. By tomorrow he'd probably be satisfied that he'd met this chick who made out with him – who didn't live here and wouldn't be pursuing and calling and game-playing and wanting to go down the whole dating lane.

'You have a message,' Harriet said accusingly the next morning after I'd gotten out of the shower, holding out the phone to me so she could replay the voice mail. She'd turned off the ringer so we could try to sleep off our hangovers.

I clutched the towel close. Harriet didn't like public displays of nudity, no matter how close the friend. 'Okay, I'm going to call him back and get this over with,' I sighed. He wasn't there, and I left a long message – wonderful to meet you, you're very sweet, I really can't meet you again because I just don't have time, will get in touch again sometime – rambling away until Harriet drew her finger across her throat. I hastily said goodbye and hung up. Harriet whisked her hands together in a 'Well, that's that' motion, and we got dressed to walk around Venice Beach for the day.

If only it were. Later that afternoon, Tim left another message. And another. Harriet, in between listening to messages from her clients, would calmly hand me the receiver then punch the rewind button on the phone, with a look on her face that said, *See?*

Twice more the next evening, and twice the next day. 'Please do something,' Harriet said. 'The voice mail is going to break down. My clients won't be able to get through. Just call him again. Just tell him you can't meet him. Anything.'

'I did call him,' I said, frustrated but also embarrassed. 'For God's sake. I told him I couldn't see him again. It was a kiss, Harriet, not a vow of marriage. I'm not going to pander to this.' We peeled off in the Geo Metro in a huff to have a gardenia cocktail at Trader Vic's.

'He called again,' Harriet said flatly when I opened the door to the room the next morning. I'd been breakfasting by myself at the counter of Swingers in order to give Harriet some time to work in peace, as well as give a token glance to my own work. 'I talked to him. I said, "Listen I know she thinks you're a really nice guy. She was attracted to you. But she's incredibly busy. And it was just a fun kiss. Can't you leave it at that? She doesn't even live here."'

I sat down, exhausted. 'I can't believe this. Well, what did he say?'

'He said – no, he *sneered*, "Oh did she say that to you? How incredibly *convenient* for her."'

I put my head in my hands.

'He also said,' Harriet continued over my groans, 'that he'd try you at work in San Francisco since he doesn't have your home phone number.'

'What work?' I asked incredulously. 'You didn't give him my home number, I hope.' Harriet shook her head briskly. I lay down on one of the queen-size beds. 'Maybe I am being very naive, or very sexist, but I do not get this. One would think this is the kind of situation every man is looking for. He meets a girl at a party. She finds him attractive. She kisses him – really kisses him, even though he himself seems to be a little wary in his tongue action. And then, she leaves town. My God, trust me to sniff out the one male in an entire party that will respond this way.'

'Actually,' Harriet said, examining my scuffed sandals with some distaste, 'if you want to deal in sexual roles, you're being the guy here. Again. You go out looking for a one night-stand, find one, use them for that night, don't want to deal with them anymore, and are uncomfortable when they look for some kind of commitment.'

'It was a kiss!' I shouted. 'It wasn't even a grope! Or a feel-up over clothes!'

'You do know you are playing the Rules, inadvertent though it may be,' Harriet said, ignoring me, examining her nails. I could see this was all very amusing to her. 'But he is getting a little mad. He said you were a coward—' She stopped as the phone started to ring. We looked at it as if it were a foreign insect who'd just crawled into the room and made its presence known. 'You know I don't normally say this, but maybe you *should* have slept with him,' Harriet said. I started to squawk. 'No, wait, listen. You're up for free sex, aren't you?'

'Within reason,' I protested. 'Nothing about this is reasonable.'

'Well, okay, but if you'd slept with him, there wouldn't be all this urgency. If he'd had an orgasm anywhere near you, on you, inside of you – then this wouldn't be happening.'

I sat up. 'Harriet! I can't believe this is coming from you, of all people.' The voice mail kicked in and Harriet lay back against the headboard of her bed, hands behind her head. She flicked on CNN and said cheerfully, 'You said you were looking for trouble.' She tucked her feet under her and reached for the nail polish remover and some cotton balls. 'Well, you got it. Just not the kind you were expecting.'

'At least I didn't sing,' I said.

CHAPTER 5

I was trying to decide between a blue rayon shirt that wouldn't wrinkle on the plane or an extra-large cotton t-shirt that used to be white, which would be comfy but also lend me that slacker look. I'd vowed on January 1, 1997 not to look like I worked in Starbuck's every single day of the year but so far I hadn't been doing a very good job. Despite just getting back from LA, my mother and I had decided at the last minute to grab this extra-cheap fare to London. 'You have a computer that you can bring, don't you?' she asked. 'You could work on the plane.'

The flight was ten hours, which was good and bad – good because it would give us ten uninterrupted hours in which to talk and 'catch up'; bad because it meant spending ten uninterrupted hours talking and catching up. She knew as well as I did that I probably wouldn't open my laptop at all, but here she was offering to pay for part of my flight. 'You don't need to do this, Mom,' I said, when she began writing me a check. I wondered at what age did it become morally suspicious to accept cash from one's parents. But she was visiting Andreas, the overseas boyfriend, and though she didn't say so, I sensed she needed some sort of moral support – at the very least, just knowing that her daughter was in the same city, because it was unlikely we'd hang out together once over there.

The ten-hour journey also meant that my hair and attire would be scrutinized. My mother was from the old school of

97

dressing up for a plane trip, and though I wasn't in the mood for a wardrobe critique, I rebelliously put on the white t-shirt anyway. I added a baseball cap – a fashion trend my mother has never understood – and then put on a gray sweatshirt with a hole in the elbow that was nonetheless particularly cozy. So much for my determination not to look like a character out of a Richard Linklater film.

'What,' Marie snapped into the phone on the first ring. 'I mean, hello, Curl Up and Dye.'

I stopped clicking a pen between my teeth. 'Marie? What are you doing answering the phone?'

'I gave Eve the day off,' she said shortly. 'Hi Courtney. What's up?'

'Any chance at all today?' I asked, trying not to sound desperate. Sometimes courting Marie could be tricky. It was sort of like chasing boys – you didn't want to appear too anxious or call too many times. 'Just a semi-permanent. I'm going to London and I can't have a faded color over there, now can I?'

'No can do,' she said. 'Sorry. That'll take three hours, and I'm short-staffed today.'

'Then why did you give Eve—' I started to say, then stopped. 'Well, okay. I did have this little story I wanted to share with you, but never mind.'

'Have a good trip,' she said, and started to hang up.

'Wait! Marie! How late are you open? Maybe I'll just run down and get some of that curl enhancer to take with me to London.'

'London,' she said slowly, as if it were an exotic dessert. 'Well, lah dee dah. Fine, but come in soon. No, come in an hour. I'll give it to you wholesale, because they're discontinuing that whole line.'

'Well, you don't have to do that,' I said, 'but thanks a lot.' She was silent, and I stopped rooting on the floor of my closet, searching for a certain skirt that I hadn't seen in a while. I sat back on my haunches. 'Is everything okay?'

'Everything's fine,' she said evenly. 'I have a story for you too. See you soon, then.' I heard her other line ring and the crash of some trendy music bursting through her cavernous salon. And a tiny wail from Davia, her baby, before she hung up.

I gave up looking for the skirt and looked over at the white cat, who was kneading with fierce determination a pile of black clothes that was lying on my bed, ready to be packed.

'Good timing,' Marie said, waving her hand toward one of the electric yellow chairs in the shape of a hand when I showed up an hour later. 'The baby's down for a nap in the back room. Sit.'

'Well, I'm in efficiency mode. You know how it is before a trip. Just keep crossing things off the list.'

'No, I can't remember. I haven't taken a trip in quite a while.' She had one foot on her hair trolley, and seemed to regard me a little absently as she rocked it back and forth.

'Uh, how's everything?' I asked. The salon was silent – probably because of the baby's nap time. A faucet dripped in the background. 'How *is* the baby? Gavin?' I said. She was bending over a box now, rummaging through the contents. 'It's the Rusk stuff. Thanks for doing this. I guess it is important to have the correct products, what with all this humidity lately.'

But Marie wasn't listening to me. 'Here,' she said, tossing me a tube. 'Knock yourself out. And you can have it for free. In fact, take two, three.' She threw a few more in my direction, and one skated across the lavender floor, under the sink.

'God, thanks, Marie,' I said, and got up to retrieve it. This hair product wasn't cheap. I started to pick up my backpack in a motion to leave, but she perched herself on the ledge by the mirror and protested, 'Hey, stay, stay. I want to hear your story.'

I sat back down in the yellow chair and gave her an

abbreviated version of The Kiss. 'And do you know what Harriet said?' I concluded. 'She said that if there had been any semen released in my vicinity, he wouldn't have been on such a mission.'

'Oh, I don't know about that,' Marie commented darkly. She'd sat listening with her legs crossed, bobbing one stiletto-heeled boot, her chin resting on her hand. Gray-blue circles ringed her eyes and I noticed that her cranberry-colored hair looked a little dirty, lying flat on either side of her face, and not pulled up in the usual series of complicated ponytails and hair implements. 'Guys get an idea in their head about a chick, for whatever reason, and sometimes there's no stoppin' 'em. You probably *should* have fucked him. Why not? It wouldn't have made any difference anyway, and you could have had a great time. He was probably married or something.'

'What?' That sounded awfully cynical, even coming from Marie.

'Sure. Why *didn't* you fuck him?'

'Because . . . because . . . I guess because I didn't want to, strange as that may seem. It seemed too complicated.'

Marie snorted, and I shrugged. 'Didn't you have a story for me?'

'Oh, yes,' she said. 'Well, just to bring you up to speed, business is fine. I'm filing for divorce. Davia just got a new tooth last week, so she's been cranky.' She stopped swinging her foot and yawned. 'Do you want a cup of coffee? I just made some.'

I stared at her. 'Marie?'

'Gavin's been fucking someone. A cocktail waitress from the bar. For the last six months. Since the baby was three months old. Do you take cream?'

'Wait a minute, wait, wait.' Marie and Gavin couldn't get a divorce. They'd been together forever, through everything. They had the best relationship in the world. She was sane, he was calm, they were mirror images of each other. 'But, but, I thought . . . okay. Jesus, what happened? He told you he was sleeping with someone?'

She went in the back room, and returned, handing me a steaming, lime green ceramic cup. 'Oh, no,' she said with exaggerated seriousness. 'No, that would be too normal, too healthy. No, I had to have one of our friends drop me a hint that they'd seen him and this chick together. Many times. In his car. And then Eve comes in here the other day and starts bawling her head off when I say that Gavin's acting weird. So I squeezed her for information and she tells me that her brother thinks that something's going on. Her brother works with Gavin at the bar.'

'And then?'

'So I confronted him. And he admitted he'd been seeing her, and sleeping with her. So I said, "Okay. Fine. Now you need to end it. You should have told me before, but end it now." And he says to me no. Just like that. *No.* And then *he* gets all fucking emotional, and says I hadn't been having sex with him and what was he supposed to do? And then he says: "*Baby, I think I'm in love with her.*"'

'Hang on,' I said. 'I'm totally confused. I thought you said he could have an affair. That you even talked about who he would do it with.'

'I said he could have an *affair*,' she spat out. 'I didn't say he could fucking fall in *love*. I didn't say he could sneak around, behind my back! So I said, "Listen you asshole, whaddya mean you think you're in love? You aren't fucking *thinking* at all. What about our daughter, you jerk? You're gonna give up your daughter for this thirty-year-old cocktail waitress with a tongue pierce who lives with her mother and drives an early '80s Toyota Tercel with license plates that read "Dream On"?'

I shuddered. 'She doesn't really.'

'Oh, yes she does.' Marie sat back quietly. She unsheathed her scissors which had been lying next to her on the ledge and began opening and closing them in the air, listening to the metallic *wheeak-snip, wheeak-snip.*

I was mute. 'You've stunned me into silence, Marie. You really have.'

'It gets worse. "Her or me," I said to him. "Decide." And he says, *"Baby I don't know if it's going to work between you and me, I can't give her up."* Then he says he'll try. And for two weeks, he doesn't see her, so he says. And one night, I'm home, waiting for him. It's 2 a.m., and nobody's answering the phone at the bar, and I'm going nuts. So I start trying all these different passwords on his voice mail. I'm obsessed, see?'

'I see.'

'And the first password I try, I get in. See, I know Gavin. I know how his mind works. And there's all these messages from her! Gooey, love crap: "Baby, it was so good to see you yesterday and I love you so much too." He'd been lying to me the whole two weeks.'

I was starting to feel ill.

'So I confront the asshole. Three separate times he changes his voice mail password, and three separate times I break in. He says to me, incredulous, "How can you keep figuring out my passwords?" And I tell him, *"Because I'm smart and you are so fucking stupid."* The first one was part of our home phone number. The second, his social security number. The third, I'm thinking *Hmmm, what does Gavin think about if he's not thinking about work or sex?* Of course: S-O-C-C-E-R. Bingo. Now he's disconnected the voice mail altogether.'

She heaved herself off the ledge and began to spray Windex on the floor-to-ceiling mirrors. 'But the last straw was finding out that he's been fucking her in his car! Now that was it.'

'Oh, God,' I groaned. An image popped in my head of Gavin and this woman, her breasts heaving up and down, trying to negotiate themselves around a pesky hand brake. 'How did you find *that* out?'

'I asked him,' she said flatly. 'The chick lives with her mom, so I wanted to know where he'd been doing this. And I tell you, that really did it. I said to him: "Not only are you a liar and a snake and a dumb jerk, you're also *cheap*. You could have at least rented a motel room." I just told him today that I was filing.' She jumped up, trying to wipe the tops of the mirrors. 'Anyway. I thought you might find this interesting.'

'Well, yes . . .' but also uncommonly sad and disgusting. 'Marie,' I began, 'I'm on your side here. But you did tell him to go have an affair. Remember? You kind of set this up.'

'I did not set this up. There was a time when I wanted nothing more for Gavin to stop hassling me about sex.' She sat down, and picked up her scissors again. *Wheeak-snip, wheeak-snip.* 'If this chick was a fuck, I could let it go. But this love stuff – forget it. I don't need it and neither does Davia.' As if on cue, the baby made a gurgling wail. 'I was just reading Emerson the other day, something along the lines of be careful what you wish for, because you most certainly shall receive it.'

'Yeah, well, gotta hand it to those poets.' Marie reading poetry – things really had gotten out of hand. I took a sip of my coffee and sighed sympathetically. 'I'm really sorry, Marie. This is just . . . well, it's terrible.'

'I'll live.' She was fixing a ponytail on top of her head, looking in the mirror, and suddenly stopped, staring at her face and her defiant expression, I imagine. With a finger, she traced her jawline up to her silver earrings, as if she were being introduced to the new planes, gentle angles and smooth skin of a new lover. She caught sight of me watching her, and embarrassed, went to the back room to retrieve a sobbing Davia.

That night, my mother and I were sitting on what must have been the most crowded flight in United Airlines's history, on our way to London. Luggage poked out from every seat, babies screamed, flight attendants stepped over the sprawled legs of passengers. My mother was adjusting the ear piece of her headset, trying the volume and channels, and I was languidly flipping through a magazine, trying not to dwell on Marie. We'd already had one fight in the taxi on the way to the airport, and now my mother was giving me the silent treatment.

'Who's taking care of Zippy?' I asked, trying not to appear too terribly concerned. I worried about that bird, even though I'd successfully put off retrieving him from that House of Chaos. It would be just like my mother, in an ill-thought-out burst of goodwill, to take on something or someone – a pet, a piece of furniture, a stray friend in need of a bed – and leave them to fend for themselves.

'What?' she asked loudly.

'ZIPPY,' I said, just as loud.

'Conchetta's keeping an eye on him. When do you think you're going to pick him up anyway?'

'When I've figured out the subtext behind this gift of a cockatiel.' I turned a page.

My mother shrugged noncommitedly. 'Suit yourself,' she said, then glanced at my forehead. I raised my eyebrows at her.

When had we slipped into the sunset years of mother/daughter relationships? It was a constant internal struggle – whether to get into a giant confrontation about some small point, or to just let it go since they, the moms, are not going to change anyway. In the cab, right in the middle of my telling her about the Museum of Jurassic Technology, she had begun staring at the left side of my head. I knew what was coming, but I tried to ignore it. No such luck. She gently tried to pull some hair out of my ponytail as I backed into the corner of the cab and hissed, 'Just what do you think you're doing, Mom?'

'Your hair is all plastered on that side,' she said, taking her hand back, and looking a little guilty, 'and it's just not as flattering as it could be.'

'So what,' I said irritably, and losing the battle against

confrontation. 'I'm thirty-one years old. It's my hair. I'll do what I want with it.'

I flipped through my magazine a little more aggressively, wondering just what it was about mothers and hair. Or more specifically, what it was about mothers and foreheads. I'd mentioned this to Harriet once, who replied she wasn't allowed to wear her hair up in a clip or a bun around her mother. 'She frowns and mutters "take it out, take it out." And then she tries to fluff up my bangs.'

Harriet didn't even have a broad forehead. I've long since stopped wearing bangs, but every once in a while when at Marie's, I look into the mirror and see what my mother sees: a big forehead, and a jagged, assymetrical hairline. 'Don't do it.' Marie says, reading my mind. 'You have an okay face and good hair.' Marie has often said her job would be a breeze if it weren't for all the seeds of doubt sown in the heads of daughters everywhere.

But my mother didn't say anything now on the plane. Thinking about Marie again made me sigh, and I lay the magazine down on my lap and looked out the window.

'What are you reading?' my mother asked, apparently in an attempt at rapprochement. She'd taken off her headphones and was leaning convivially toward me. 'Huh. Penis size, I see. "Is Bigger Better?" ' she said, reading over my shoulder. I smiled at her with mock cheerfulness, as if we were two girls poring over Good Housekeeping, reading a recipe secret together. Then I leaned back and put the magazine up to my face, blocking her out.

Long ago, my mother and I began talking about sex, spurred in part I think by the desire not to imitate her own Irish Catholic, repressed relationship with her mother. She accommodated my pre-adolescent questions with a great show of openness, talking to me about menstruation, breast size and intercourse in a matter-of-fact tone as she put on her make-up or brushed her hair. She herself had been divorced for many years now, and growing up I'd seen a few boyfriends come and go, tiptoeing out of the house in the pre-dawn hours, looking pale and guilty in their black dress socks and rumpled, untucked shirts.

If anything, it was me that was the prude when it came to sex talk with my mother. Yes, we were honest, but we were not blunt. Skirting around the periphery was fine with me – yes, she knew I slept with men and a good number of them by the time I was thirty, but she did not need to know more than that. Details were not asked about, nor were they provided. I wasn't even certain if she knew exactly what I wrote about, although I had overheard her once at a cocktail party say something about her daughter, 'who scribbled some kind of urban life sex thing.'

'Well?' she asked, frowning when the titles of *The Mirror Has Two Faces* flashed on the poster-sized movie screen.

'Well, what?' I said. 'You want to talk about the importance of penis size with me? Go ahead.' I shifted in my seat and got a little hot in the face.

'Penis size *is* important,' my mother said. She was still fiddling around with her dials. 'Don't you think it is? Any woman that says that it isn't is lying,' she continued, and not particularly quietly either.

'Mom, could you keep your voice down?'

'Why? Does it embarrass you?' she shouted.

'Ssshh. For God's sake, at least take off your headphones,' I whispered. 'No, of course it doesn't. You and I can talk about anything. How is your Intel stock doing, by the way?'

'In fact, I think penis size is *very* important. I think it directly affects the way a man treats a woman, how big or small he is. You and I have never talked about this, have we?' She still was trying to tune her headset, frowning and not appearing to pay very much attention to our conversation at all.

'No,' I said, shifting around. A man burping a baby glared

106

at me. 'Maybe there's a good reason for that.'

She said matter-of-factly, 'Men my age are completely hung up on their penises.' She took a careful sip of her Diet Coke. 'Then again, so are the women!' Giggling suddenly, she began, 'Have I ever told you about going to that nude beach with your father—'

'Okay, Mom, that's it.' I sat up. 'This discussion is over. I refuse to hear that P word and my father in the same sentence.' I plugged my headphones in, determined to catch up on *The Mirror Has Two Faces*. From what I could tell, Lauren Bacall and Barbra Streisand were having the same conversation.

'Well!' my mother said. She pretended to be a little huffy but I could see she was highly amused. 'When did you become such a nervous Nellie? I was only going to say in the 70s, we used to always go to the nude beaches and look at all the different sizes. There really is an amazing range.' She opened my magazine, and began poring over it.

I wouldn't see my mother very much in London. She would be swept up in the lifestyle of her European boyfriend – a man I'd only met a few times, and who needed a lot of female attention, like most men her age, it seemed. I waved goodbye as she peeled off in a black cab, feeling relieved and abandoned all at the same time.

That night I sat with a group of my English friends in a loud, skinny, minimalist restaurant off Piccadilly, the type of which seemed to be taking London by storm. It was designed by one of the Conrans, I was told importantly – the Conrans being a kind of UK Mafia in the world of cool, as far as I could tell. We sat in a large circle at the bar, waiting for our table, and I was glad my mother wasn't there – it gave me time to acclimate in the drinking zone without being eyeballed about my alcohol intake. My English friends drank glasses of gin and tonics as if they were pleasant little fizzy sodas. There were ten of us, but I sat between Mary and Jayne, gazing at them like a little girl in between gulps of my cocktail.

The talk on the plane with my mother, or rather the non-talk, had pricked at me all day. Maybe Gavin had a small penis. Maybe Sir did too. But the small penis/big ego correlation had a Harrietesque whiff of simplicity, and I wondered how Mary and Jayne would weigh in. My English girlfriends were all a very open lot, much more so than their American counterparts. I still couldn't even bring myself to talk about Jemma in any great detail with Harriet.

The fact that I had this snooping tendency in the arena of sexuality amused Mary and Jayne to death. It was all 'so American'; it showed how uptight we Yanks really were. Sitting with them, I was suddenly struck by the peculiarity of the BritChix. They were like a different species: giant exotic birds, glossy, dressed in black, with graceful fingers and fashionably clunky shoes. So much more overt, less conservative, and so much more sexual: Jayne with her bare shoulders, in her bias-cut dress, Mary in her clinging Ozbek turtleneck, the way they threw back their heads and laughed, the slight parting of their lips when they listened. They'd asked what I'd been snooping around about lately, and when I replied 'penis size,' they nodded knowingly, as if I'd said 'tax reform.' The men, on the other hand, regarded me with polite curiosity.

'I would like to know,' Trevor interrupted in his most perfect BBC accent, 'why people talk about penis size. The question shouldn't be how big or how small the man is. The question is, how small is the woman?'

'Trevor,' Jayne said languidly, leaning over to kiss him loudly on the ear, 'Anyone who talks about anchovies, women and oral sex in the same breath is a misogynist. You're just digging yourself deeper.'

'I never said that. That was Mark. I was merely recounting his anecdote.'

'Actually, women have surgery all the time to make their

vaginas tighter,' Mary put in. 'They just don't talk about it. It's one of those things that women don't talk about with each other.'

'This is news to me,' I said. Mary, with her women's health magazine background, was not to be dismissed. 'What other things do women not talk about with each other?'

'That's true about the surgery,' Jayne said. 'After childbirth, or just to be smaller. It's a very simple operation, it takes no time at all apparently.' She and Mary nodded as the men drifted into rugby talk. 'I don't know why women don't talk about it. I haven't had it done. Have you?' she turned to Mary.

'No. I know someone who did. It's really not a big issue.'

'Whatever happened to Kegel exercises?' I asked.

'Spoken like a true Yank. Why do a load of exercises when you can just have a simple procedure?' Jayne asked.

'Women don't talk about masturbation in the States,' I said. 'There still seems to be some sort of shame attached to it. But I asked an English friend of mine about it recently, and she was, well, frank. She said when she's anxious, she masturbates about four times a day. She works at home, you see.'

'Why would there be shame attached to masturbation?' Jayne seemed genuinely surprised. 'Such a conservative observation. Trevor bought me a vibrator. I use it all the time.'

'She also said,' I continued, warming up to the subject, 'that she hadn't yet had a boyfriend who didn't connect her frequent masturbation to her feeling like she wasn't getting enough sex in the relationship. Whereas, she said, the two had nothing to do with each other. It was just a tension easer.'

'Women don't talk about Bartholin gland cysts either,' said Mary. 'Although something like 70 per cent of all women get them at one time or another. My gynecologist told me that, and he's a man.'

'We also don't talk about multiple orgasms,' declared Jayne. 'I'm not sure why that is. I would like to know, actually, how my girlfriends count their multiple orgasms. For instance, does anyone have one right after another? Or is it within the space of five minutes? Or ten? And if so, does that count as a multiple orgasm?'

'Another drink?' the waiter asked.

'Yes,' we all cried.

'But we all know you lot talk about our penises,' Trevor interrupted, in that deeply serious way that Brits only employ to say something deeply unserious. 'That's something I think you should stop talking about. It's very private.'

Jayne patted his hand in pretend sympathy, as he turned back to sports talk. She finished the last of her drink and crunched some ice. 'Maybe we Brit girls need to get on the Internet. We need to find out from the Americans what it is that we all don't talk about. I will start by saying that I have one orgasm per sexual session. That's it.'

'Let's have a round robin,' Mary said eagerly, rubbing her hands on her shoulders. 'Let's all talk about one thing that we've never talked about with girlfriends. I'll start: I lust after a woman at my office. Now you,' she said to me.

'I can't top that,' I said. 'You know my life is an open book. Let me get back to you on this.'

Jayne and Mary groaned. 'You can take the Yank out of the country,' they said in unison.

I was staying at Jayne and Trevor's – a tall, thin, rickety house near the Isle of Dogs in East London. They'd bought it ten years ago when the real estate market was momentarily depressed, and proceeded to excavate, knock down, haul, rebuild and repaint the entire interior, so that entering from the shabby, litter-filled streets was a little like stumbling into a jewel box. Each room was expertly and trendily painted in hues of aubergine, cucumber and periwinkle with contrasting curtains and duvets to match (those damn Conrans, again) and unlike any London couples I knew, Trevor and Jayne actually had spare rooms and storage space. They loved to entertain, and so despite the incredibly inconvenient and inaccessible location of their neighborhood, their home became a party central for all their friends living in shoeboxes and bedsits scattered throughout London.

And like many English couples I knew, they'd been together for several years and had no plans of ever getting married – a refreshing switch from the Noah's Ark procession to the altar that I was encountering so often. Jayne said this was because her mother was French and encouraged her to do things differently to what might be expected from an English woman. Trevor attributed it to his rich Welsh parents' messy divorce when he was five. Whatever the reason, they were blissfully unaware of the marital guillotine that was threatening to slice through the reality of every person I knew on my side of the pond, male or female.

'Did you ever meet Nigel?' Jayne asked me, the day after our dinner at the expensive minimalist restaurant. I was lying across the dove-colored chaise longue in the kitchen, wishing I hadn't drank so much gin the night before. Jayne of course looked absolutely unsullied and untouched by the previous night's debauchery, and even now was pouring herself a little Campari, having just strolled in from her day's work as a television producer. 'You're sure you won't have one, then?'

'Ugh,' I replied, my hand over my eyes. I felt like Camille. 'No thanks. Nigel who?'

Jayne added an expert splash of club soda to her glass, and dropped a slice of lemon in with a fizzy plop. 'Mmm,' she said, taking a sip. She lit a cigarette. 'I think you may have met him at one of our parties. You'd find his story very interesting,' she said. 'He's more classic of the blokes here, I think. He works with Trevor at the firm, but they went to school together. When Blair got in, they all went out in a huge group together to celebrate – you know that Trevor's firm is tight with Labour?'

'Uh huh,' I said, wondering exactly what it was that Trevor did, since he never explained it past 'political consultancy.' 'Are you trying to set me up with Nigel?'

Jayne chortled and added some more Campari to her glass. She draped herself over a stool next to me and kicked off her Prada mules. 'Good God no. I wouldn't be a very good girlfriend if I did that.'

I lifted a hand to scrutinize her with one eyeball. 'How come?'

She blew smoke toward the ceiling. 'Let me tell you about our Brit boy Nigel.'

It wasn't the sort of thing he usually noticed, but Nigel couldn't get over her skin. Kath was fifteen years younger than him, and she had that flawless, creamy complexion that you only saw on soap commercials and supermodels. Her hair was shiny and straight, and she spoke with a Glaswegian lilt that alternately charmed and befuddled him. He asked her if she liked Lloyd Cole; in particular, did she like that song 'Perfect Skin'? No, of course not, she'd be too young to remember who the hell Lloyd Cole was. Kath laughed a tiny tinkling laugh, and pushed a few strands of hair carefully behind her ears.

At thirty-six, Nigel was tired – no, exhausted – of the London dating scene. All the women he met seemed normal enough at first, but after two or three months it became clear they had an agenda. Marriage, kids, flat in Hampstead, the whole lot. He couldn't blame them, really; after all, he'd wanted kids too, someday at least. Kids sounded good as a concept. His brother Barry had three boys and he said marriage was all right, apart from the fact that he, Barry, never had sex anymore. Anyway, these London women drove Nigel right round the bend, with all their silly hysterics about careers and biological clocks, chattering away on their mobiles in the middle of Jaeger and Harvey Nicks. They all looked like a version of Princess Diana, and he was bored with them and their plotting.

Maybe it was her youth, but Kath seemed different. She laughed at his jokes, she liked her job at a popular women's fashion magazine and she seemed perfectly happy with Nigel just the way he was. She'd come from a huge Catholic family in Glasgow and, overlooking the odd temper tantrum around the first days of her period, she wasn't like those moody bitches he used to date. True, the sex wasn't very interesting (lights out, him on top, occasionally if she were very drunk she'd go down on him but that was rare), but maybe that was the price you had to pay.

He had to woo her. It didn't take very long – maybe two months of getting his secretary to send her flowers once a week – but in the beginning it seemed like an eternity. There were days when he'd sit in his office in the City, chewing on his hangnails, wondering when he'd see her again and what she was doing and if she was seeing anyone else. She was distracting, this Kath bird; his mates thought he'd lost his mind the way he was mooning over her like some lovesick dog. In the pub at lunch, he'd try not to talk about her – he was starting to disgust himself, for God's sake.

Then, suddenly he bagged her. He didn't know how or why, it was just that one day he realized that he was in control again. She returned his calls, in fact she'd begun calling him all the time. When she met him at a restaurant, or when she'd arrive in a cab at his flat late at night, she'd throw her arms around his neck and kiss him numerous times, leaving half-moon crescents of her brown lipstick all over his face. He realized he didn't really think so much about Kath during the day as he used to.

After eleven months, they were a couple, an Official Couple. They were Nigelandkath, or Kathandnigel; they had mutual friends and were invited everywhere as a twosome – to weddings, parties, drinks and the like. At first it was wonderful – to be swept up in the frenzy, to have his friends be envious of his regular sex, to just have another person be there when he left work. And then, just as suddenly, it was not so wonderful. Nigel found himself wondering what it felt like to be a single bloke; he couldn't remember. He knew he should probably marry Kath and somewhere he felt that she was waiting for him to ask. There was, after all, no reason why he shouldn't: she was pretty, lively, she was perfectly presentable. His friends all liked her, and she'd mentioned in passing one time that she wasn't in a rush to have children.

But sometimes he would wake up in the middle of the night and stare at her sleeping form beside him, wondering if this was the way he was supposed to feel. People always say you knew if it was the Right One, and while he couldn't be certain if Kath was the Right One, he felt he also couldn't be certain if this was the Wrong One. It was all a leap of faith anyway, or at least that's what his brother Barry said. If it were left up to the men, nobody would ever get married and the human race would die out. What did he want, Barry asked – to be middle-aged, sitting in a pub alone every night in his checkered cap drinking a pint with his dog sleeping at his ankles? Well, no, Nigel said, but did his relationship with Kath have to be so predictable and . . . well, **public**? *Every fight, every reconciliation, every holiday, every event they attended was noted and discussed ad infinitum by their little group of friends. He didn't know how it had gotten this way; he couldn't remember a time when it was just the two of them, foraging around in each other's minds, finding out their respective likes and dislikes.*

So he broke up with Kath. He didn't even feel he was that serious about the break-up, it was just something he wanted to try on and not really own, like a friend's father's cardigan, or a Stetson hat. Kath, by all accounts (he'd of course get daily updates about her through the grapevine), was devastated. She was crying, she was sick – how could he have done this to her? He was just about to ring her up and get her to meet him in a West End pub, and maybe try out a reconciliation, when he went to a drinks party in Chelsea one evening and ended up fucking some woman in the bathroom.

Why did he do it? Anna was loud, funny, talkative, smart – not at all the kind of woman he was normally attracted to. She was the same age as Nigel and had an important advertising job in New York dealing with celebrities; Nigel was sheepishly impressed. Most surprising of all, Anna was fat. Well, not fat exactly, but definitely plump. He'd never gone out with a fat woman before even though he himself was a little soft around the middle.

But the sex – well, he couldn't believe it. She'd actually dragged him into the bathroom, stuck her tongue in his mouth, put his hands on her enormous breasts, and then fucked him right there and then against the sink. He looked at Anna's buttocks – huge, round, like giant grapefruits – reflected in the mirror as she sat on the edge and he was ramming inside her, and briefly a vision of Kath's skinny little bottom floated through his mind.

He fully intended to never see Anna again. He wasn't attracted to her; she was too smart, too old, and not the sort of woman he would ever date, much less become involved with. No, Kath was better. Much better. This was it – a sign, he decided. He phoned Kath the very next day and they reconciled on the phone after forty-five minutes of tears. He didn't think she'd hear about Anna – nobody would dare tell Kath, and not that many people knew anyway. But Anna stayed in London a few weeks longer, and as hard as he tried, he couldn't get that image of her buttocks out of his mind. He found himself phoning her desperately, and arranging to meet her: Today? Tomorrow? The next day?

What on earth was the matter with him?

'We haven't shagged yet,' Mary was saying, 'because I've had that horrible premonition that it's not going to be ...' She examined her cuticles. 'Oh, bollocks. Never mind.'

'Yes?' Jayne asked impatiently. 'Not going to be fantastic?' She waited while Mary fell silent, smoking her Silk Cut like a film star from another era.

As usual, I felt like a little girl, listening to the grown-up girls talk. Normally it would be I who would press my friends into a confessional, adding here, jousting there, but Mary and Jayne were different. Since nothing was sacred – from multiple orgasms to terrible oral sex to glandular cysts to preferential clitoral manipulations – I'd learned early on that if I just sat and listened, eventually every sexual subject would be covered, ad infinitum. In one week they'd told me more about female sexuality than all of my American friends over my lifetime.

Now if Mary was hesitating, it must really be something interesting. 'That's never stopped you before,' Jayne was saying. It was two-thirty in the morning, and the three of us were sitting at a late night Chinese restaurant in Soho, picking at Singapore noodles. We'd just been tossed out of Jayne's horrible dive of a private drinking club, that being another facet of the London nightlife that startled me. So much for the repressed Brits.

'He doesn't kiss properly,' Mary said. 'I know that shouldn't be a factor, but I can't help it. I feel it may be a sign.'

'That is a sticky issue,' Jayne said, lighting a cigarette as well. She blew some smoke abstractedly and considered. 'There may not be a direct correlation though, from kissing prowess to cock prowess. You can't just write the poor boy off.'

'That's just it, I think there is a correlation. If a man is a sensitive kisser, he is a sensitive lover.'

'Not true.'

'And if he's a rough kisser, he will be a rough lover.'

'Absolute rubbish.'

'I'm telling you, I've tracked this sort of thing,' Mary insisted. 'You could do your own personal test, and you'd come up with the same results. Remember when I kissed Russell? He was a dispassionate kisser, all tight and withdrawn. Never used his tongue, never any sensual wet kisses, ever. And he was exactly the same way as a lover.'

'As we all know,' said Jayne, pouring some tea into my cup, 'Russell was a dispassionate, tight and withdrawn *man*. It's not just his kisses. It's his entire being. You couldn't even get him to buy you a bar of chocolate much less give you a tender kiss.'

They argued some more, and I watched them as one would a tennis game. Harriet and I had often said that kissing was as important as you could get. A warm, tender, moist kiss with the tip of the tongue just probing the inside of your mouth, or a passionate wet kiss that seemed to devour your very soul and made you feel light-headed, or a playful light nipping of the lips in between the sucking of tongues – foreplay didn't get much better than a great make-out session.

The LA debacle popped into my mind. 'I had a mediocre kissing encounter recently,' I piped up. Mary and Jayne suddenly looked at me. 'He was very tentative. You know, like *peck, peck, peck . . . pause . . . pause,* then gentle *peck, peck, peck.* I felt like I was kissing a hen.'

'Tentative is not good,' Jayne allowed.

'No, it's not,' said Mary. 'Although, I will say that sometimes men need to be given a chance to warm up, like an old car. They need a little initiative, a little goosing of petrol from the driver.' She picked up an errant shrimp with her chopsticks and examined it, frowning. 'But just based on what you said, I'm willing to bet he was a lousy lay, as you Americans put it.' Jayne snorted.

'Was he?' Mary pressed.

'I don't know. We didn't do it—' Jayne groaned loudly, and I continued over her, '—it wasn't right. I was drunk, he was tentative, it was LA . . .'

'Now you'll never know,' Jayne said severely. I poured some tea in her cup.

'Oh, shush you old committed bag,' Mary said gaily. 'Easy for you to criticize. She did the right thing. If he can't even be bothered to give her a nice, deep, *Casablanca*-style kiss, what makes you possibly think that he will take his tongue anywhere near the vicinity of her clitoris? You've just forgotten all this, you have.'

'I agree with Mary,' I said. 'What other clothed act between two people can express so much with such economy of movement?'

Jayne said, 'That's awfully poetic of you.' She sipped her tea thoughtfully. 'I do remember that I always thought American men were lovely kissers. Irish men, too.' Now it was my turn to snort.

'Oh, never mind me,' I said, as they looked at me, amused. 'I'm jet lagged. I don't know what I'm saying.'

'But you've been here for over a week,' said Mary. 'Still?'

'And you're leaving tomorrow,' Jayne said.

'I don't know how you girls do it.' I wondered if all the alcohol was catching up on me. 'I just don't get how you can live in this incredibly expensive city and have all these *things* and drink so much. I can't keep up with you.' I meant it more as an observation but it came out more as a lament.

'What things?' Jayne asked.

'Well . . . houses,' I said. 'In my city, people my age have about as much chance of buying a house as they do buying the Grand Canyon. In fact, I'll bet the Grand Canyon would be more affordable.'

'Gentrification!' Mary muttered darkly.

'Poor sweetie,' Jayne cooed at me, and rubbed my head as if I were a little furry animal who'd lost its way. 'I was telling her about Nigel and Kath,' she said to Mary.

'Oh, God,' Mary groaned. 'Did you tell her about Sabine?'

'No,' she said. She patted my hand sympathetically. 'We'll save that for another day.'

I perked up. 'Of course, now I have to know. What happened after that?'

'Well, this might give you a little insight into the way Nigel sees things,' said Jayne.

Once, ten years ago when Nigel was in his mid-twenties, he was engaged to be married. Sabine was French and he'd met her at Harrod's, of all places, where she was helping him pick out a fountain pen for his then-girlfriend. He'd selected a Parker and Sabine, behind the counter, had wrinkled her nose, and said (rightly) in her impossibly sexy accent, 'You must not think very much of this woman.'

He fell intensely in love with Sabine, and one night, six months after the pen comment, after they'd downed three bottles of Pomerol, he asked her to marry him. It seemed the right thing to do; he even got on his knees in the middle of the Kensington restaurant. He loved that time, that initial period when everything seemed possible and the sex was great and boredom was like an advert on the television, starting and leaving in quick short bursts. It would be wonderful to be married and have pretty little children who spoke French and a wife who looked at him adoringly when he roared up the lane in his Land Rover.

The wedding was to be in Aix-en-Provence, where she was from, and her family was hosting the whole huge affair. Sabine came from a large family and she was the first to be married; her mother had cried on the phone when Sabine told her. The machine was set in motion, the prenuptial snowball gained speed and momentum daily. Sabine flew to Paris to have her wedding dress fitted, and had marathon conversations with her mother on the phone. She worried about the flowers, went on a Champagne tasting to select the vintage for the wedding breakfast, bought fountain pens (Récife, not Parker) for the groomsmen. The invitations were sent out. The dress was ready. The honeymoon had been paid for (non-refundable). And suddenly, a week before they were to fly to Aix, Nigel looked down at Sabine's sleeping face and her prominent, Gallic nose, and knew he wasn't in love with her anymore.

He woke her up and told her and that was that. Sabine cried and screamed and eventually she refused to talk to him. A month later he'd heard she moved to Paris, and when he tried to call her parents to apologize – he wasn't a complete bastard, after all – they hung up on him. Nigel never spoke to Sabine again.

He didn't think very much about this event for years. After all, things happened, sometimes it just didn't work out. Better that he broke it off than go through with the wedding and live in complete misery for the rest of his life. He never mentioned it to Kath – what was there to tell? That he'd fallen in love and it seemed right and then one day it was suddenly . . . not right?

But, ten years on, he found himself thinking about Sabine and what had happened. He was back with Kath now, the relationship was fine, so why in the hell did he keep thinking about something that occurred so long ago? Kath was nothing like Sabine, so it wasn't that. It didn't take long before he realized that what he recognized was his own panic, resurfacing like an old friend, clapping its hand on his shoulder.

To make matters worse, there was Anna. She was still lurking around London, staying over at his flat once in a while, sneaking out with shoes in hand early in the morning (Kath occasionally dropped by before going to work). He simply could not understand what it was about this woman that he fancied – she was fat, she was loud, she was not his type at all, at all. She drank too much and smoked too much and there was no way in hell that he'd ever give up sweet, skinny Kath for this cow. But the odd thing was, Anna didn't seem to give a fuck. He found it quite curious that she never even asked him about Kath or what he thought he was doing, screwing around with the two of them.

He wondered if it was an act, if she were following that Yank book *The Rules* that he'd seen (he'd found a copy of it lying around Kath's flat, and leafed through it one day). No, that wasn't it. Finally, it dawned on him that Anna simply viewed him as he viewed her: a good fuck and a good time. That made him feel a little, well, **used**, but he tried not to think about it too hard.

But sometimes at night, after Anna had left (he could never be sure when she would stay the night; Anna was nothing if not whimsical) the thoughts crowded in his head and his heart began pounding. Sabine, Anna, Kath, the girl he bought the Parker pen for ten years ago (what was her name?) – all of them yammering at him, looking at him, some hurt, some angry, some distressed and some just plain bored. He wondered if he needed psychiatric help. Maybe this was how madness started. He couldn't sleep on those nights. He tried to put them all out of his mind, these women. They all wanted something from him, and he didn't know what it was, only that he would fail all of them.

After a month of this, he decided to talk to his brother Barry. Barry always had an opinion on everything, from New Labour to Geri Halliwell's tits to Nigel's women. 'You know what yer problem is,' Barry drawled, poking a finger in Nigel's chest as they sat in Barry's local pub, 'You're a sex maniac, you are. You just don't know when to stop. Give it a rest, mate. Stop fucking the fat one, get married to Kathy. She'll give you no problem at all, and it's time you started thinking about settling down.'

Why did he even bother talking to Barry? He could have saved himself a trip down to Essex and read a self-help book instead. All this whingeing and whining . . . all he knew was that he wasn't happy with

Kath, and he wasn't happy without her. And that he couldn't seem to stop fucking Anna.

Anna would tell him to do things. 'Get on your knees,' she'd command. 'Lick my pussy. Shut up and start doing it.' Sex with Anna was like the movies; sometimes he felt that they even had an audience. (They probably did, since Anna insisted they leave the curtains open and the lights on when they fucked). It was nothing like anything he'd ever experienced. They'd fuck once, twice, sometimes three times in one night. He even liked the fact that she was fat.

So maybe that was it. Maybe he was a sex maniac like Bill Clinton, just like Barry said. Maybe there was just nothing he could do about it, maybe it was something that he just had to accept in himself. And as long as Kath didn't know, it couldn't hurt her. She was the right one for him, anyway – she was all the things that he'd envisioned in his wife – pretty, social, not too difficult. He loved her, he did. He just didn't really like to fuck her the way he did with Anna. It was only sex after all, not unlike eating or sleeping or breathing, really. Anna was a sex maniac too, now that he thought about it. And if the situation was okay with Anna, and okay with him, and okay with Kath (and it was, as long as she didn't know), then where was the problem?

As he fell asleep that night, he briefly wondered why women, apart from Anna, were always so pissed off. Men and women were just different, and thought about sex differently. Apart from Anna. And she was a bit nuts.

CHAPTER 6

'This melatonin stuff is all a ruse,' I said to Harriet. I was sipping my tea – a hangover from my London jaunt. I added some more milk and looked out the kitchen window. The same grayness, a vague cloudy cover amassing the sky, identical to the one I'd just left in England greeted me. San Francisco summers – it was like living inside a giant gray pearl. 'I woke up with a start – *bing*! – staring at the ceiling at 4 a.m. The cat was stretched out across my legs, snoring away. My feet were asleep, my cat was asleep, the whole damn *world* was slumbering away and there I am, wide awake and racked with jet lag.'

'Did you buy any perfume at the Duty Free?' Harriet asked mildly.

'Another ruse,' I fumed. 'I don't believe all this Duty Free thing. It's the same price, I tell you. It's just that Americans are too lazy and stupid to calculate the exchange rate. They see twenty six pounds, and think, "Oh, that's around twenty six dollars. Or at most, thirty." '

'I don't do that. I have a calculator in my purse.'

'You're different,' I told her. 'You're thrifty.'

'You mean I'm cheap,' said Harriet. 'I know you think that I am.'

'No, I don't. Just because one time I said something about your dial phone.' I opened the window and stuck my head out into the airshaft, peering up at the sky. 'I think it's charming that you must hold for an operator while the rest of the world is pressing pound for more options.'

Harriet said, 'Did you get any work done?'

'No. Well, yes. I started researching a story about the return of the Goth music and fashion. But then Trevor and Jayne said that Goth hasn't returned – it just never went away. I figure if I wrote about it though, it would look like a trend, just by the mere fact that it was being written about. How about you?'

'I finished that health insurance job,' she said. 'Now I have a client who wants me to write a brochure about a new kind of toenail clipper that he's trying to sell to hotel chains. God, it's so muggy here today.'

'Yes, and while I'm thinking of it, what is going on with this world weather? I just left this miserable sogginess in London. Now it's followed me here. And don't tell me it's El Niño, either.'

Harriet sighed. 'It's hot as hell here. I'm depressed. I woke up and felt so discouraged. I don't know what's the matter with me.'

'Did you eat a banana?'

'Several,' she said, and I heard her shuffle her way down the creaky hall to her closet-sized kitchen. 'Now I'm having my third cup of coffee. But maybe you just need some fresh air.'

I climbed out onto my window sill, so my butt was hanging off the edge as I held onto the sash, still looking up at the sky. 'Hang on,' I said, and grabbed my sunglasses which were lying in the fruit bowl. I returned to my perch and tried to tuck my nightshirt around my thighs. 'I'm taking your advice. Now, have you and Just Jerry had a fight?'

'Not really,' she said and sighed again. 'You know, you have no idea how long it took me to train him out of saying that. You and I laugh about it, but it's only just recently that he's stopped saying that on my machine.'

'Well, good,' I said. 'You've been going out with him for

what – two years? If he were a dog, you'd have to give him an extra-big treat.'

'If only it were that easy,' she said severely. I heard her kettle whistle in the background. 'Two years! I don't know how much longer I can take of this.'

'Of what?' I asked, disingenuously. I knew exactly what Harriet couldn't take much more of, although from my – albeit limited – perspective, they seemed to be coasting along amicably. They were the typical Manhattan couple, going out for dinner and meandering through museums and patronizing the ubiquitous East Village old-man bars. They saw an endless supply of movies on the weekends. Certainly they never fought, which would be against Harriet's code of ethics anyway.

Harriet responded, 'This! This . . . dating thing, going along like we're in our twenties. I mean, what is he thinking? I'm almost *forty*. I want to start thinking about children. I want to have a family and a bigger apartment. We've been going out for two years, and I think it's time. I want a proposal.'

'You mean, like, of marriage?' I leaned further out the window.

'Yes, "*like, of marriage,*" ' she repeated. 'What do you think I mean? A proposal that as individuals, we should floss more? Yes, a wedding proposal. This is ridiculous, carrying on like this, with no discussion of the future, like we're kids.'

'Okay, okay, calm down,' I said. 'Didn't you just have the where-is-this-going conversation on Valentine's Day? After the flower incident?'

'Oh, yes,' she said. 'That's why I think, why bother talking about anything? We're just sailing along in the same old way, no different from a year ago. Oh, sure, we have a good time and we still have nice sex, but since he travels all the time for his stupid job, I don't want to wreck the times we do have together by bringing up all this serious stuff.'

'So – what had happened when you had the where-is-this-going discussion before?' I persisted.

'Don't you remember?' Harriet said accusingly. 'He agreed with me that we should start to have a plan and then we never brought it up again. The worst part is that I think he *likes* it this way. I think if it were up to him, we'd just keep going along like this, seeing each other three or four nights a week, holding onto our teeny rent-controlled apartments, going away on weekends once in a while – until we were eighty.'

'I think so too.' In fact, I didn't think – I knew. Just Jerry was nice enough, certainly a better mate prospect than Clark, but he had the backbone and purpose of an amphibian. As if reading my mind, Harriet said, 'I want him to want me. I want him to be a man. I want him to pick movies. I want him to decide where we're going to eat. And I want him to propose to me.'

Just Jerry proposing! I almost fell out the window. There were so many issues I didn't know where to begin, but perhaps for now, it would probably be better to table the minor discussion of whether Harriet was even in love with him.

Certainly she never spoke of him in passionate tones, not anywhere near the way she used to talk about Clark. But Harriet herself said she would 'never go through again' what she'd 'suffered' at the hands of the cavalier Clark – a man who, among other dastardly deeds during their five years together, had managed to hit on virtually every one of Harriet's girlfriends at one time or another. Clark was a mildly successful performance artist who, in addition to being charming and charismatic, was always flat broke. But as much as I hated to admit, Clark and Harriet did have a certain chemistry that was undeniable. He made Harriet laugh like I'd never seen her laugh before – big, giant, belly laughs from the bottom of her gut – and when he wasn't secretly phoning her best friends the minute she stepped out the door, he actually seemed quite devoted to her. He held her hand, laughed at her jokes, and made her recount stories that she'd told him. He was one of those kinds of men that women talk about in a pitying, wistful way – 'He'd be such a great guy if he weren't so fucked up' – and I could see there was a certain dark, likableness about Clark. The few times we'd engaged in a deep conversation (for whatever reason, Clark reserved his more caddish behavior for Harriet's other female friends), I sensed he was genuinely unhappy about his less-than-stellar track record with Harriet.

And my best friend had been so remarkably patient over the years. His screw-ups, she'd explain, sprung from a deep sense of insecurity or alternatively, Attention Deficit Disorder. Either way, he was 'powerless' to change it, despite a decade of 'working on it' in group therapy. (In that venue, I suspected if Clark was working on anything, it would be his stand-up act rather than any peccadilloes.) After many tortured years, even Harriet saw the light and they had a ragged, hurtful break-up that lasted for over two years . . . which is not to say that I wasn't still half-expecting him to pop up in the picture again.

In the meantime, there had to be some happy medium between Just Jerry and Caddish Clark. 'Why don't you propose to him?' I asked in what I hoped was a reasonable tone.

'Because I don't want to,' she said petulantly. 'I want to be proposed to. I know it sounds archaic, but that's what I want.'

'Well,' I foundered. This proposal thing had always confused me, even when I was a little girl. This whole idea of 'popping' an important question – when it seemed by that point the issue would have been discussed or at least alluded to by both parties – was completely bizarre to me. 'You know what I think. You know I think you should talk about it. At least then you'd know where you stood, Harriet.'

'The Rules say, "Never make ultimatums unless you're prepared to back them up," ' she said.

I groaned. 'Well, there you go, then.'

'But we had a nice time last night.' I sighed now, and closed the window on my thighs. 'I was talking to my cousin about it, and she's all in favor of Jerry. She liked Clark, but she didn't feel I was safe with Clark.'

'Well, safety is one thing you could count on with Jerry, that's for sure.'

'I know you think we're mismatched,' Harriet said.

'I never said that.'

'You don't have to.'

'Now, that's not true,' I protested. 'I just think that Jerry is the deer that happened to stumble into your matrimonial headlights.'

Harriet sniffed. 'Timing *is* everything,' she said. 'It's just — okay. For instance. He could make so much more money at his job if he wanted to. And he never asks to be moved up, he never asks for a raise, he never complains that they send him around the world traveling one week out of four so when he comes back he's exhausted and doesn't want to do anything. He's too tired to get his resumé together, and they know it and they just walk all over him.'

'He works with, um, technology?' I asked hopefully.

'Finance,' Harriet said stiffly. Apparently she didn't know all that much about the specifics either. 'And . . . I don't know if I should be a fishwife and nag him about it, but how can we move into an apartment together if neither one of us has enough money? We can't live in these tiny apartments together. And I'm not going to make enough money in PR to get us a bigger apartment — I mean, it's just not going to happen. He should be thinking of this stuff.'

'And he's not,' I said. The recently married yuppie couple who lived across the airshaft were staring at me from their kitchen. The guy waved, and the girl smiled, but they both retreated nervously after seeing their neighbor hanging out of the window in her nightshirt.

'And he's not.' I heard Harriet's kettle go again, which was a bad sign. Harriet drank coffee in the morning like alcoholics turned to their first drink of the day.

'Harriet, this couple across the hall from me just got married,' I whispered. 'Remember I was telling you about them? The Siamese Twins?'

'Oh, yeah. The couple where you can't tell which one is the man or the woman because they look exactly alike.' Harriet, in spite of herself, chuckled.

'You can't imagine how often the UPS man comes a day,' I whispered, cupping the mouthpiece. 'And the stuff they get! You would never know where to put all that junk – all from Williams Sonoma, Crate & Barrel, Banana Republic, Pottery Barn. It's another one of those dumb marriage things that I just don't get. I mean, what are people thinking? Do they really think that a combined couple in this day and age doesn't own a toaster between them by now? A CuisineArt? A set of mixing bowls? What era is this? I'll bet her dad gave her away at the altar.'

'What's wrong with a father giving away his daughter at the altar?'

'Nothing, if you're a prize heifer.' A few drops of rain plopped on my head and I edged closer to the window, almost dropping the phone four stories down the airshaft.

Harriet sighed again. 'They're probably not getting toasters, or if they are, it's the $400 kind from England. In addition to all the sets of All-Clad cookware, bread makers and vintage bottles of specially pressed olive oil from Tuscany.' She took a gulp of coffee. 'I should eat a billion bananas today.'

'Well, speaking of bananas,' I downshifted, 'I saw an interesting program last night. It was *Dateline*, or *20/20* or one of those so-called news shows. They had this psychologist on who was talking about what makes a happy and long-lasting marriage. He'd done all these studies, and what he came up with was that the couples who have the best rate of success are those that have similar interests, a shared sense of humor, the ability to laugh in the face of adversity and a common value system.'

'Shocking,' Harriet said in a monotone.

'But wait. This psychologist – I forget his name, he looked exactly like Gabe Kaplan from *Welcome Back, Kotter*, so admittedly it was a bit hard to take him seriously – said the best indicator was when the husband literally *adored* his wife. The way he put it was, "You know how men always think they can get a better car? When a husband thinks his wife is the Cadillac, then the marriage is almost destined to succeed." If he praises her unprompted, if he puts her up on a pedestal. He said, "If he really thinks he got the best banana in the bunch." '

'Huh,' said Harriet thoughtfully. 'I don't know if Just Jerry thinks I'm the best banana in the bunch. I know *I* certainly spend a lot of time picking at his little bruises – to his face and behind his back. What did Gabe Kaplan have to say about that?'

'There's the interesting part.' I knew Harriet would warm to this story. It was another one of those nuts she could store for use during the cold winters of confusion. 'He said it doesn't necessarily go the other way. That wives could feel they had a Nissan, say, or just a good old yellow banana with maybe a bruise here and there, and they would be fine with that. They didn't have to feel that they'd gotten the best there was out there.' The sun had made a brief appearance behind the gray gauze and I squinted up at it. Climbing back inside my kitchen, I jumped down and shut the window. 'I just thought you might appreciate that little factoid.'

'Oh, I do,' she said. 'Now I have to figure out how I'm going to use it.' Her call-waiting beeped. 'Maybe that's Just Jerry,' she sighed. 'I guess I should get that, even though my mother counsels that I should pull back and let him figure out that he has to fight for me.'

Oh, poor Just Jerry. He had no idea. 'Don't eat anymore

bananas, Harriet,' I said. 'Go buy your own set of balsamic vinegar and extra-virgin olive oil. Let's talk tomorrow night.'

'Will you be home?' she asked fretfully.

'I think so,' I said, thinking, *I hope so*. Because Jemma had left me a few messages the week after I returned, saying I should 'come along' to the Power Exchange on Saturday night – she had arranged it all with Sir and Ellen.

A series of phone calls went back and forth between Jemma and me the next day before I was to accompany her to the Power Exchange. Despite my earlier confidence that she wouldn't break the date, now that the night was here I was fairly convinced that she would live up to the old Jemma and flake out. After thinking and ruminating and obsessing and trying to imagine what was in store for me that night, I half hoped that she would.

I tried to put myself in her shoes. What would she say to Sir? 'I have this friend who wants to watch us at the Power Exchange and would that be all right with you?' 'I have this friend who has an obsessive curiosity about other people's love lives and I want to help her understand what it's really like to be a submissive and would that be all right with you?' Or, 'I have this friend who has a secret desire to be topped because of all the passive men she's encountered recently and this could be her entry into being a love slave and would that be all right with you?' I didn't know how Sir felt about my tailing Jemma, pestering her with questions, but from what little I understood about their relationship I couldn't imagine that it would be positive.

That was another thorny issue. I was trying to keep an open mind about Sir, but a few things Jemma had said during our lunch at Elroy's worried me. At one point she darkly alluded to the fact that he was 'much less open' about their sexual arrangement than she was. 'I think he would prefer if I were a little more careful, because I have a big mouth,' she said. 'I talk too much.' What would he do to her if he disliked me and my investigations? The last thing I wanted to do was to piss off a sadist – and a big, burly, pirate-y looking one at that.

The next night, precisely at 9 p.m., I stood waiting outside the Power Exchange. For once in my life, I was actually on time, having decided to get dressed early in order to feel fully prepared. What does one wear to a sex club? I didn't want to be mistaken for an active participant, but at the same time I certainly didn't want to stand out, wearing vanilla attire. The regular fall-back uniform for all alternative or semi-alternative events won out: basic black. Black t-shirt, black jeans, and black boots. No make-up, since I wanted to blend into the crowd. That day I'd gone on a long bike ride up and around Marin County, and as per usual I'd braided my hair in two severe Heidi-like plaits that fell on either side of my face. I'd decided to keep it that way, despite the slightly Fraulein air it lent, and probably wouldn't have thought twice about it had I not gone to the grocery store that evening. In line behind me was a slightly disheveled young man, staring at my plaits with a tiny grin on his face. My insane-man radar was going into the red, counseling the average response which of course was to just ignore. Nevertheless, the man kept staring until he finally said to me, 'Nice hair.'

'Thanks,' I said neutrally, swiping my debit card.

'Did you braid it yourself?'

I sighed. 'Yes.'

The man edged a fraction closer. 'Can I touch one?'

Again, I sighed loudly. Maybe I ought to rethink this hair thing tonight – if it was causing a ruckus among the slightly addled in the supermarket, what would happen at the Power Exchange? I eyeballed the guy as I took a mental check – did I have the energy to make a big fuss? Maybe it was a little test, a G-rated version of what was in store for me later. I fixed him with an icy stare and tried to shame him into retracting his request. 'Go ahead,' I dared, glancing at the mild-mannered, mustachioed cashier who was waiting for me to press 'Enter' in the debit machine. If anything outrageous happened in the next thirty seconds, he looked like he could be counted on to vault over the conveyor belt and take matters into his own hands. But undaunted, the young guy timidly picked up a plait, and then dropped it. 'Thank you,' he whispered.

Still, the braids were in place. There I was, clad in my leather jacket, my black garb, my pale, cosmetic-free face – I felt like a German mime.

'Hello,' Jemma breathed, seemingly coming out of nowhere. For a split second, I didn't recognize her. She wore elaborate eye makeup, shiny, ruby lipstick with a dark lip liner, and her two-inch long hair was gelled to perfection, sticking straight up. She was followed by a large, Nordic-looking man carrying a black canvas duffle bag and a strained, mousy-looking woman teetering in high heels. Both Jemma and she were wrapped up in what appeared to be furry cloaks, the kind that I imagined Anna Karenina to don before setting across the frozen steppes of Siberia. Admittedly, there was something, if not Tolstoyan, then downright dramatic about the setting, with the moist fog tumbling under the freeway overpass and the red bulb above the door shrouding everything in an x-rated glow.

She introduced me to Sir, who gamely shook my hand. He was wearing a frilly white shirt, much like the pictures I'd seen, and his long shoulder-length hair was brushed back, leaving a boyish lock that tumbled into his eyes. All in all, he reminded me of a Danish Oliver Reed.

'And this is Ellen,' said Jemma. Ellen smiled at me weakly but remained silent. Because she was lower on the feeding chain than Jemma and Antonia, I hadn't paid much attention to what Jemma had told me about Ellen. She was small and thin, with a flighty edge, and frosted blond streaks throughout her light brown hair, and minty-green, Maybelline-type cream eyeshadow. She looked like one of the Financial District secretaries that stood in line at the deli after four o'clock to get a half-priced tuna sandwich with their Diet Coke.

We walked up the three stairs to a large, heavy door, and into a small alcove lit again with a dim red bulb. There were various signs posted at eye-level: safe sex at all times, no touching unless mutually agreed upon, no alcohol and no drugs. 'Hey!' a young man wearing a leather vest exclaimed. He was standing behind a makeshift counter, talking to an enormously obese man, and both lit up with grins as the trio came into view. 'Hi Gray,' Jemma said. 'How are you doing tonight?'

'Great, great. Can't complain.' He shook Sir's hand and said hello to Ellen.

'Gray is the doorman,' Jemma explained to me. 'Gray, this is our friend. She's with us tonight.'

'Welcome,' Gray said warmly. 'How's it going?'

'Oh, fine,' I said.

'Were you here late last Saturday?' Jemma asked Gray. 'How was it?'

'You know, the usual. I had to deal with Howard—' Gray jerked his thumb in that direction and lowered his voice. '—he's already here.'

'Oh, God.' Jemma and Sir groaned in unison. Sir bent down and whispered something in Jemma's ear, and she nodded. She turned back to me and said, 'I'll explain in a minute about Howard.'

'Okay,' I said. So far, so good. I wasn't sure what I'd been expecting, but at this rate I felt as if I were going to the movies.

We went into a darker larger room that was behind the double set of doors in the alcove. Loud, techno-industrial music shook the walls, and a red and white strobe light lit the dark interior. When my eyes adjusted, I could see the small jail cells that lined one side of the room. Each cell had its own light source from a dull bulb overhead, and there were various benches, stools and contraptions that looked suspiciously gynecological in every cell. All of the cells were empty, but Jemma had told me the whole of the club would be that way because it was so early. They needed to stake their claim in what she called the Medieval Room.

I followed them down a narrow corridor lit by a black light, and turned left into a large, spacious area known as the famous Medieval Room. There were fake coat-of-arms and shields on the walls; on one side of the room was a long, King Arthur-style dining room table, running about fifteen feet, complete with a plaster-of-Paris roast boar on a platter with an apple in its mouth. On the far side was a dais with a majestic throne in the center, flanked by two smaller thrones. Next to that and between the dining room table and the dais was an imposing brick 'fireplace' with plastic logs lit from underneath by an electric bulb. In the center of the room was a ten-foot-high wooden X, a sort of Joan-of-Arc stake, and cordoned off by heavy rope from the other half of the room. On that side, opposite the throne, was a king-size platform bed, on which a man with thick eyeglasses and a Paul Bunyan-ish red beard sat fiddling with a small riding crop, smiling beatifically to himself.

There were small, handwritten signs tacked on the door frame. 'Free Flowers with Every Flogging,' they cheerfully offered. 'Free Floggings on Request.' Jemma groaned under her breath and patiently led me across the room, where Sir and Ellen were already unloading the duffle bag onto one end of the oak table. More heavy rope cordoned off the main area of the room from the side where one entered – presumably the spectators' area. There were a few chairs and a bench on this side of the room, but apart from our group, Gray, the enormously obese man and Paul Bunyan, no one else was at the club yet.

I looked around, uncertain of where to plant myself. I'd

taken off my jacket and was standing next to the dais, watching as various tools, whips, contraptions with cords, ropes and strings were being carefully arranged by Sir. Both Jemma and Ellen had taken off their cloaks; Ellen was wearing a shiny black teddy made of some man-made material, and Jemma wore what looked to be almost a black leather bikini top with a matching butt-skimming mini-skirt and fishnets. She was extremely tall, and I looked down to see six-inch patent leather stilettos, the sight of which made my bunions ache. I wondered if she and Ellen were cold.

I gravitated over to the other side of the room, wondering if I should seat myself in the spectators' section, trying to memorize the room and all its components. Paul Bunyan looked up and said, 'You can sit here.' He patted a part of the bed.

Not wanting to appear like a ninny, I reluctantly sat on the edge. Jemma caught sight and immediately strolled over. 'Um, why don't you come with me? I have to get Sir a Coke. He's hurt his eye and you can have a look around.'

I followed her out into what was a lounge, with a sofa, coffee table, chairs and a soda machine. On the coffee table, in a large bowl, lay a pile of not individually wrapped candies but brightly colored condoms. It was a bit quieter out here, without the industrial noise emanating from every speaker in every corner. 'Sorry to pull you out of there,' Jemma said, shaking her head.

'Did I do something wrong?' I asked fearfully.

'Oh my God, of course not. It's just Howard. He's the freak that puts up those signs. He's a total and utter loser. He has no life, so he gets here early every weekend, and cordons off his little area, which incidently you're not supposed to do, since the place is open to everyone. Ugh. He's just weird.' She was unfurling a sweaty dollar bill that evidently had been folded up in her bra.

I asked, 'What's wrong with Sir's eye?'

'He thwacked himself with the bull whip on the way over here. It sometimes happens. He was curling it up, and the end of it just hissed in the air and went into his eye. He'll be all right – I'm just going to get something cold to put on it.'

I sat on the end of the sofa. 'What a good submissive you are.'

'Thank you darling. I'll take that in the manner it was offered.'

She tried to feed the bill in, but nothing was happening. 'Great,' she said sarcastically, looking behind the machine. She picked up the plug, and searched around for a socket. 'Now why would this be unplugged? I guess I'll have to get Gray to go over to the gay boys' side and get me a cold can. Hang on a second here – or you can go to the other room, if you want.' She teetered off as I gingerly poked my head into the next room.

Here was the aorta of the club – a large, brightly lit area with sofas and chairs scattered around, and a long snack bar with a revolving hot dog machine and fresh popcorn on one end. Across from the cash register was a clothes rack with rubber, Lycra and plastic accoutrements, and a sign above, 'All Rubber 25% Off.' A Japanese person of indeterminate gender and a turquoise mohawk was chatting cheerfully with the obese man. In the glass case under his/her elbows was every kind of candy imaginable, including Skittles, Hershey bars and, yes, licorice whips.

I wandered back to the Medieval Room. Ellen was standing against the wall next to the fireplace, hands behind her back, eyes cast downward, the very picture of submission. Jemma was holding a Coke can to Sir's eye, who was alternately laughing and saying things in a low voice to her, who would smile or laugh back.

I sat down on the edge of the dais. It was either there or in the spectators' wing where, curiously enough, you couldn't see all that well since the stake was facing toward the back of the room. There was a silence in the air, among Sir, Jemma and Ellen – or at least, no one was shouting to be heard over the pounding music. Paul Bunyan was still calmly fingering his riding crop, sitting on the edge of the bed, looking as if he could have been waiting in line at the DMV to register his car. Jemma smiled at me and said something to Sir, who glanced over at me and shrugged. There was a shift in mood; apparently, play had begun.

Jemma unhooked her bra top and, now topless, walked across the room to stand against the wooden X. Now I saw that she had a pierced navel as well as a pierced breast, with two heavy silver rings that were connected by a chain. Why had she not told me she had a pierced nipple? I could almost hear her cheerful retort, 'Well, you never asked.'

Sir had led Ellen out from against the wall. She bent her head a little and he took a handful of her hair and carefully but assertively pulled it back so she looked at him. She had an intense but passive expression on her face, and he gently turned her around. Taking off the rope that was curled around his waist, he began to painstakingly knot and twist her wrists together, looping the rope back around, and knotting again. Now I understood about the Japanese knot books that Jemma said Sir studied religiously. He adjusted and wound it around her tight body, so after about fifteen minutes she was elaborately tied up with a network of precisely intricate knots and ties. It was rather beautiful looking, although she did bear a certain resemblance to a Thanksgiving turkey.

Next it was Jemma's turn. He had backed Ellen up to her original position against the wall, so that she was facing Jemma. He wound some more cord around Jemma's wrists, knotting and tying her to the stake. Her ankles remained free, but she spread them, so as to form an X. Throughout this both she and Ellen maintained a serene and, well, submissive expression to their faces – and Sir just looked like he was concentrating.

He had picked up a shorter whip and was lightly tapping her on the inside of her thighs. I wondered if I looked part of the scene, since I was in essence sitting right at the top of the room, in their space. I got up and moved to the other side of the room, to the spectators' side. For the next fifteen or twenty minutes or so, Sir picked up various implements – floggers, ropes, etc. – and tried them out on her, gently whipping her breasts or thighs or arms. She kept her eyes shut for much of it, apart from when Sir would back up and seemingly consider what he was going to do next. Then she'd open her eyes, they'd look at each other, and murmur back and forth. The music – 'Firestarter' by Prodigy – pounded fiercely, and Sir looked annoyed at one point, wondering out loud if there wasn't something else they could play.

I strained to hear what they were saying. She didn't look like she was saying any 'yes, sir,' or 'no, sir' or 'three bags full sir' – if anything, they all looked like they were sharing a private joke. And indeed, they'd laugh to each other, and direct something to Ellen (who kept her eyes downcast) who would also make a quip and they'd all laugh knowingly to each other.

Just when I was starting to get used to this whole strange spectacle, even feeling a tad bored, Sir hauled off and slapped Jemma across the face. Hard. Jemma gasped and I immediately cringed. A large red welt appeared on her left cheek. At this point, a few other men had wandered into the room and were standing near me, watching as well. They were young Latinos, and they were craning to see Jemma's large breasts without actually stepping inside the scene. They seemed nonplussed by the slap, but I had to get up and move. For some reason, amongst all this prelude talk of being whipped, burned, humiliated, shocked, cut and mock-raped, I'd forgotten about the garden variety hand-to-body physicality. I looked at her carefully: she still had her eyes closed, and looked as if she were concentrating very hard. Sir was now rubbing her face gently, but I shifted around, looking at the audience. There were about ten of us now, all men except me, and a couple in their mid-forties who wore denim jackets and sneakers, who looked like they just stumbled in after a day at Fisherman's Wharf.

At this point I decided to go investigate the rest of the club. I wondered if Jemma could see me leaving – if it bothered her, or Sir, or Ellen even for that matter. Ellen was still standing, trussed as a turkey, looking demurely at the floor. Sir was now doing the fire trick on Jemma – lighting her back from one point, and quickly putting it out as it traveled up the length of where he'd applied the rubbing alcohol. Then he'd wipe more alcohol on, set it alight, and put it out. She gasped a little every time, but I remembered her words in Elroy's as she described it to me ('No, it doesn't hurt – it feels hot. It's a shock more than it's painful') so I tried to feel unconcerned.

I followed a set of narrow stairs down to the dungeon. It was a large open space, in half-light, with the same industrial music crashing through the walls. Still, no one was there to occupy the large leather slings, or to lay upon what looked like the gynecological exam tables. My footsteps echoed down the length of the room. There were a few false walls set up here and there, about six-feet tall, topped with cyclone fencing, presumably to give the space a cosier feel. I tried to imagine this basement teeming with people and spectators and masters and slaves, since at this point, it was a little like wandering around a museum after hours. On one end was another set of rooms with circular windows at eye-level in each door. On the other side was a narrow closed hallway with a bench running along its length. I went back upstairs to the Medieval Room.

Now there was more of a crowd, and there seemed to be some sort of excitement or humor in the air. Even mousy Ellen was cracking a smile. There were a few murmurs, and when I got closer, I heard Sir speaking in above-normal tones to Jemma, who was responding with some hesitancy. She was turned around again, facing him, but her bare buttocks now sported huge red welts across them, and criss-crossed over the backs of her thighs.

Sir was winding his bullwhip in a circle. I thought I heard him say something that sounded like 'Alaska,' and Jemma immediately replied 'Juno.' He nodded approvingly. He then said something that I couldn't catch, and I saw Jemma hesitate, before saying 'Cedar Rapids?'

Craack!! The whip sang out into the air, snapping near Jemma's belly. Everyone jumped. Sir was shaking his head in mock disgust, and Jemma and Ellen I could see were trying hard not to giggle. He was coiling the whip again, stepping back, when he saw me. I'd moved to the head of the crowd and was standing with my arms crossed, looking, I'm sure, like a cross between Miss Muffett and Eva Braun.

'South Dakota,' he called over. 'Courtney.'

'Me?' I squeaked. *Oh, no.* 'Okay, hang on a second.' *Come on, come on* – of course I knew the capital of South Dakota – my grandmother *lived* there, for heaven's sake. 'Umm. Well, it's not Fargo,' I finally said weakly.

'Nope,' said Sir, drawing back his arm, priming the whip.

'That's North Dakota,' a man on one side of me added helpfully.

'Sioux Falls?' I guessed.

Craaaacck!!! The whip lashed out and returned, screaming through the air. Jemma flinched again, but as far as I could tell, she hadn't been touched. 'Pierre,' Sir said matter-of-factly. Jemma glanced at me and I mouthed, 'Sorry.' She shook her head, and the three of them laughed.

'Nebraska?' Sir said, picking up a shorter, multi-tailed flogger.

Jemma closed her eyes. 'Lincoln.'

He examined one of the tails of the whip. 'Connecticut.'

'Hartford,' Jemma said without hesitation. Jesus, I thought.

He was now gently tossing it in the air, and grabbed it quickly.

'New York!'

'Um. Um. Hang on, I know this,' she murmured. *Albany*, I thought. Albany. Albany. Come on Jemma, *Albany*.

'I don't know it.' *Whick-shee*. A slap on her stomach with the flogger and she winced – but smiled at him through closed eyes.

At that point they must have decided that a little break was in order, because Sir approached Jemma, untied her wrists, and stroked her head with surprising tenderness. She walked to the side of the room by the duffle bag, and put her bra top back on, speaking quietly to Sir. Ellen now was led in the middle of the room, and Sir was carefully tying a black leather blindfold across her eyes. Waiting, Jemma whispered something to Sir – who was considering his array of equipment on the table – and he nodded without looking up. She made her way over to me and the mostly male crowd of twenty or so automatically parted, as if greeting a celebrity.

'So,' she said, as we went into the smaller lounge area with the coffee table and soda machine. 'Do you want a drink?' She fished around her bra.

'Yes, but not the kind they're serving here,' I said.

'They have juice in the other snack area—'

'That wasn't really what I meant, but sure, let's go get a juice drink.' Ignoring the men's stares, she led the way to the candy counter and greeted the Japanese mohawked man/woman.

'What do you want?' Jemma asked me.

'I'll pay,' I said, thinking that's the least I could do. 'A Ruby Red Grapefruit Juice Squeeze, please.' I turned to her. 'I'm sorry about getting that capital wrong. Or should you be thanking me? I'm not really certain.'

Jemma chuckled, taking a large swig of her lemonade. 'I'm just glad that we weren't doing state flowers tonight. Or birds. Then I'm really in trouble.'

'I can imagine,' I said. 'You're not even an American.'

We sat on one of the foam-filled couches. Jemma was breathing slightly heavily, as if she'd just come from a workout, which I guess in a sense she had. She inspected me closely. 'You okay? Everything all right? Still have jet lag?'

'Oh, yes,' I said, but cheerfully. The last thing I wanted was Jemma to worry about me – it seemed she had enough to think about. 'That whip – it wasn't hitting you, was it?'

'The bull whip? Oh, no,' she said cheerfully. 'It just makes a very loud and scary noise.'

I toyed with the twist-off cap in my hand, breaking off the little aluminum bits. Another couple – this time, the man in jeans, the woman in a leather dress which barely contained her – came in and began perusing the sale rack of rubber clothes. 'Do you ever wonder what these guys do when they go home, Jemma? After they watch you? The guys in the audience?'

'What do you mean? As in, do they jack off?'

'No, that's not really what I meant,' I said. 'I mean – you have the advantage of being a bit educated about all this. You know it's consensual, you know that it's a complex arrangement. But – do you ever wonder about some of these young guys? Some who come from particularly macho cultures, who come in here and see this and see you being, um, whipped or slapped in a . . . a . . . sexual way? I was just thinking that maybe they would get the wrong idea and maybe go home and, um, practice on their girlfriends or wives or whatever.'

Jemma considered. She finished her juice and wiped her mouth. 'No, I don't think about that.'

'I was just wondering if maybe you felt like you had some responsibility in all that.'

'No. No.' She read the ingredients on the back of the empty bottle, and set it on the white linoleum table. 'I think you could say the same thing about seeing a particularly violent movie, or a graphic porn film. That – if they're going to do that stuff and do it as assholes and not be responsible and be consensual – well, I think they would have done it otherwise. I don't think we plant a seed in their brain, if that's what you mean.'

'Well, no,' I said uncertainly. 'But you can see why some people – well, maybe women, maybe women who've been beaten up by their lovers or husbands or boyfriends or whatever – wouldn't think this was such a great thing to be doing. That it wasn't setting a particularly good example for, um, the menfolk, who – who wouldn't understand that it was consensual and pleasurable for you too.'

'I see what you're saying,' she said slowly, 'but really, I don't think it's my responsibility to set good examples in the S/M world. I mean, for one thing, if it wasn't me they were watching, it would be someone else. You know?'

'Ye – es,' I said. What I didn't say was that her answers reminded me – pretty much word for word – of all the apologias given in these contexts: violence in the media, snuff films, graphic pornography and the like. And I felt the same type of dissatisfaction upon hearing them again – that there was a logical piece of the puzzle missing from their words that I couldn't quite put my finger on. 'It was just something I wanted to ask you,' I said weakly, examining her eye make-up in the brighter light. 'How long does it take you to put on all this stuff?'

'Hours,' she smiled, fiddling with her bra strap. 'Maybe you'll have to ask me about the philosophical things later – it's hard for me to think about, particularly in here.'

'I'm sorry.' I said immediately. 'It was just a thought.' Good God – sometimes I had about as much tact and diplomacy as Rush Limbaugh.

CHAPTER 7

The experience of the Power Exchange left me befuddled for weeks. I phoned Jemma a few times, hoping she would debrief me, as if I were an international hostage who'd just been sprung. But when I heard her polite lilt, her warmth flowing through the phone lines as she breathed happily 'Hullo, darling!' I simply couldn't bring myself to talk about the more disturbing elements, feeling that I might upset her with my tone – a tone that would probably come across as accusatory and judgmental. She would happily recount her latest exploit with Sir and Ellen, and I would listen, trying to voice an encouraging 'that's nice' and 'how funny' here and there. I still hadn't told anybody about my little foray because, oddly, I felt protective of her and her lifestyle.

'Something's happening to me,' I said to Harriet one Sunday night, not long after the Power Exchange soirée. 'Slowly but surely, I am dissolving into thin air and disappearing.'

'What are you talking about?' she sighed.

'I can't quite understand it,' I said. 'Get this: Last week, I sent Marco a birthday card. I haven't talked to him in, oh, two months or so. Nothing too unusual.'

'He's probably in the throes of a new Ms Trouble,' said Harriet. 'You know how he gets. Give him a month, and he'll be disillusioned and frustrated, back to where he started. And calling again.'

'Okay, sure. But I send him a birthday card in the mail. The *mail*, Harriet. You know my feelings about the US Postal

Service. So, I send him a card, just because I happened to remember that his birthday is around Labor Day. And . . . nothing. No phone call, no response, nothing. I thought maybe it got lost, but no, because then Adam told me he'd mentioned it. Next, my grandmother.'

'The one in the Midwest?' asked Harriet. 'The one who just got thrown over for a sixty-five-year-old?'

'The very same,' I said. It had been a devastating story that my mother had revealed last week: my eighty-three-year-old grandmother had been dumped by Hank, her seventy-year-old widower boyfriend of the past one year. He'd confessed that he was still in love with his dead wife, Flossie, and he hadn't gotten over her. Unbeknownst to my grandmother, he'd been seen around the small Midwestern town with a sixty-five-year-old hussy, driving a red sports car. My mother further added, much to my displeasure, that through this Hank, my good Irish-Catholic grandmother had apparently discovered what the big fuss about sex was after all this time; also, that my great uncle Ernie had 'disapproved' of his sister sleeping in the same motel room as her boyfriend, and had made his displeasure heartily known throughout the Irish clan, thus driving the boyfriend away. Heartbreakingly enough, my grandmother – not normally an expressive type – had proceeded to read my mother a poem she'd written for Hank, and concluded the conversation by saying she had nothing left to live for.

'So I sent my grandmother some flowers,' I said. 'Just a little arrangement, saying that I loved her and I was thinking of her.'

There was a pause on the other side of the line. 'I hope you didn't send that anonymously,' said Harriet cautiously. 'It doesn't matter what age you are – a dump is a dump. And imagine how she felt when she saw the delivery man standing there, beaming, with a vase of flowers in his hand.'

'Of course I didn't send it anonymously,' I said crossly. 'Do you take me for a total heartless fool?' Privately, I had to admit that I hadn't really projected that literally into the future, so as to imagine my grandmother's hopes when she flung open the door. 'So, are you saying that's why I haven't heard anything from her either?'

'No, of course not,' said Harriet. 'But think of her disappointment when she read the card.'

'Thanks a lot, Harriet. Now I feel much better.'

'Oh, I'm sure she got over it really quickly,' Harriet added. 'What else?'

'Well, I went on that organized bike ride this weekend around the Bay Area,' I said.

'I don't know how you can do those things,' she said, not for the first time.

'What things? Exercise?'

'Well, yes.'

'Okay, so afterwards, I'm standing at a food booth, trying to order a sausage sandwich. There are three people working behind the counter, all laughing and chatting, all ignoring me. I'm saying "Excuse me? Excuse me?" and they still go on talking. Finally they look up and start asking all the people around me – beside me, even in *back* of me – "Can I help you?" "Have you been helped?" I get this one man's attention and he says, "Oh, you can't order from me, I just take the money. But I'll tell them what you want." And he stands there and does absolutely nothing. I tell you, at one point, I looked down at my shoes to see if I was still there.'

'The Invisible Woman,' Harriet commented.

'That's me,' I said. 'Besides the fact that the phone has not rung at all this weekend. Apart from you. Isn't that pathetic?'

'Yes,' she said seriously. 'But you have been away an awful lot.'

I suddenly remembered. 'How was your weekend in Woodstock with Just Jerry?'

'Great,' she said, without irony. 'No, I really mean it. It was

147

so relaxing. We barbecued and ate and drank like fish. I think I drank a bottle of wine a day.'

'You didn't talk about stuff?'

'No, of course not. We were staying at Patricia's house. There were five other couples that weekend. No place to talk.'

'Of course,' I said. 'You know, maybe this Invisible Woman thing – is it because I'm not part of a couple? That there aren't two people to answer to?'

'Don't tell me *you* are getting bitten by the husband-hunting bug,' said Harriet, incredulous.

'No, silly.' I thought for a moment. 'But maybe everyone around me is. I notice it more when I'm out with Aidan – I get paid attention to by service staff, at the dry cleaners, at movies. But if I'm alone, *poof*. Even my own mother has given up trying to find me a partner, settling instead for a bird named Zippy.'

The bird cocked his head. He seemed to want to peer at me out of both eyes, to get a straight-on view. But the perches inside his cage were placed at a diagonal, and I was timidly standing to the side of him. I poked a finger between the bars and he began racing back and forth on the length of his wooden perch, doing a little nervous dance. He raised the cherry-hued feathers on the back of his head, fanning them out in ire. I took my finger away.

'He's getting more aggressive,' my mother said. We both regarded him with trepidation. 'He didn't use to do that when I first got him.'

'Maybe it's because he's alone a lot,' I said. Zippy's cage was on top of a mantel in the middle of my mother's house, in a drafty hallway. 'Does he see people very much?'

'All the time!' my mother practically shouted. 'People are walking in and out of this house all day. The contractor, the painters, those men who sand the floor—'

'I mean, like, people who know him. I don't think the

construction crew for your kitchen really counts.'

'They've been here for a year,' my mother pointed out. 'Zippy should be familiar with them. God knows I am.' I'd come over to use my mother's fax machine, not expecting her to be home, yet here she was in the mid-afternoon, regarding her unpacked suitcases spilling out with dirty clothes with some curiosity, extracting this and that newly purchased London item and holding it up to herself, saying, 'What do you think of this jacket/sweater/brooch/scarf? It was horribly expensive.' Then she'd throw it to one side, adding, 'You can borrow it if you want.'

I crouched down next to the fax machine and punched some numbers in. I heard the number ring, and a secretary's voice answer perkily 'Hello? Can I help you?' before the fax screech on my end would kick in. Obviously I'd written down the wrong number. I tried a few more times then gave up, as my mom watched me in a jet-lagged fog. I'd been home for over a month now, but she'd extended her trip, accompanying Andreas on a teeth-chattering business trip to Oslo.

'Did you have a good time in London?' she asked me as we went in the hall to look at Zippy.

'Sure,' I said. 'It seems so long ago.'

'Well, it was,' she said. 'Weren't you going to get your hair done there?' she asked, which, translated from mother-daughter-speak, actually meant 'You really should have gotten your hair done there.'

I decided to ignore that, and said instead, 'You know London. It's a blast while you're there, throwing around that exotic Monopoly money, dashing around in black cabs, and then you come home to rack and financial ruin.' My mother nodded knowingly.

I waggled my finger again at Zippy and he hissed at me. We turned away from his cage and I looked for somewhere to sit down, but all the furniture had been removed from the front part of the house, piled into the living room and covered with plastic tarps. This was the house I grew up in, but as each year went by, I felt more and more detached each time I visited – as if I were attending an art show in a familiar old museum. 'When did you decide to get the floors re-done?' I asked.

'They talked me into it.' My mother leaned against the wall like a forlorn girl at the sock hop who hadn't been asked to dance yet, her hands behind her back. 'They said, "Listen, Peggy" – and why is it that people your age are so familiar with you, throwing your first name around like they've known you for years? It's "Peggy this," "Peggy that," all the time now – anyway, this contractor whom I don't know from Adam says, "Peggy, since we're re-doing your kitchen, why not sand these floors too? And while we're at it, we could repaint the hallway." When he said it, it made sense. But I didn't want to give him the satisfaction. I replied, "Look, Mr. Williams, will it make you finish the kitchen faster? Because if the answer's yes, then do it." Do you know that I have not had a stove for eight months? My toaster is in my bedroom. I plugged it in behind the chaise longue. I've been surviving on toast for the last year.'

'Well, don't forget to eat some fruit once in a while. Otherwise you'll get scurvy.' I leaned on the wall too. 'Did you have a good time in London? How was it with Andreas?'

My mother gave a sniff. 'Andreas and I are not seeing one another,' she said coolly. 'This going back and forth is not working. I can't move to London, and Lord knows he can't move here. I decided as I was freezing my toes off in Oslo that I will put all this excess energy into getting this house in order, and making it a really great house – the kind that I've wanted to live in.'

'God,' I said, startled. I looked at her curiously. She certainly didn't look very shaken up, apart from a few deeper circles under her big brown eyes, which were probably due to jet lag more than anything else. Ever since my mother's divorce from my father some twenty years ago, it seemed that nothing would shake her again to the core of her soul like that had.

And I'd had my doubts about Andreas for some time, classifying him as one of those wily and smooth European men who probably had a few families stashed around the globe. I gestured around the bare house, at the stripped walls and dusty wood floor. 'So now it's just you and Zippy?'

'It's always just been me and Zippy,' my mother pointed out calmly. 'In a manner of speaking. And Conchetta. And the dog. And the cat. And now all the contractors and work men.' She ran both of her hands through her hair and eyed me with a weak smile. 'It's nice to make your nest comfortable. Maybe you should start entertaining more. Having friends over for little dinner parties, that sort of thing.'

'There's nowhere to park in my neighborhood,' I said lamely. 'And all my friends are . . . scattered.' I tried to imagine Jemma, Sir, Marie, Cheating Gavin, Harriet, Just Jerry and Aidan all sitting around my tiny kitchen table, talking about . . . what? The skirmishes in the former territories of Yugoslavia? The fall TV line-up? Our work? 'It's not really like when you were my age, Mom. Like when you had cliques with all your married friends.' I glanced at Zippy, who was doing his little anxiety dance again. 'Unless you're one of those A-list society people that you read about in the paper, I think almost everyone could be called a victim of the postmodern urban diaspora.'

'What does that mean?'

I thought for a moment. 'It means that we spend a lot of time on our own trying to figure out how not to be that way.' I wanted to tell her a little about Jemma, or Marie, or even Kath and Nigel, but decided I couldn't put their messy relationships in a neat little box that would make an uncomplicated, hallway story. It occurred to me that one of the beauties of my mother's upbringing was her firm belief that things were either *this* way, or *that* way – and people must act accordingly. It was from this simple philosophy that another belief of hers sprang – that she and André Previn were meant to be together, that he was her perfect man, and that the only blockage to their happy future was the minor fact that they had never actually met. 'When did you and Andreas decide this?' I asked.

'When I was over there,' my mother said, seemingly off-hand. 'Oh, I'm sad about it. But I have so much going on right now here, what with my work and my house. And it really cuts me off from other opportunities. When you're my age, great people are hard to find. They're either married or dead. It seems like they're hard to find at any age, though, now that I think about it.'

'That's true,' I said. 'Lots of good friendship material though.'

My mother kicked the floor a little as she spoke. 'How did my generation raise you kids to be so afraid of commitment?'

'I'm not afraid of committing, Mom,' I told her. 'I just can't seem to make an intimate emotional connection.'

That little statement hung between us like a helium balloon, and my mother sighed again. She was wearing tiny French jeans and a yellow button-down shirt – she looked like an urban cowgirl. 'We could get you little buffet plates,' she said. 'That's what you need to do: have a little buffet every so often. We'll buy you twelve buffet plates, twelve little forks, twelve cute, bright Provençal-style napkins.'

'How about twelve, cute little chairs, too? There's nowhere to sit in my apartment.' My back was starting to hurt with all this leaning and I knelt down on the floor, as if we were two cowgirls conversing by a fire. 'Mom, you are really sweet to think about this, but honestly. I just can't imagine all my friends coming together and having anything in common. There's my hairdresser – she's got a baby and a cheating husband. There's Jemma – she's, um, a nanny and uh . . .' I paused for a second. 'Well, I think her boyfriend wouldn't really feel comfortable.'

'Why?' my mother interrupted. 'What's the matter with him?'

'Nothing,' I said, thinking about a recent conversation with Aidan. Aidan finally said this 'have-his-cake-and-eat-it-too' situation of Sir's was ridiculous, and it was, moreover, ridiculous of all of us to pretend that it was just a perfectly reasonable arrangement. Giving me a significant look, he asked me if I thought Sir was an 'asshole' for putting Jemma in this untenable position? I'd tried to explain about Jemma's consent, consent, consent comment ('What's the three most important words in real estate?' she'd asked me. 'Now think about my arrangement. What's the three most important words?'), but Aidan just waved his hand away. 'You could say that about any woman in an emotionally abusive situation,' he said. 'They're always free to walk away. If I ever meet this guy, I'm going to have a real problem being nice.' No, it wasn't possible to throw Sir in the mix. I finally said to my mom, 'He's a sailor. He'll probably be out at sea.'

'Well, fine, he won't be able to come then.' My mother knelt down on her haunches too, against the mantel, so we were right under Zippy's cage.

'And Harriet – well, she's in New York. She can't come obviously. Although she is making a little trip out here soon.'

'Good,' my mother said, brightening. Harriet and my mother had always gotten along well. Sometimes I suspected them of having secret rendezvous lunches, coordinating their dating strategies and notes, so similar did they sometimes sound. 'Is she bringing that Mr Trouble with her too? Courtney! Remember that terrible story about the home movie?' My mother shook her head and I resisted pointing out that my mother had her own history of Mr Troubles as well, up to and including my very own father. Harriet and my mother and I had once drunk martinis at Café des Artistes in New York and Harriet had made the mistake of telling my mother the sorry saga of Clark and all his transgressions. 'Then my friend Ted made a home movie about it,' Harriet had said, nibbling her cocktail onion. 'He made me re-enact when I found out that Clark had been secretly phoning one of my girlfriends, trying to go out on a date with her. I rolled around the floor of apartment, clutching my hair. I had to do several takes, writhing around on my carpet with Ted saying, "No Harriet, look more upset. Can you cry on cue? Now, roll this way, to the camera." '

'She doesn't go out with Clark anymore,' I told my mother. 'Now she goes out with a mild-mannered, even-tempered decent man named Jerry. She's plotting and scheming about getting a ring out of him. I keep waiting for her to tell me she's back to seeing Clark.' I sneezed violently and Zippy let out a loud squawk. 'Allergies,' I said. 'Suddenly I'm allergic to my cat. That's another thing – the cat would have a heart attack if all these strange people started tramping into my apartment. I don't think she could survive it.'

'Shut her up in the bedroom,' my mother said impatiently. 'How old is that cat, anyway?'

'Uh, four. No, five. I got her four years ago when Michael turned allergic and she was one then.'

'Good God,' my mother said, and started to laugh. 'Cats live into their twenties. You could have that cat for a good seventeen more years. Till I'm seventy-five. You'll be forty-eight, living with your cat! Isn't that something?' I sighed and started to laugh as well, but I stood up, stretching my legs. 'Isn't there somebody you're interested in that you could invite too?' my mother asked, looking up at me.

I locked eyes with Zippy. He was frozen, watching me. 'Him,' I said, pointing. Besides not thinking of anyone else off the top of my head, Zippy would at least not cause any stress between Aidan and me.

'Are you still friends with that cold, short lawyer?' my mother asked, her face darkening. 'I hope you got your shirt back.'

'I did,' I said. 'No, not friends.'

'What about any editors? Writers? Artists?'

'No, no, and no.'

'What about that adorable boy you went to high school with?'

'Marco?' I said, and wrinkled my nose. 'Mom, no. I don't want to go out with Marco. Really, it's okay. I'll think about the buffet thing. And I've got to go home and clean now, because Trevor and Jayne arrive next week for a day before they go to Las Vegas.' At that point, a paint-covered man in overalls and a Coors baseball cap rounded the corner of the hallway, practically falling over my mom who was still kneeling, picking a piece of navy lint off her yellow blouse. He nearly shrieked, which gave me time to appraise him – he had a long nose and a lock of dark hair falling into his eyes. He stepped around me, carrying paint cans and excusing himself. I shot a look at my mother. We looked him over, and then shook our heads in unison.

'Where are you going to be?' my mother asked. 'You could come stay here if you want! It would be nice to have you home for a while. And I'll help you plan a buffet if you want! Maybe I could even come.'

I inspected her closely. She looked like an eager little girl, kneeling the way she was, a big smile on her face. 'What's going on, Mom? Why are you getting all maternal on me? It's really not like you.'

'I just want you to be happy. Is there anything wrong with that?'

'No, I'm kidding Mom,' I said hastily, although I wasn't. 'I *am* happy. And I'll just sleep on my sofa. I was going to stay at Aidan's, but it seemed ridiculous just for one night.'

'That's true,' my mother said, and I could see the question

of where I would sleep at Aidan's apartment bouncing around in her mind like a green tennis ball, until she finally whacked it out.

'Mom?' I said suddenly. 'Are you sure you're okay about this breakup with Andreas?'

'Oh, yes,' she said, and waved her hand as if she were saluting a general. She was reminding me every minute of the little Peggy, the Peggy I'd seen in tiny scalloped-edged black-and-white photos, squatting down in the dirt as she dug in her mom's vegetable garden with a stick, a determined look furrowing her dark brows. She must have been a funny little kid, one of those that could drive you crazy with their dogged questions and plucky inquisitiveness.

I clucked at Zippy, kissed my mother goodbye, and waved to the paint guy, who was on the other end of the hallway by the kitchen. 'I'll think about the party,' I said. 'Maybe when Harriet's here.'

'Okay,' my mom said, standing up. She tried to arrange my hair a little and I let her, liking the feeling of her cooled, ringed fingers brushing my ears and cheeks and forehead.

Two days before Trevor and Jayne were to breeze into town, I was pushing my bike up a steep hill in the direction of my apartment. It was one of those windy but hot autumn days in San Francisco, and not for the first time, I thought about how I didn't remember any of these kinds of days when I was growing up. Twenty years ago in San Francisco, summer meant fog. Autumn meant a chill in the air. Winter meant rain. And spring – well, spring was just more fog and some blue sky and occasionally an eighty-degree day here and there.

I'd jumped on my bike in a well-intentioned fit of organization, determined to get down to the last day of the sale at a sports store. 'All of this bike riding is great, but my butt has been hurting for days,' I'd told Aidan, refraining from the actual specifics of my pain, which naturally had nothing to do with my butt.

'Do you have proper cycling shorts?'

'I have some tights that I cut off at the knee,' I said. 'That's not good enough?'

No, it wasn't – I needed to get special leggings that had a nice, cushy chamois pad in the seat. At the sports store I tried on a pair, felt like I was wearing diapers, returned them to the rack and then glanced at the price tag. Good God – no wonder poor people were out of shape, because how could anyone else afford all these exercise accoutrements that were described as *absolutely necessary* by those in the know? As I stood there, wondering if I could just sew a dishtowel into the seat of a pair of old tights, I caught sight of my old friend Lizzie.

'Hey!' I said.

'Hey!' she said – the standard greeting, it seemed, nowadays.

'What are you doing?'

'Just looking at trail running shoes,' she said, in such a depressed tone that I could have sworn she was about to burst into tears. But she smiled at me forcefully, and said, 'And you?'

'Wondering if I have to get these things,' I said, waving the shorts at her. 'I heard about this new kind of bicycle saddle that has a hole cut in the middle, and I was thinking maybe my money would be better spent on that. It's called "The Liberator." Isn't that funny?'

'You're so athletic,' she said sadly. Now I noticed that Lizzie, normally one of my truly beautiful friends, was a lighter shade of gray.

'Not really,' I said. 'No, what I am is impatient. I can't stand driving around the block forty times looking for a parking place.' I returned the shorts to their place and said, 'Are you okay Lizzie? You, um . . .'

'I'm fine,' she said, and her eyes filled with tears.

We talked for half an hour that day on the sidewalk outside, and as she told me of her recent dissolution with her boyfriend, I began recognizing with unease that same furrowing of brows, that catch in the voice, that vision that washes the world colorless. I hadn't felt that since Sean, and now seeing it again, up close and personal like this, made me hugely uncomfortable. I tried patting Lizzie on the back, giving her a hug, but I could see she was far from being consoled. We made promises to see each other soon, and I watched her as she went back in the shop, her shoulders slumping.

I got back on my bike, clipped in and rode slowly away, barely seeing the pedestrians crossing in front of me or the cars barrelling out their driveways. It was going to take a lot to get me into a place where I could risk feeling that kind of despair again.

Then, I rode two more blocks, where I was blown off my bike. Literally blown off, as I had rounded the corner of Sutter and Hyde, and struggled to get up the hill until the wind began gently tapping me back like an invisible hand. And slowly, slowly, I tipped over. It probably served me right for getting those fancy-schmancy clip shoes that *locked* you into your pedals (another ungodly expense) which Aidan said were a virtual requirement for riding on the hills of the city. Naturally I'd heard no stories of him being blown over or unable to clip out before crashing to the ground.

I lay on the road for a moment, still clipped in and attached to my pedals, as if I'd been riding a horse and we'd both been shot. A car carefully veered around me.

I was about four blocks away from Marie's, and as I examined my knee (ragged skin, bleeding, full of little pieces of black asphalt as if I'd landed in a pile of pepper) I wondered just how difficult it would be to breeze in and check up on her, and maybe, if I were lucky enough, get her to do something about this mess that my mother so gently pointed out was in need of assistance. The imminent arrival of the Cool Couple was another incentive, but I really was curious if this Gavin storm had blown over.

I rounded the corner and began heading back in the direction of Hayes Valley. Maybe I'd just pop in and say hello. Maybe she'd have some good news – he would have gotten the little hussy out of his system, and everything would have returned to normal. Marie, I knew, had a great propensity for forgiveness.

Now how I would know this, I wasn't certain. I hiked the bike up over my shoulder once I was buzzed in, and crept my way down to her windowless lair. Marie was silently dabbing blue bleach into a well-dressed woman's scalp. The woman was intently studying *Vogue*. Marie wore a huge, shapeless rubber smock which made her look like a black haystack, and she was frowning at the bleach – but perked up when she saw me lugging my bike down the stairs.

'What happened to you?' she said, staring at me. She'd changed into a platinum blond since I'd last seen her, with huge ropey hair extensions falling down the length of her torso. The woman changed her hair color like most people changed their shoes.

'I fell down,' I said. 'Could I wash my knee off in your bathroom?'

'Sure,' she said. 'I meant your hair. What the hell happened to the color? Talk about dishwater. Ick.'

'Oh,' I said. 'Well, that wasn't really why I was here, but now that you mention it—'

'No.' Marie said this with some conviction. 'This time I really mean it. I have to pick up Davia in an hour. I've had to put her in day care since this whole Gavin breakup.'

'Oh dear,' I said. 'For some reason I thought you'd have worked this out.' Marie shook her head and barked a comical 'Ha!' But she did seem in a good mood, humming a little here and there, smiling at my head with mock horror. I said, 'I'll just wash my knee and be on my way—'

'Hey, stay! Do you want a glass of wine? Get the bottle. It's in the fridge on the side of the bathroom. The glasses are in the cupboard above the sink. Diana, you'll have some, right?'

'No, thank you,' said the woman, who actually bore some resemblance to Princess Diana. She even had an English accent. 'I'm not drinking these days. Part of my therapist's advice.'

'What a terrible thing,' Marie said severely, as if Diana had just revealed she had cancer. She dabbed the last of the bleach into Diana's hair, and carefully brushed a gloppy lock away from her cheek. She picked up an egg timer and cranked it. 'Okay, well you just sit tight for fifteen minutes, and I'm going to have a glass of wine over there.'

I leaned my bike against the receptionist desk. Everything was neatly in its place, the pencils sharpened, the appointment books carefully filed between two large cement blocks. There was a yellow Post-It note with a list: *Buy zucchini, lamb, mint, red wine – marinate 1 hr.* I went in the black bathroom that smelled like lavender, washed my knee off with some electric-yellow soap and found a half of a bottle of sauvignon blanc in the tiny fridge. I grabbed some water glasses and plopped next to Marie on the fluorescent pink foam-filled sofa. She looked tired, with some lines I hadn't seen before around her mouth. But her eyes were serene, eyeing my head with disdain.

'Please stop looking at it,' I said. I filled her glass almost to the brim and handed it to her. 'Cheers. I'll make an appointment soon, I promise. Maybe tomorrow. How does tomorrow look for you?'

'I'm booked out to do my own hair,' she said. 'Eve'll be here too.'

Eve! I thought with interest. The one who had spilled the beans. 'Maybe we can go out for lunch,' I said, wondering where that came from. Marie and I had never had lunch together – it wasn't one of the things that we did.

'Stop in,' she said, clinking my glass in a little cheerful toast. 'If you have time. Maybe we can work something out. Don't you work, for God's sake?'

'Not when there's human dramas to hear and absorb and comment on.' Marie grunted and leaned back against the cushions. She glanced at my head again and said, 'It's not so very bad. It was just a semi-permanent, right?'

'I think so.'

'Not good for your hair. You need permanent color. Your hair is like a *sponge*. It'll absorb right away, and float right out again.' Some tinkling bells whispered from nowhere and a low moan filled the salon.

'Is this the chanting monks that I've been reading about?' I asked.

'Culture Club Live,' she said, taking a large gulp of wine. 'I'm tired of all my music. I decided to go backwards. Are you still seeing the guy that you were seeing before you went to London?'

'Uh, who?' I said breezily. 'I don't think I was seeing anyone then.' It wasn't like her to forget a fact like that, but the woman obviously had more on her mind nowadays than to keep up with the romantic comings and goings of all her clients.

'The Irish guy. You were friends with him —'

'Oh, Aidan.' I took a sip of wine. 'Yes, we're friends. Sometimes we sleep together though —'

Marie's face darkened. 'I told you not to do that. Now why are you?'

'Lust?' I said hopefully. 'It's really okay. We're on the same page about it.'

'Not possible.' Marie drank a huge gulp and sighed. 'I would have thought you'd know that by now. You're too old to be doing things like that. No one is ever on the same page. There's always somebody who wants more, when the other person is trying to get out of their grasp, like that PePe LePew cartoon. You know the one I mean? The girl cat that PePe

161

thinks is a skunk, and he's always clutching on to her and kissing her, while she's sliding away, trying to hide and get away from him. That's what your friend's boyfriend is doing — what's her name? The one who practices the Rules?' I saw Diana's head snap up at that mere mention, before returning to her magazine.

'Harriet.' I looked in my glass, and chased a little piece of cork around with my finger. I wondered if that's how Sean had felt. It was certainly the way I had behaved when Aidan got too gooey with me. But he kept his cool distance now that we were in the just-friends mode. 'She's coming to visit soon. And I'm not sure Just Jerry's slithering away from her. He just doesn't really know what's going on, from what I can tell. I'll find out more when she's here,' I said brightly. 'And I like your hair, by the way.'

'This?' Marie fingered a dreadlock. 'They're just extensions. I'm getting rid of them. *And* I'm getting this tattoo lasered off. The last treatment is tomorrow.' She rolled up her black t-shirt to reveal a network of Band-aids covering her bicep.

'How come?'

'Because I'm sick of it,' she said.

'What was it?' As usual, I felt like a mall chick getting advice on how to be hip like the Big City Girls.

'Just a tribal sign,' said Marie.

'Oh.' Typical: when I'd begun to merely consider a tattoo, they'd gone and become low-rent and over-used on me. There was just no point in trying to keep up with the Joneses nowadays.

'But hey! I want to meet Harriet. Bring her in, will you?' Marie asked, patting my knee. 'And, I don't really know what I'm talking about, in terms of your Irish boy.'

'You don't?' This was an unnerving admission from her.

'*Anything* is better than what I've been going through.' She took a long slug of her wine and sat back against the persimmon-colored cushions with a groan.

'Well, what's happening?' I said. 'You really aren't getting back together?'

'Uh uh. No way. Not after all this. I mean, did I tell you any of the details?'

'Not really.' I tried to fill her glass again but she waved me away with 'I'm driving.' I put the bottle between my legs and shivered a bit. I moved it onto my knee as Marie craned her neck to see the egg timer.

'Ten minutes. Okay. I told you that Eve told me? That she started crying and everything when I'd been complaining that Gavin was acting so weird lately? Her brother works with Gavin at the bar, and the word was out that he was having an affair with one of the cocktail waitresses. Her brother even confronted Veronica, that bitch, and do you know what she said to him? He goes, "Are you having a thing with Gavin? Because if you are, you should know that he's got a wife and a brand new baby." And she apparently says to him, "No, I'm not having an affair, but Gavin's situation is very complicated." *Complicated*! I'll show that bitch complicated.' Marie laughed a little and leaned over again to see the timer.

'So, I canceled all my clients, and I called him on his cell phone. He's in a job interview, because he's been hating the bar lately. And I said, "I'm coming down. You better meet me out front." He says, "I'm in a job interview." I say, "You leave the job interview. You meet me outside and you're gonna talk to me." He says, "Well, what's going on?" I said, "You'll see when I get there."

'So he comes out of the interview, all pissed but also really nervous looking. I say to him, "Who is this chick Veronica?" and he says nothing is going on, they're just friends. He's like "I love you, we just had a baby, you're crazy, nothing's going on." And then I sort of settled down. Because you know, Gavin does have a lot of female friends. And maybe the information just got mixed up.'

I took a giant gulp of wine. Always a bad sign when you try

to convince yourself that the gossip is mixed up. I'd had enough of that to make me never want to be a part of a clique again.

'But nope. So after that, I went home and I called up the bar accountant. I said really sweetly, "Listen Pat, I really need Veronica's number. I have to talk to her." And Pat muffs it. She gets completely nervous and says, "No Marie! I can't do that! I'll get fired!" So right there I know something is up. I told her, "No, you won't get fired. I promise. Now give me that number. Right now." I wasn't exactly *threatening* her, but—'

Marie's face was getting red. 'I got the number.'

'You *called* Veronica?' I said.

'Yup. I said, really politely, "Hello, this is Marie Moore, Gavin's *wife*, mother of his *child*, what are you doing with my husband?"'

'Was she nervous?'

'Well, no, at first she was just kind of surprised. And she replies, "Nothing! We're just friends! I just started working there and he was showing me the ropes, and we're there so late . . ." and da da da da da. And I said, "Well, there are rumors." She goes, "Nothing's going on, I swear! He showed me pictures of your wedding, of your baby – there's nothing going on between us, we're just friends." And that's when I said to her, "If there's nothing going on between you and him then you should come meet me. I'm pretty cool, I have a lot to offer somebody as a friend. And I'm friends with most of the girls that Gavin's friends with. So, you know, let's go have coffee tomorrow. I'll bring Davia, you can meet her."'

Marie grabbed the wine bottle and dumped the thimble-full that was left into her glass.

'What did she say?' I asked.

'She completely blew it. This girl – she's not the brightest bulb on the tree. She goes, "Oh, no no no no no, I can't do that. It's not right." And I knew of course, from there on out. That's when I said, "*Bitch.* You stay away from my husband."'

And that's when I got really threatening with her. I told her, "You have messed with the wrong person. You are jeopardizing my daughter, and you better grow eyes in the back of your head because you'll never know when I'm coming. I know where you work, I know where you live, I know what you're little car looks like, I know what you look like." She got a restraining order against me.' Marie chuckled at this. 'Hey Diana! Are you having fun listening to this?'

Diana nodded gravely. 'That's how I remembered it.'

'But Marie!' I spouted. 'You told him to go fuck someone! You told him!'

Marie looked at me and shook her head. 'I've said this before to you. This was different. This was him sneaking around, sleeping with someone, and then denying it and calling *me* crazy. Besides, that was just a joke of mine, and he knew it! And obviously, if he's denying and denying it, he's shielding her for some reason, which means he's in love with her. Which he *eventually* admitted to, but not before lying to me for months and acting like it was over with her, which it never was. She has fake tits. Did I tell you that?'

'No, you didn't.' I finished my wine. Diana calmly turned a page. 'How did you finally find out about the affair for sure?'

'I called the cell phone company and got them to fax me the bill here at the salon,' Marie said evenly. 'Her number was all over it, at all hours of the day and night – three o'clock in the morning, four o'clock, six o'clock. And on Valentine's Day, *really* a lot.' God, that day again. It caused so much angst. 'So I called him up – remember, he's still denying all this to me – and said really nicely, "Gavin, I've got something to show you. I'm coming down to the bar." He's like, all fearful, like maybe I'm going to get a gun. "Well, what are you doing? You sound really crazy, Marie." That *word* again. I *hate* when men say that about women – it's only when a chick's making him feel uncomfortable. I went to the bar and said "Where's Gavin? Where is he?" And they looked all scared, saying, "Uh, he's upstairs, Marie." And I stood in the middle of the bar and said, "I just want everyone to know that my husband is a cheating, fucking bastard. And I gave birth to his daughter." '

Marie glanced at my reaction, but her eyes strayed to the top of my head. 'You really need to do your roots.'

'What did the people at the bar say?' I asked.

'They all just looked at me. But you know, Gavin *still* denied it. Or rather, he said it had ended. *That's* when I cracked the code to his voice mail.'

'I didn't tell you before, but I have, um, vast experience in this area. I don't think—'

'Best thing I ever did,' Marie interrupted. 'Because when I heard that, I thought, Okay I'm not crazy and jealous. This is really happening. It was a real relief. Didn't you feel that way?'

'No,' I said. 'But maybe my situation was different.'

'I've done that too,' said Diana suddenly. 'I found out that he *wasn't* having an affair. So I could relax.'

'Did he ever find out that you listened to his messages?' I asked. 'Because don't you think anything you find out that way is sort of . . . invalid?'

Marie and Diana looked at me as if I were a moron. 'No,' they said in unison.

'Okay, well,' I said lamely. I turned to Marie. 'So that was it then.'

'Well, he did confess then,' Marie said, and stood up. 'And we tried to get back together, which we did for about a month. But he just had to lie to me one more time.' She walked over to Diana and scratched a little patch of bleach. 'About a minute to go, okay Diana? I said to him, "You used condoms, right?" He assured me that they did. But I called up Veronica and asked her—'

'You were *still* calling her?' God, never get on the bad side of Marie. Talk about a pit bull.

'Yup. I'd called her up to tell her that Gavin and I were

back together and she better fucking *back off* because I was nice the first time – the next time, I might not be so nice. And then I tricked her into telling me what they used for birth control, and she said she was on the pill. I said to her, "Well, you are even a bigger fool than I thought – because how do you know who *I've* been with over the years? Go get an AIDS test, you idiot." ' Marie put her hands on her hips, as the timer went *ping*.

Despite the nature of the story, I couldn't help feeling there was some lesson to be learned for me here. Marie was downright refreshing, now that I thought about it. No whining and wheedling and passive-aggressive behavior for her, no sir. It was *action*, and lots of it. 'I said to Gavin that night, "You know what? This is really the end. You just had to lie one more time to me didn't you?" And that's when I punched him in the face.' She released the lever under Diana's chair and she floated toward the floor.

They walked across the salon to the sinks as I watched them. 'But,' Marie said suddenly, 'Here is the real news: I have a boyfriend. Can you believe it? He's a snowboarder.'

'No,' I said incredulously.

'He's got a great body,' she said. 'He loves Davia. His girlfriend died in a car accident last year. Can you believe it? You know that ad for the opera that goes, "People Die. Husbands Cheat. Women Cry." That's me in a nutshell.'

I shook my head as Marie adjusted the water temperature on sprayer nozzle, and said what Harriet had often said to me: 'You lead the most dramatic life of anyone I've ever met.'

That night, I tried to give Harriet some wardrobe tips. She'd been vaguely down for some time now, citing this work problem and that Just Jerry tiff, but something else was going on too, although I wasn't sure even she knew what it was. After some cajoling, she finally declared that yes, she did want to go out to San Francisco and cavort in 'this small town with big buildings,' as Marie and I called it.

'Okay, do you have a pen?' I asked. 'First: Raincoat. It's hot now, but that means Arctic conditions are around the corner. Um, a pair of pants that aren't too heavy. But not too light either. And no sandals. Sandals never work in this city. It's either raining, or too cold, and then your feet get dirty—'

'That's okay. I don't wear sandals,' Harriet interrupted. 'Remember?'

'Oh, that's right.' Ever since the photo of a newly-wed Carolyn Bessette Kennedy emerging from the island chapel was splashed around the world, Harriet could never bring herself to wear any cute, strappy sandals – so depressed she was by Carolyn's perfect, corn-free feet.

'I saw her, by the way,' Harriet said. 'Carolyn. In person. She was at this restaurant in Tribeca, having dinner with a girl and two guys. Where was her husband is what I want to know.'

'Working?' I suggested. 'Maybe the magazine was going to bed, or to press, or whatever it is that they call it. How did she look?'

'Great,' said Harriet unenthusiastically. 'She had her hair pulled in a pony tail with all these perfect little strands hanging down. She was wearing a white tank top with a black jacket thrown across her shoulders, and she looked happy and relaxed. And not too skinny, either.'

'Well, good for her,' I said. I heard her scratching on a pad with one of her smelly indelible markers that she was particularly fond of, and imagined her sitting at her paper-filled desk, lit by the circle thrown from the '50s-style lamp that Clark had given her for her birthday one year. She sighed lightly, and I said, 'We're going to have a great time! The last time you were in San Francisco, you'd just started going out with Just Jerry. I can't believe it's been that long.'

'Neither can I,' Harriet said, and I could tell she was trying to sound more cheerful than she felt. 'You were obsessively checking voice mail. But we went to that great restaurant with the hard benches.' She shuffled some more papers and I heard her chair scrape across the floor. 'What did you do today?'

'I actually got a full five hours of work done,' I said proudly. 'I am really happy about this. I haven't taken a nap with my computer in, oh – weeks now.' It was eighty degrees in San Francisco – a mini-heat wave. All the windows in my apartment were open, and I sat in boxer shorts and an undershirt, fanning myself in my lemon-yellow kitchen. The cat wound herself around my clammy legs and I shooed her away. 'And I saw Marie, which I'll fill you in on when you get here.'

'Oh, God! You got more details?' Harriet stopped pacing.

'Uh huh. It's like a traffic accident – I can't stop looking at it. I'm one of those people that everyone hates on the freeway: slowing down to see the blood.' I opened the refrigerator, peered inside, and closed it again.

'She must be devastated,' said Harriet in a hushed tone. 'I don't know how she can work at all.'

'Actually, she's surprisingly – well, okay about it,' I said. 'She started laughing today, saying, "I can't believe all the times I drove all over the city at 3 a.m. like a crazy woman, trying to find Gavin after I'd paged him 35 times! Good God! What an idiot I am! And what an asshole he is!"'

Harriet gasped. 'Laughing? Well, that *is* heartening. Right on.'

'Is that phrase coming back in style?' I asked her. 'Marie said that today too. Um, let's see – then I took a walk. I put on some sneakers and walked up and down the hills, trying to appreciate my city. And just when I was getting a little bored, wondering what it is that people enjoy about walks, an interesting thing happened.'

There was a silence while I heard Harriet closing drawers and banging cabinets. 'What?' she asked. She began crunching a tortilla chip, or something of that texture, which meant she really was distracted. Harriet never ate anything while talking on the phone, or if she did, it was accompanied by profuse apologies.

'Remember how you were saying that there are days in New York when you run into just about every single person you've ever known?' I asked. 'Well, it happened to me today. Which proves to an even greater degree my theory that our worlds are colliding at a faster and faster rate. No more of this six degrees stuff. We're all down to two degrees, three at most. Today I figured out I am *two degrees* away from Madonna, Harriet! What does that tell you?'

'It tells me that you spent some time in New York and San Francisco in creative fields,' she said mildly. 'That you know a lot of frustrated film-maker types. Who have wound up working – probably making coffee – on the set for commercials, in major urban metropolises.' She crunched again.

'Harriet, you're no fun anymore.' There was that little petulance of hers again. It had been cropping up for weeks.

'Anyway, I would think you'd run into people all the time in San Francisco,' she continued. 'If I went back to El Dorado, I'd see people I knew too.'

'Actually, I don't,' I admitted. 'I wish I could brag to you that I know every single person in this teeny claustrophobic little town, but I don't. So today, I ran into this girl Tricia,' I went on. 'I'd given up on having a meaningful, meditative walk and off I went to the All-Star Deli to get a cup of coffee. She was in front of me, trying to get the little old woman behind the counter to make her a generic version of a Chillini, or whatever you call those frappe-y things.'

'Who's Tricia again?'

'She's the friend of my sister's – the young one. The one who still goes out to nightclubs and meets guys. You remember! The funny one. The one who still lives with her parents.'

'Okay, now I know who you mean,' Harriet interrupted. 'Helena Bonham Carter lives with her parents too, I read. But what about this Tricia?'

'Well, she's fallen in love,' I said. 'This is the girl who said she'd never been in *like*, much less in love. She said, and I quote, "When I look at the back of his neck, I get weak at the knees." ' I paused. 'When was the last time you got weak at the knees looking at some guy's neck?'

'God,' said Harriet in a stunned voice. 'Have I *ever* felt that way about a man? It's been a really long time if I have. How about you?'

'If I have, I've blocked it,' I said. 'I told that to Tricia, and she said, "Well, I was the same way. I was starting to think there was something wrong with me." Now she's met this guy who's in his first year at med school, and she's leaving for Baltimore for grad school in a month. It really sounded rather tragic.'

'She's young,' Harriet responded, crunching. 'She'll get over it. Who else?'

'Lizzie,' I said. 'I went to grammar school with Lizzie. She was standing in this sports store, buying a pair of trail running shoes. I almost didn't recognize her because she's lost so much weight. I mean, a lot. Maybe twenty pounds.'

'That *is* a lot. Does she have an eating disorder?'

'Well, get this. I finally said, "Jesus, Lizzie. You look like Ally McBeal. Are you okay?" And she said, "That's what happens when you have a broken heart." '

'Oh, no,' said Harriet. 'When did her relationship fall apart?'

'Seven months ago. I know I told you this. He was the bartender who was driving along and all of a sudden turned to her and said, "Elizabeth, sometimes when I'm with you, I'm filled with ennui." '

Harriet gasped. 'No! I've never heard this! That's terrible.'

'I know,' I said. 'I told this to my mom in the car, and she almost hit a lamppost. I'm *sure* I told you that story.'

'No, I'd have remembered that line,' she said with conviction. 'How can you forget a line like that – *when I'm with you,*

I'm filled with ennui.' She stopped crunching momentarily. 'He's got a pretty good vocabulary for a bartender.'

'My mother said that too. Anyway, Lizzie's completely broken up about it. Aren't you just dying to get here?'

'Okay, one good man story and two bad man stories. Anything else?'

'Nope, that's it.' She crunched again, and I finally said, 'What *is* it that you're eating?'

'Oh, sorry,' she said hastily. 'Carrots. I need to lose weight. I decided this weekend when I was in the Hamptons with Just Jerry. I need to change my whole life, actually, but this will have to do for now.'

'Dieting? You? I thought we had a pact.' Harriet and I had had many a weight discussion before, and both of us had agreed that the dieting industry was an evil conspiracy cooked up by bored, misogynistic, post-Cold War CIA agents. 'I thought you were doing that Cindy Crawford workout video that you liked so much. And you live in New York, so you must walk like, what? A marathon a day?'

'I can't walk any more than I already do,' she said crossly. 'I can't stand dieting, but I didn't like my bathing suit on me. I'm not going to wear it until I lose some weight in my butt. You're an exercise freak. How long does it take to drop poundage in the butt?'

'Not as long as the stomach,' I said. 'But I'm not a freak. Riding a bike around the city and falling off isn't worthy of being called an exercise freak.'

'How about those horrible runs you used to do?' Harriet said accusingly. She seemed really stuck on that time in my life. 'When you played those games to keep yourself from going out of your mind with boredom? You have to admit you were pretty thin then.'

'That was last year.' Running reminded me of feeling lonely. Somehow riding a bicycle seemed more companionable – there was at least something, if not someone, else enduring the effort.

'Anyway, I'm sure you look fine in your bathing suit,' I said, trying to sound cheerful. I felt guilty that I'd forgotten that she had gone away with Just Jerry over the weekend. Obviously it hadn't gone so well. 'Uh, well, other than your butt dissatisfaction, did you have a nice time?'

'Does it *sound* like I had a nice time?' Harriet snapped.

'Well, no,' I said, feeling a bit hurt. The cat jumped up on the windowsill, looked down the airshaft, and settled down on her haunches, blinking. 'What happened?'

'I'll tell you what happened: Nothing. Not a thing. We had a very lovely time, went out for dinner, stayed in this cute little inn, walked on the beach, had sherry in the afternoon, read books in the sun, got up late, had great sex.'

I waited. 'And? Yes, this does sound downright diabolical.'

'Wait. I'm not finished.' Her call waiting clicked, and she said, 'Hang on,' before clicking over, and then coming back on the line. 'That was him,' she said, gritting her teeth. 'I told him I'd call him back.'

'And you will? I thought the Rules said you couldn't call men back.'

'That's only in the first six months. Or maybe the first three. Anyway, we're past that point.'

'Oh,' I said. 'Did you tell him you were talking to me?'

'Of course not. Why would I offer that kind of information?'

'Well, I don't know,' I said airily. 'He's only your boyfriend for the past two years. I was just wondering if this Rules stuff had a statute of limitations.'

'Never,' she said, as if I'd asked her to burn the flag.

'Okay, go on.' I settled down in the kitchen chair and fanned myself again. 'You were telling me about your God-awful weekend full of great sex, soft sand and gentle surf.'

'Well. After all this wonderfulness, did he say one word about our future? Even hint around it? No. I'm becoming so obsessed with a proposal that I can't think about anything else.'

I imagined this. It probably was not unlike any of the other obsessions and neuroses that I went through, like Caller ID, or breaking into voice mail trying to find out a horrible truth. But Harriet's obsession was dependent on Just Jerry taking some action, and behaving in the way that Harriet thought he should. Reading my mind, Harriet added, 'A dating commitment is not enough anymore. Not when forty is right around the corner.'

'It's hardly around the corner.' I tried to think of some little pithy comment of comfort but couldn't come up with anything – mostly because, for better or worse, I simply couldn't see myself sitting around *waiting* as patiently as Harriet had. I was the type of person who couldn't stand to wait in line at a post office, never mind waiting for my boyfriend to understand something complex and unspoken.

Maybe her homespun roots had something to do with this 1950s fixation of getting the ring. 'Are you afraid your mom is not going to see you walk down the aisle?' I asked suddenly.

'My mamma?' Harriet hiccupped a little. 'Good Lord, no. She doesn't want me to get married, not to anyone.'

'Really?' This shocked me. How had I got it into my head that Harriet's mother was the brains behind all this ring strategy? I imagined a wall map with colored pins and arrows, an altar at the center, with Harriet and her mother the Colonel coldly marking Jerry's progression across the frozen tundra of the matrimonial landscape. 'I guess I just assumed that she'd been giving you tips all along.'

'No, not really,' Harriet said. 'She just doesn't want to see me get hurt, so she tells me not to give away too much. But married? No way. And she *likes* Jerry.' She resumed crunching. 'It's sort of funny too, because she and my dad had a great marriage by all accounts. She thinks I'd be better off with my freedom. I'll bet your mom feels the same way about you, huh? Career woman that she is.'

'Well, no,' I said, thinking about the buffet dinners my

UNZIPPED

mother was happily conspiring and plotting for me. 'I think
she would really like me to have a partner, and of the human
variety. And she had a really crappy marriage. There must
be some psychological kernel of insight to all of this but we
can save it for another day.' I stopped fanning myself and
pulled the window shut. 'Harriet, seriously – you didn't really
expect him to get down on one knee this weekend, did
you? That doesn't really sound like him, from what you tell
me.'

'Yes, but not even a *hint* about it. Case in point: We're in
this little seaside gallery. I'm complaining about health
insurance, about how I can't quit doing PR because I need the
health insurance from one of my clients. Now, you know I
want to do other things – write, teach maybe, go back to
school. He knows this too. So I'm complaining and complaining about this health insurance issue. And does he say
anything like, "Maybe someday you'll be on my health
insurance," or even, "Maybe someday it won't be like that"?
No. Nothing! All he says is, "You don't hate PR that much.
You can stand it." '

'God, Harriet,' I interrupted. 'I'm sorry, but I can't imagine
that even you would want a marriage proposal on the heels of
a discussion about health insurance. Yuck.'

'Case Number Two,' she said, ignoring me. 'I'm talking
about going away with my mother and my aunt to Nice next
summer. You know we always take that one trip together
a year? So I'm talking about it, and I say, "It sure would
be nice if you could come, but you know how my mamma
is about unmarried couples sleeping in the same room.
She wouldn't put up with it." And do you know what he
says? "Yeah, I've always wanted to go to Nice. Oh well,
then." '

'Well, that doesn't sound too bad,' I put in.

'Whose side are you on? Case Three: We're walking down
this lovely shaded road, with all these beautiful Victorian

175

houses. Big wide street, cool breeze, lazy trees hanging across the road. We come across this darling little church at the end of it. There's a wedding in progress: a big sign on the door. You can't miss it: WEDDING IN PROGRESS. We stand there looking at it. And do you know what he says?'

'Nothing?' I guessed.

'Nothing! Not a word! Not a hint, not even the merest hint of a suggestion.'

Was this the way proposals were prompted nowadays? By health insurance discussions and appealing to the sensibilities of the old-timers? If so, then I really needed to get out there more. 'Just to play devil's advocate here for a moment,' I speculated, 'what did you want him to say in all those circumstances? I mean, that wouldn't be completely and ridiculously unromantic? "Maybe this would be a good church to get married in *if* and *when* I ever get around to asking you to marry me"? Some little bone that he throws in your matrimonial trough?'

'At this point, a piece of kibble would be appreciated,' Harriet said unhappily. 'I don't mean to be crabby. But what are we doing here? I'm going to have to crank the Rules up a notch, I think. From now on, no going out on Friday or Saturday night unless he calls by Wednesday. And maybe I *won't* return calls – he can't always think I'm so available all the time.'

'What if he spends the night on Wednesday but doesn't ask you about Friday until Thursday morning over coffee?' This was one of the Rules that Harriet and I had debated long and hard in the past. Now, I refrained from pointing out that, if we were to strictly follow these trap-a-man guidelines, Jerry was not supposed to be spending the night at Harriet's anyway. Or maybe I had made that up – at this point, if I forgot the exact Rule all I had to do was think of what my grandmother would do in similar circumstances.

'I'll take it on a case-by-case basis.'

'Wouldn't you prefer him to just ask you to marry him when he's certain?'

'That's just it! He's not certain. He's not even really thinking about it, as far as I can tell. I've been thinking about what you said about the Cadillac, and I think I am just a Suburu to him. He's not certain, and that really annoys me.'

Obviously the man was not certain. 'But, um, Jerry is hardly the go-gettum type of guy,' I tried to point out gently. 'I mean, he seems to me – and I don't know him very well – to be pretty content coasting along if all is right with the world. You know, the if-it-ain't-broke-don't-fix-it type. How long has he been at that job that he says he doesn't really like?'

'Fourteen years,' said Harriet with a sniff.

'Are you crying?' I asked. 'Because if you are, we're hanging up and I'm flying out there tonight. I may not know what it feels like to be lying in wait for a proposal, but I sure remember how I felt during the Incident at Flying Saucer.'

'No, no, I'm fine. You're sweet.' Harriet hiccupped again. 'Thank you.'

'You sure?' I said cautiously. I had to remember that just because I had frozen myself out of the marriage loop, for no good reason other than fear and loathing, not everyone felt similarly. In fact, it seemed like the more together the woman, the more she was willing to admit that wanting to get married was not the venial sin against feminism that it had been made out to be lately. 'Just follow my argument here for a moment. How long has he been living in his little shoebox apartment?'

'Twelve years.'

'Okay then,' I said. 'Maybe you shouldn't take this non-proposing thing so personally then. He just doesn't sound to me like the kind of person that makes major life changes unless there's a gun to his head.'

'Great,' she said, sniffing again. 'The bad paying job. The average, rent-controlled shoebox apartment. And good ole girlfriend Harriet to round out the picture! Oh, I feel wonderful now.'

'Do you really love Jerry?' I asked. 'I mean, really love him—'

'I think he would make a good husband,' said Harriet. 'And I've really thought about this. I love being with him, I think we're good for each other. But do I have the gut-wrenching, writhing-on-the-floor thing that I did with Clark? No. And I think that's a *good* thing.'

'But shouldn't you be really in love—' I persisted, closing my eyes.

'Aha! The romantic rears her ugly head!' Harriet interrupted. 'That sounds really great on paper, but it's just unrealistic. I don't think marriage is like that anymore. The ones that last, anyway. It takes more than just being crazy in love now.' She coughed, and then added, 'Life is too hard.'

I lay down on the cool linoleum floor, wondering about my mother in her perpetual-state-of-disrepair house, and Zippy. 'Maybe,' I allowed.

'Clark called me last night,' Harriet suddenly said, as if she could see my position under the table.

'Oh, yeah?' I opened my eyes. 'I didn't know you were really speaking to him, since you've been on the marriage campaign trail with Jerry.'

'I *don't* really speak to Clark,' she said. 'Well, only on e-mail. And on the phone. His dad's sick. And I really liked his dad. He was a Texan too, I don't know if I told you.'

'No, I don't think so.' I wondered how long this had been going on. Harriet was rarely coy about anything, but this took me by surprise. Historically, this would be just the time that Clark would swoop in and grab Harriet by the scruff of her vulnerable neck, carrying her off to the land of unbridled passion and an unreliable future. 'Well, I know something will happen with Jerry, Harriet. Maybe we can cook up some scheme to trap him into saying those four little words. We've steamed mail open in the past. This isn't that different.'

'Uh huh,' she said.

'Well, don't sound so enthusiastic,' I said.

'No, I was just thinking about something.'

'What?'

She sighed, then began crunching in rapid-fire chews. 'Just something you told me about a long time ago. You probably don't even remember. It was something about a friend of your mother's, about how she was waiting and waiting for this man to come around. They were going out for years and years, and she'd finally just had enough. So she dumped him, and the very next month she met someone else and now is married. Are they still married, do you know?'

I thought for a moment. 'Yes, very happily. With two kids.' I had no idea who Harriet was talking about. 'They have a house in Tahoe, and a house here in the city. She's a city politician. She's never been happier.' Maybe this was laying it on a bit thick. 'Anyway, I hear stories like that all time, don't you? How about in that Weddings page in the *Times*? I'd say ninety-nine percent of the stories start out like that.'

'I guess so,' said Harriet doubtfully.

CHAPTER 8

The next morning, as I was leaving the apartment to meet Marie, I dialed Aidan's number. 'Can I call you back?' he said immediately when he heard my voice.

'Sure,' I said. His voice seemed a little high, and I asked, 'Is everything okay?'

'Oh, yes!' he said enthusiastically. 'I'll call you later.'

'Okay. I should be home later in the afternoon because I have an assignment due tomorrow, but I'm off to meet Marie—'

'Uh huh,' Aidan interjected.

'Oh. Well, um – do you want me to get you that special girlie gel that you like?' I asked.

'Fine, fine,' he said shortly. 'Talk to you later. Bye.' Click.

Hmmm. A tiny bubble of annoyance and jealousy floated up in my throat. Definitely a female lurking around . . . an idea which was startlingly repellent to me. I stood in the middle of the living room, staring at the phone in my hand. Then I grabbed my keys and my wallet, pulled a sweater on; and tried to put that abhorrent thought out of my head. As I locked my apartment door, I made a mental list of the places near the salon where Marie and I could have lunch. But my mind kept jumping back to various Aidan events and theories.

About six months ago, I had lain in bed writhing around with a cold. It was the kind that started as a tickle in the throat, and a mere hour later had progressed into a full stage five, complete with sneezing, headache and weepy eyes.

We had been planning to see a movie that night – it was his

turn to choose. (Aidan and I had very clichéd, strictly gender-delineated taste in films: he'd suffer patiently through all my costume dramas, while I would sit stonily through the latest Hollywood offering involving varying degrees of extra-terrestrial life, Bruce Willis and explosions.) But this night I called him at work to cancel. I expected a reminder about how I made him sit through that subtitled Iranian movie the previous week but instead, he said 'You do sound terrible.' Aidan never got sick, as he always pointed out to me, and didn't have much respect for colds or allergies. Now he even sounded a little concerned. 'I'll come over anyway and bring you some juice.'

'I'm fine,' I said, trying not to sound plaintive.

'No, I'm coming over,' he said, hanging up.

Aidan had a strong mothering streak in him – he'd claimed, during the brief months we'd dated, that he was the 'woman' in our relationship. I wasn't sure what that was supposed to signify for him, being brought up in a place that, like many Catholic countries, had a powerful mythic attachment to the female while simultaneously keeping her down at heel in everyday life. I had a feeling it meant all those things to him: that he felt at times weak, at others powerful but most of all, just plain confused by my ambivalence.

'Just use your key,' I yelled from my bedroom when I heard his knock. 'What's all that?' I asked. He was holding a large grocery bag and sighed when he saw me propped up in bed, listening to my clock radio tuned to a classical station, wads of tissue surrounding me.

'Stuff to make you feel better,' he said. 'Some coffee frozen yogurt. Juice. Diet Shasta Cola – it was on sale. Oh, and flowers.' He reached in the bag and waved a cellophane-wrapped bouquet in my direction. 'I know this is just a ploy to get out of seeing Lethal Weapon Part 1000, but you didn't have to go to such great lengths. I'll go put this stuff down.'

'You are so cute,' I called as he shrugged his way into the

kitchen. I heard him shuffling around, opening cabinets and drawers. 'Thank you,' I continued. 'You didn't have to do all this. I'm quite a baby when I'm sick, I'm sorry to admit.'

'I know you are.' He returned and sat on the edge of my bed, handing me a glass of grapefruit juice and three puke-green echinacea capsules. 'Your eyeglasses are absolutely filthy.'

I took them off and wiped them with the edge of the blanket. My hair was piled on top of my head in a ponytail, and I was wearing a faded pink t-shirt that I'd had since college. My skin was oily and my eyes felt the size of peas. I reached for his hand. 'You really are so cute,' I said.

'Stop saying that word,' he said.

'You are – you're . . .' I gulped down the echinacea and winced. 'Adorable. You're going to make some girl a lucky wife.'

Aidan gave me a withering look. 'Gee, thanks.'

'I mean that in the nicest way possible.'

He took a pillow and tried to smother me. 'Stop saying that or I'll have to kill you.'

'Don't.' I sat up. 'No, I'm serious. I have a phobia about things covering my face. Once a boyfriend tossed a shirt on my head while I was sleeping. That was the last he ever saw of me.'

Aidan hugged the pillow to himself. 'Which boyfriend was that?'

'Doesn't matter.' I sat back and tried to rearrange my blankets.

'You know, you're a woman with a lot of dislikes,' Aidan observed.

I stopped rearranging and looked at him. 'What do you mean?'

'Well, you don't like your face to be covered,' he began. 'You don't like to be held in bed all night, because you don't like to be hot. You also don't like to be cold. Uh, let's see, you don't like people who wink. You don't like the lace curtain in my bedroom. You don't like beds on the floor, because they remind you of a college dorm – no, wait, a frat house. You don't like any purple clothes. You don't like running shoes worn with jeans. You don't like my music, but you really don't like Jim Croce—'

'*Especially* Jim Croce,' I told him. 'I'm really not a fan of the 70s, as a whole.'

'You don't like science fiction. You don't like my e-mail software. You don't like napkins on plates after one's finished eating. You don't like salmon, green bell peppers, balsamic vinegar, salad without onions, any poultry that's overcooked, wine not in a wine glass—'

'Wait a minute,' I said. 'Now that's not exactly true. What I said is that I don't like wine in a plastic cup. It doesn't taste the same.'

'Okay,' he allowed. 'You don't like t-shirts worn inside out, dark oak furniture, *Trainspotting*, needless sentimentality, that writer who tried to kill his wife or girlfriend or whoever—'

'Norman Mailer.'

'Yeah, him.'

I waited. 'Is that all?'

'Isn't that enough?' he asked. 'Give me a moment and I'm sure I'll come up with some more.'

I pulled my blankets up to my chin. 'I guess I'm just more vocal about what I don't like than what I like. I have a lot of likes, too, you know.'

'Such as?' Aidan wanted to know.

'Well,' I said. 'I like nice white cotton sheets.' My voice trailed off as I tried to come up with something else. 'And – um, snorkeling. I like to snorkel. And you, of course. I like you.'

'That's true,' he said. He replaced the pillow behind my head and fished around for my hand. 'You *like* me.'

'I do,' I said. I felt my eyes getting wet and hot. 'I wish it was more, but it's just not. I'm sure that makes me an idiot and very probably a bitch. But that's the way it is. And I do like lots of things – I just can't think of any right now.'

Aidan looked down at me, and put his hand across my forehead. 'Ssshhh. You're sick. I know you like a lot of things.'

'You do?' I sniffed. 'Like what?'

He patted my hand. 'You like your cat. You like Harriet. You like vacuumed rugs. You like margaritas. You like beating me in running. You like that tragic writer – um, the one who makes everybody's life out to be a disaster because of some stupid choice they made at one time—'

'Oh,' I said. 'Thomas Hardy.'

'You like strong men. You like strong women. You like your space. You like when I'm not gooey, when I'm not clingy or needy—'

'That's not really a like,' I told him. 'That's a negative being expressed as a positive.' I sneezed harshly and Aidan leaned over and pulled out a Kleenex, handing it to me.

'And you like that really depressing band, Dead Can Dance. Actually, you like any depressing music, from what I can tell.'

'I know.' I blew my nose. 'That may be part of my problem. I should listen to more upbeat, happy stuff – like country music. Something that's not always in a minor key.'

Aidan stroked my hair sympathetically. 'I'll always be your friend, Courtney. I'm not sure why, but I will. I wish it wasn't like this between us, but it's okay. I can live with it. And maybe you're right – I do deserve someone who *really* likes me. Plus you do drive me absolutely insane.'

'I'm sorry.' I turned over and clutched a pillow to me. I peered up at him through my grimy glasses. 'See, you thought you were getting out of a chick flick tonight, but here it is – live and in color.'

'That's okay,' he told me. 'There are a lot of Christmas blockbusters coming up.' He got up and went into the living room, returning in a moment with the TV in his arms, groaning as he said, 'Where do you want me to plug this in?'

Humph, I thought now, as I plodded down the hills toward Marie's salon. Now which chick would be distracting him? One of the snappy, wise-cracking, impossibly pretty waitresses at his restaurant? Or possibly a fellow line cook-ette, who could exchange sympathetic tales of burnt fingers and screaming executive chefs into the wee hours of the morn? *You are a small person, Courtney Weaver*, I thought as I crossed against the light at Bush Street, narrowly missing being creamed by a postal truck.

I was telling Marie how Aidan had rattled off all my dislikes like he had memorized them from a script. Picking up a bottle of conditioner, I unscrewed the top and sniffed. 'Kiwi – very nice.' Marie nodded in agreement, and I added, 'That's another thing I don't like: supermarket shampoo and conditioner. They all smell like old lady perfume.'

I wondered why Marie and I hadn't done the girl-lunch thing before. I'd known her for a long time, after all – nearly eight years. We were the same age – although, ironically, I always thought of her as younger – and we'd gone through the Goth/punk stage at the same time, in our early twenties. In those days she worked at a hip yet expensive salon that catered to the Pacific Heights matriarchs, run by a screaming control-freak of a man. She had jet black hair and incredibly intricate, beautiful tattoos circling her thin ankles, and peeking out from under her sleeveless t-shirts. Marie was the only hair colorist – then and now – who really understood what I meant by 'red' hair – not natural red, not fire-engine red, not burgundy red, but somewhere all in between.

In those years, our social paths would very occasionally cross. We'd run into each other at parties or Sunday picnics or barbecues. Marie was friendly, always convivial, but she had a toe-hold in what I called 'the dirty life' that I couldn't and didn't want to match. Like most people in her industry, her social circle was vast and megalithic, usually wrapped up in the alternative music scene.

But then Gavin came along, and Marie went the domestic, if slightly alternatively domestic, route. She still had little clues that belied her wild past – the rubber bracelets, the eight holes in one ear, the tattoos that still slid out from under sleeves and hemlines. Now she was a mother and, once upon a time, a wife, and so had moved into another realm of existence of which I had some knowledge but not much. On the one hand it was surprising that we hadn't socialized before, but on the other there was something not quite natural about it, like lunching with your therapist.

When I tiptoed down the dark stairs into her salon, she was standing over Eve, dabbing blue bleach into the roots of Eve's short white hair. Both of them were facing the mirror and wore serious expressions – one would think they were discussing the future of the global economy. Marie was swathed again in that huge plastic shapeless black smock that reached her knees. Her long, extension-free hair was covered in strips of foil and stuck out at odd angles from her head, and she looked exceedingly strange to me. I realized I'd never seen her with her hair all covered in dye, pulled unflatteringly off her face, even though that was normally how she saw me. It was a little unnerving, like realizing the Wizard of Oz was a withered old man sitting behind a curtain, or seeing your mother cry for the first time.

'So why aren't you with that guy?' Marie wanted to know after I told her about Aidan's list. 'There's not many guys who would remember *my* dislikes. I don't even think Gavin could name four or five.'

'Maybe you don't have as many dislikes as I do,' I said. 'I think I need to work on this. May be I should read Norman Vincent Peale.'

'Who's he?' Marie scraped the bowl around with the brush.

I picked up another bottle and sniffed. 'Father of self-help books. This minty stuff is nice.'

Marie swatted her hand through the air. 'Pah! You don't need any self-help books. As long as you're getting your work done – that's what I always say. Things happen for a reason. You *are* getting your work done, right?'

'I suppose,' I said. 'In between naps and talking on the phone.' I snapped the bottle shut and replaced it on the glass shelf. 'When did you get rid of your hair extensions?'

'This morning. You just snap them right off. It's not a big deal.'

'It *looks* like a big deal,' I told her. 'You look completely different.'

'Yeah, well,' Marie said with a circular motion of her hand, which I guessed meant that change was par for the course in the hair world.

I squirted a golf-ball size of mousse into my palm and dabbed it into my cowlick. Now the little lock of hair stood straight up from my head, like a curly antenna. Mom would love this, I thought. 'Aidan wears sneakers with his jeans, Marie,' I turned to look at her. 'What do you think of that?'

'What do you think I think?' Marie eyed me with exaggerated patience. 'Shoes make the man. I've told you that. But he does sound like a sweetie pie, from what you're telling me. How's the sex? Does he have a nice penis?'

'He does. I have a feeling someone else is getting to know it quite intimately, however.'

'Huh?' Marie stopped dabbing bleach into Eve's scalp. 'What does that mean?'

'Nothing,' I said. 'Just a feeling I have.'

Marie eyed me for a moment, and resumed her dabbing. 'Oh well. Use condoms. I can tell you're not really into him, though.'

'But I *should* be into him,' I said. 'There's nothing wrong with him. Any woman would be happy. I should just leap into the abyss and take my chances.' I leaned against the mango-colored wall while Marie sighed.

'When's your divorce final?' I asked her.

'I haven't filed,' she said, scrutinizing the bowl.

'I thought you said you were doing it right away,' Eve piped up.

'And you have a boyfriend,' I added.

'Yeah, well . . . it's just going to have to wait. I don't have the $2000 to do it right now.' She said all of this matter-of-factly and Eve and I exchanged worried looks. 'You're too nice,' Eve finally said. 'You feel sorry for him. And you shouldn't.'

'I'll get around to it,' she protested defensively. 'It's just . . . oh, never mind. I don't want to talk about it right now.'

A waft of bleach floated over to me and I wrinkled my nose. I heard a deep drum beat and then wisp of a men's chorus. 'I love this CD,' Marie said, shifting gears. 'Except, I can never figure out which is the name of the band and which is the title. Oh, well.'

'Is this the Bavarian chorus that you've been listening to for years?' I wanted to know.

'Karma,' said Marie flatly. 'Or Delirium. Pick a name, any name.' She sneezed and set the bowl on top of her towel-covered trolley. 'I have to sit down,' she said flopping down in the chair on the other side of me. Now the three of us were all lined up parallel to one another, staring into the floor-to-ceiling mirror. 'So – this boyfriend of mine.'

'Yes, a snowboarder. Is he smart enough for you?'

'Hmmm,' she said. 'Well, he's not a brain surgeon, by any means. But you know, that's okay. We have great sex. *Great* sex. I do like him a lot, I have to say. Gavin is *not* happy.'

'Remember my friend Harriet?' I examined my hair in the mirror. Marie was right – it looked awful, particularly in this setting. 'Um, she would have a lot to say about this. I mean, if you wanted to get Gavin back.'

'Is that the Rules chick?' Marie demanded. 'What *would* she say? And no, I don't want him back. I like my snowboarder.

COURTNEY WEAVER

Even though Gavin calls me all the time now, saying how much he loves and misses us.'

'As the World Turns,' I mused.

'I want to read that Rules book,' Eve interjected in a small voice.

Marie scoffed. 'Ah, it's such bullshit.'

I turned to Eve. 'Basically, it comes down to this: men are the hunters and you are the hunted. And you need to make yourself as unavailable and unattainable as possible if you want to land him.'

'Oh,' said Eve, disappointed. 'Well, I've heard that before.'

I'd given up on lunch with Marie that day. After the bleach had been washed out of Eve's scalp, and Marie suddenly exclaimed that she'd look much better as a raven-haired goddess than a white-haired angel, I bade them goodbye and told Marie I'd take her out to lunch some other time. As I trudged up the stairs, it occured to me that our relationship had shifted yet again. Now I had become the Father Confessor and she the penitent – the structure of many of my friendships nowadays, it seemed.

I walked back up the hills, but right on Franklin, just half a block from the salon, I saw a great pair of pants. The pants were walking down toward me, and they were filled by someone with the color of hair I'd always tried in vain to describe to Marie. The pants hit right on the hips, and had a slight flare (but not too much) at the ankle. They were the kind of pants that would look good this year and looked good five years ago and would look good for the next five years. You could tell they were expensive pants and that the angry-looking woman inside took good care of them – they didn't have any little faint, mysterious food stains, or white cat hair or pill-y build-up on the hips where bookbags or handbags would rub them. They were just great pants. I smiled at the pants, and the angry woman smiled back, surprisingly cheer-

33333

ful. I wondered if I could tear them off of her and scamper up the street, jumping into a passing cab.

And I wondered where *my* one pair of great pants were – it seems that I hadn't seen them in months, maybe even *years*.

I'd been fully intending once I got home to open the computer and actually put my fingers to the keyboard, and not just take a nap with it or use it as a platform on which to work a crossword puzzle. This had become my new obsession – crossword puzzles – because I'd read in the 'Science' Tuesday section of the *Times* that it was a good brain exercise for memory and word recall, particularly for those suffering from Alzheimer's. Since it was only a matter of time before Alzheimer's would be a concern – and with the disappearance of my one pair of great pants, maybe it should already be a concern – so I might as well get a jump on it. It also further proved to me that I was becoming everything that I used to make fun of when I was a teenager: a crossword-working, Teva-wearing, exercise-partaking and nap-loving woman.

'What's a five letter word for burden carrier?' I asked Harriet an hour later.

Harriet was silent for a moment. 'Beast,' she said finally.

'Thank you,' I said, writing it in. 'What is a flunky's response? Three letters.'

'Yes,' Harriet guessed.

'That's it,' I said. 'Is Innsbruck the capitol of Tyrol?'

'Why aren't you working?'

'I can't,' I said. 'I tried to find my favorite pair of pants, and they're not here. I looked everywhere. I called Aidan – I even called Julian. They've completely disappeared. And that distracted me so much that I thought I'd just get this crossword puzzle in.' I didn't mention that I'd called Aidan for another reason – namely that I wanted to know who the Little Missy was that was taking up his attention this morning. But the phone rang and rang, without even his machine picking up.

'Maybe they're at the drycleaner's,' said Harriet. 'Or Sean's. Did you try him?'

'No,' I said. 'I can't. I will sew myself a new pair of pants before calling him to ask.'

'Can you sew?'

'Nope,' I said. 'But this seems as good a time as any to learn.'

'Don't you ever have an urge to call him?' she asked. I heard her tea pot whistle, and her steps down her minuscule hallway.

'No.' I peeked into my refrigerator, and then closed it.

'Never? Even when you're drunk? And feeling maudlin? And you want answers?'

'No,' I said. 'Do you ever feel like you want to call Tom?' Tom was one of Harriet's boyfriend's several years ago, when she and Clark were on one of their legendary hiatuses. He'd dumped her in an extremely hurtful and obvious manner – by simply never calling her again. Then he spread it through the grapevine that he was in love with someone else, whom he ended up marrying a mere three months later. Harriet and I rarely talked about Tom; he was a romantic episode that even we could not yet joke about.

'Okay, I understand what you mean, then,' Harriet said quickly. 'I never did get my socks back from him. These dumb, gray cotton socks that probably cost me two dollars. But they were my favorite socks. At least you got your shirt back from Sean.'

'Oh, that,' I said.

The comparison was apt. I'd liked that shirt about as much as I liked my favorite pants, but with a few crucial differences – for one thing, I wasn't a lunatic breaking into private voice mail systems anymore, and for another, there was quite a different reason why I'd obsessed on the absence of my shirt.

We'd only been broken up for an hour or so, when I called Sean back and said, 'By the way, I'd like my shirt back. I think that's the only thing of mine at your house.' An image of my cute little silk top hanging in the closet next to his starched dress shirts flooded back to me, and my eyes filled with tears. 'Maybe we can do this "friends" thing some time in the future. But not right now. And I really want that shirt. You could mail it, if you want.'

Sean had sighed, wishing out loud that we could have the 'give-me-back-my-stuff' conversation at a later date.

'Certainly,' I said. 'But I want my shirt back. Fed Ex?'

So a few days passed. Then a week. For the first time, I felt us drifting, unable to gauge what was going through the other's mind. I'd had my Defining Moment on the Isuzu-counting run – I wanted to put this behind me, I told myself. But as our silence stretched into two weeks, I could feel us getting in our respective corners, and moving into the territory I dreaded but knew was inevitable: Dumper v. Dumpee.

I fell silent, brooding. I thought about my shirt constantly. Voice mail messages were left by him, falsely cheerful: the newest book, the movie he'd seen last week, the article he'd read in the *New Yorker*, the local elections . . . on and on, blah blah blah. Occasionally, he'd mention the shirt, saying he knew he had to get it to me, he hadn't forgotten. After each message, I'd grimly press three – *Erase* – holding the button until the tone sang into the air.

Weeks passed, then a month. Then two months. And still no shirt.

'Why don't you just call him and say you want the damn shirt back?' Harriet had asked reasonably.

'He knows I want it back,' I said savagely. 'I have nothing to say. I don't want to talk to him. Maybe never again. But I want that shirt back.'

More time passed – days, another week, and another. By now it was clear that our dissolution had entered the dangerous stage. He continued to call, once a week now. I continued to not return his calls. I was smarting, I was bitter. But I wanted that shirt back. Like most material possessions caught in the break-up crossfire, it had taken on talismanic properties.

'Could he be wearing it?' I asked Marco. 'Is that why he hasn't sent it back?' I thought of its stretchy silk fabric, the way it exposed my collarbone, its beautiful russet color, like ripe plums. It seemed a little feminine for Sean.

'Jesus, the shirt, the shirt!' Marco groaned. 'Just forget about it! Is that so impossible?'

'Maybe that new girlfriend's wearing it,' I mused. 'I want my shirt back. It is my little Calvin Klein shirt and I paid a lot of money for it and I want it back. Why is he holding it hostage?'

But I knew why, and I had a feeling so did Sean. He and I didn't have any mutual friends, so there was no chance of getting information about the other through that channel. And we didn't work near each other, nor live in the same neighborhood. The shirt was the last link. Once it was back in my hands, that was . . . well, *it*.

Harriet had been sympathetic, citing her socks. 'But your shirt was expensive!' she exclaimed. 'Do you want me to call him?'

'No,' I said. 'He knows this shirt means a lot to me.'

'I don't think it's the *shirt* that means a lot,' Harriet said.

'You know my Brit friend Mary?' I said suddenly. 'The night Chris announced he wanted to break up, he offered to drive her and all her stuff home. Right then and there. That night.'

'Oooh, that's harsh,' Harriet said, and we both fell into a one-minute silence of sympathy. Finally Harriet said, slowly, 'I know you want your shirt back. But maybe you don't, too. If you really did, don't you think you'd call him and demand it?'

I didn't answer. 'I want my shirt back, I want my shirt back, I want my shirt back,' I hummed when I woke up each morning. It occurred to me that maybe this was how the descent into madness began, when material objects took on lives of their own.

I did get my shirt back – finally. He sent it via Fed Ex, and chivalrously enough, had it dry-cleaned. Enclosed as well was a nasty little note about how I was to blame for our break-up, and that, if I really had my head screwed on right, we could have been the best of friends. I thanked him silently for this, another Defining Moment, and looked forward to the time when clothes would be clothes again, without magical properties. Pants would be something to covet, shirts would be something to be cleaned, underwear would need to be replaced. And true to my expectations, we didn't ever speak again.

'When are Trevor and Jane coming to stay?' Harriet was asking me now. 'How are you going to get any work done if you have all these houseguests coming?'

I looked around for the cap of the pen, which seemed to have magically disappeared. 'They arrive next week,' I said. 'It's just one day. Look, the way I figure it, people in offices get the same amount of work done that I do – that is, very little. In between coffee breaks, lunch hours, doctor appointments, e-mailing, talking on the phone and trips to the supply closet. Maybe they squeeze in drafting a few memos here and there. Then before you know it, it's five o'clock and *bam*, they're out on the sidewalk, jockeying for the best spot on the bus. At least, that's the way it was when I was a temp. Have you ever been a temp?'

'I worked in a mall once,' she said. 'When I was twenty-one. I got fired after a day. They told me I wasn't aggressive enough. So I drove to the nearest supermarket and bought a bunch of bananas. Then I cried and cried, sitting in the parking lot, as I tried to eat as many as I could.'

'That's a sad little picture.' I had never seen Harriet cry, but sometimes her stories – like this one – could border on heartbreaking. Once she had told me that when she was a little girl and had a fight with her mother, she would retreat to her room and fling herself on her narrow single bed, sobbing uncontrollably. Her father would come in and just sit there with her, rubbing her back. 'He didn't say anything, maybe a few clucks like, "You know your mother loves you," and something like that. He wouldn't try to defend her, or side with me, but he'd just sit and hold my hand, ssshhing me. That was around the time that he died.' The thought of little Harriet crying her eyes out, as her father tried to comfort her, always sent pricks of tears to my own eyes. 'Did you get much work done today?' I asked.

'I'm a little distracted,' she said. 'I can't seem to come up with any bright, witty prose for this client. He's trying to market a new kind of dental floss, and he's commissioned me to write a little booklet to interest investors. There really are only so many ways you can describe floss in terms that'll hold a reader's interest.'

'Well, I have a new theory,' I said. 'If I move my laptop computer to a different place each day, brand spanking new ideas will explode in my head and flow uninhibited through my fingertips. My RAM might even be tested by all the creative juices pouring into new documents. The only problem is that, as you know, I live in a two-room apartment and so I've used up every flat surface there is.'

'There's always the bathroom,' said Harriet, and paused. I was about to tell her about my Aidan suspicions, when she said, 'Um, I have some bad news. I have to delay my trip to San Francisco for a month.'

'Why?' I said. For some reason, I suddenly pictured the little girl crying on her bed, while her father rubbed her back. I knew something like this had been coming – the day had been going in this direction from the moment I'd woken up. 'What's going on?'

'I'm okay,' she said quickly. 'Here's the deal. I went to the doctor today.'

'The doctor?' I repeated. 'What kind of doctor?'

'The girl doctor,' she said. 'I mean, he's a man, but he's a gynecologist.'

Good. Not an oncologist then. But, 'Why? What's wrong?'

'Well, here's the thing.' I heard her turn off CNN. I glanced over at my cat who was leaping around the hallway, playing with some minuscule object that I couldn't see – probably a long-lost earring of mine. 'You know those pains I've been having whenever I drink orange juice or eat tomato sauce? I've been thinking for the last six months that I've had a stomach problem, and it turns out that it's not that at all. It turns out I have fibroids. In my uterus.'

'You found this out today?' I sat down. 'Hang on. You mean those twisting, intense pains that would wake you up? Harriet! I thought you were going to see a doctor a long time ago about that!'

'I know, I know,' said Harriet. 'But at least I don't have an ulcer, like I thought.'

'How did you find this out?' I asked. 'Are you okay? What exactly *are* fibroids?'

'Oh, I'm fine,' she said, but there was a certain creepy undertone to her voice. 'They're these – *growths* that occur in the uterus. I'd seen sort of this lump in the mirror, and I though, "Well, that's strange. I'm getting fat only on one side." And then when I'd do sit ups, I'd see this little bulge that didn't go away, even when I was lying down. So I went in for my annual today, and he's feeling around and he says, "Hello, what's *this*?" So he feels around some more, and then he does an ultrasound and checks my chart, and it seems that I've got five big fibroids in there that just started growing within this year. He starts telling me their size in centimeters, and I finally just said, "Please put it in terms I can understand." He says, "Basically, you have one that's the size of a grapefruit, one that's an orange, and three apricots." '

I gasped. 'I can't believe this. How could you not feel them?

And – in your *uterus*? How could you confuse your uterus with your stomach?'

'Well, I did,' she said, a bit defensively. Obviously the doctor had given her some grief about this as well. 'I blame the Texas educational system. I thought my stomach was lower than it is. Plus, I'm surrounded by people here who have all these dumb allergies – wheat allergies, lactose intolerance, can't eat Indian food, can't eat meat products – and I just assumed that I'd become one of those food neurotics like everyone else in New York, it seems.'

'What are you going to do?' I asked fearfully. 'What did he say?'

'He said, "They're quite large." And I look at the ultrasound picture and go, "So I see." And then he says, "Are you planning on having children?" I said, "Well, someday, but not at this precise second—" He interrupted me and said, "Then we have to get rid of them right away." So he looked at his appointment book and we called the insurance company and then the hospital and I'm getting my operation next week.'

'Oh, my God,' I said. 'Should I fly out? What? Will Jerry be around? What do you want me to do?'

'My mother's coming,' she said firmly. 'And I decided that I'm still coming to San Francisco – it'll just be a bit later than I thought.'

I stood up and then sat down again. 'Harriet. I am so sorry. I – I guess I don't know what to say.' Then, I decided to take the plunge, 'You can still have kids, right? I mean, this isn't going to affect your fertility, is it?'

'Well, it shouldn't,' she said, and here her voice cracked a bit. 'They just have to get those fibroids out as soon as possible. And I feel so – weird, like I have an alien inside me. Actually, what I have is a fruit bowl. A big giant fruit bowl, growing in my womb.'

'Oh, God.' How could anyone have that many objects inside one, growing away happily in the dark, until a doctor just happened to stumble across their existence? As always in situations like these – excruciating dental pain, a mole that had progressed into a black malignancy overnight – I thought about what the cave women had done. It was a miracle that the human race existed at all. 'Have you told Jerry?'

'I told him right before I talked to you. I actually called him.'

'I hope he was supportive,' I said stiffly.

'He was,' she said. Now she was full-on weeping. 'He j-j-just said it would be okay, and that they'd get them out, and did I trust my doctor and blah blah blah.' She blew her nose and I said 'Oh, Harriet,' but she continued. 'He told me that my health insurance would probably deny the claim, because that's what they always do, right up until the point that you're ready to go to court, but that he'd help me fight it. Oh, and that he had two women friends who had them, and then I remembered that I had three cousins who had friends who had something like this too. I don't know if they w-w-want to have ch-ch-ch-children, though, someday.' She took a long sniffle. This was the worst part of a telephone friendship: only being able to offer lame, sound bites of empathy. 'And, and – I know this is stupid – but, but – it just puts so much *pressure* on our relationship now, as if there wasn't enough already. Because now there's this baby issue to think about, right up close and personal.' She blew her nose with a loud honk. 'He's coming over here in an hour.'

'That's good,' I said. 'It'll be okay. Don't worry, Harriet. We're all here for you.' Thank God Harriet had a thousand-strong network of girlfriends in New York. And thank God, I suddenly thought, that Clark was not in the picture. He'd be a disaster at responding to something like this. It sounded like Jerry was saying all the right things – well, at least all the realistic things, up to and including the inevitable evil health insurance response. 'My doctor was telling me that tons of women have them,' Harriet was saying. 'It's practically an epidemic. But it's one of those things that women don't really talk about.'

'I'll bet Mary would agree with you,' I said. I paced around, suddenly espying the cap of my pen that the cat was staring at, ready to pounce. I snatched it up and glared at her. 'You know, Harriet, I'll fly out if you want—'

'No, no,' she said. 'Really. It'll be okay. We'll have a good time in San Francisco, and I'll be over the operation at that point, and it'll be okay. I'm sure of it.'

'I'm sure too,' I said, trying to match her optimistic tone. She began to tell me about the operation in excruciating detail, and that she'd be in the hospital overnight, possibly for two days, depending on her recovery.

I realized I could barely listen to what she was telling me. I heard myself saying 'uh huh' and 'that's good' and 'all right' and 'that doesn't sound too bad' but what I really was thinking about was some horrible *ER* scenario with monitors hooked up to her arms and blinking machines and one long *wheeeeee* sound with the nurses saying urgently, 'Doctor, we're losing her!' and my eyes welled up, drops spilling over the kitchen table, and onto the crossword puzzle as the ink dissolved and flowed in tiny cloudlike pools, like a watercolor painting. I tried to cry silently, not wiping my nose or sniffing, because I didn't want Harriet to hear, knowing that the source of my tears was largely empathetic, but also due to something grittier – more personal, more disturbing, probably having to do with Aidan and Sean and the AWOL pants and even Marie and Gavin.

What if Harriet couldn't have children? Moreover, and more chillingly, what if something happened to her? Could you die from a fibroid surgery? I couldn't bear the thought. She was closer to me than any boyfriend, ever.

'Which unsuitable man are you now frolicking with?' Trevor asked me languidly, as I sped down the highway. They were in the throes of jet lag, Trevor and Jayne, and most of what they'd said since we'd stood in baggage claim, waiting for their impossibly stylish luggage to be disgorged from down below, was basically unintelligible. But now he turned toward me, and lifted his sunglasses to inquire from red-rimmed puffy eyes. 'Good God! Bloody bright in this country! Is it always like this in California?'

'Every single day,' I said. I adjusted the rear-view mirror, trying to see Jayne's newly bleached platinum pixie-cut hair. In the airport, I had walked right by her. 'How are you doing back there?'

'Horrible,' she responded cheerily from underneath her coat. 'I feel nauseated and exhausted. My teeth are aching and I feel as if I may be getting a migraine. Trevor doesn't care, do you darling?'

'Not a bit,' he answered, just as cheerful.

'Oh, dear,' she continued. 'How am I going to enjoy San Francisco and tell you all the latest gossip if I feel this poorly?'

I changed lanes, nearly driving into the side of a truck. 'Sorry,' I said, as Trevor gasped involuntarily. 'I'm a little distracted.'

'Now why would that be?' Jayne piped up. 'Have you been having lots of late nights with illicit sex? Do tell.'

'Yes, who are you sleeping with nowadays?' Trevor yawned. As always, my might-as-well-be-married friends viewed my single American girl life with a mixture of curiosity, condescension and creativity, imbuing it with far more lasciviousness than what was really going on.

'I'm in a holding pattern,' I said.

'Don't *tell* me this,' Trevor said.

'Well, I mean, not really. I used to have a standing groping date every four weeks or so with one man, but I haven't waxed my legs in a long time so that prevents us from going any further.'

COURTNEY WEAVER

'I love having my legs waxed,' said Jayne. 'Isn't the pain lovely and addictive?'

'American women don't wax very often,' I said. 'My mother thinks it's the most decadent thing I do.'

'Any other poor fools swimming around in the pond?' Trevor pressed. 'You red-haired temptress.' These comments were par for the course with him – he didn't believe a word of it. Privately, I was fairly certain he considered me a neurotic handful, the way most British men viewed American women. I leaned over and chucked him under the chin.

'What about that foreskin bloke?' Jayne asked. 'The last time we all talked was on the phone. What were you doing to that poor Irish lad? It sounded so delicious.'

'Oh, him.' I feigned indifference. In the last week, Aidan had virtually fallen off the radar – never home, rarely calling and highly nervous when he did, a certain sign the man was in lust, or otherwise preoccupied. I gritted my teeth at his vague answers and guilty tone; we'd gone to the gym the day before, and it took all my strength not to start peppering him with jealous asides as he heaved 185 pounds off his chest.

'What – there are so many men that you couldn't remember which one?' Jayne was asking.

'No, I was trying to remember which conversation that was.'

'Why are motorways from the airport so depressing and colorless?' Trevor mumbled.

In the past, or as recently as two weeks ago anyway, before a Little Missy entered the picture, Aidan would insist that what we had (whatever that was) suited him 'just fine.' But a few things – the forced brightness in his tone, the way he remembered absolutely every detail of every conversation we'd ever had – were ringing some very distant bells. It reminded me of what Harriet had counseled when I was in the throes of all my Defining Moments with Sean – sit tight, don't rock the boat, don't put pressure on him, he'll come around. And Aidan,

202

unlike me, was a lesson in patience and optimism – it would be like him to just sit and lie in wait, until I finally broke down and we slid into coupledom again. That's what it would be: a slide, not a movement forward, not a progression, just a lateral motion, like being walked to first base. But who was I to say? Maybe this was how the best relationships began. Somehow it didn't fit my idea of a mature relationship, however.

That conversation with Jayne and Trevor a few months ago probably wasn't the smartest move either. It had all started one overcast Sunday morning, when I heard the rattle of Aidan's shower curtains being drawn back, and the faucet squeaking off. 'Come in here,' I had called, feeling frisky. I had been reading, lying on my back on his bed, trying to keep my legs straight in the air, with the soles of my feet parallel to the ceiling. Aidan approached me warily. I put the book down and pulled his towel off.

'What's all this?' he asked as I inspected his warm, small penis.

'It's a new yoga position I just learned.' I lowered my legs down, and brought them back up. 'Strengthens the lower abs. But it's hard to maintain for long.' I pulled back his foreskin, touching him gently, as I drew my knees into my chest.

He sighed and looked at the ceiling. 'Why?'

I tugged on him a little bit. 'I just wanted to see it close up, in its, well, natural state.'

'And? Any conclusions?' He stepped closer.

'Nope,' I said, and rolled onto my stomach, returning to my book: the life and times of Eleanor and Franklin Roosevelt. 'Just that I don't know how you men deal with that skin issue. It is truly strange.'

Jayne had once asked me why I dated so many European – well, Irish – men and I couldn't come up with a plausible reason. 'I just seem to meet a lot of them,' I said, unconvincingly. It probably had something to do with alcohol and feeling oppressed, but I didn't want to say that to my

British friend. Jayne then remarked quite seriously, 'I think it's just that you don't like circumcised penises. That must be it.'

Could it? Clotheswise, I had always had an aversion to men in turtlenecks, but I'd never thought about the penile equivalent until that day. 'Listen to this,' I said to Aidan, who was still standing there, towel-less, waiting to see what was in store for him next. I put my book down again. 'Lucinda called me the other day. Her father, who is sixty-two years old, just got circumcised. She said that her mother had held a grudge against him for years for his uncircumcised penis and sex with him had become "challenging" and "difficult." The extra skin got in the way and it was starting to dry out.'

We both looked at his penis, now curled inward like a small frightened animal.

'Anyway,' I continued, 'the doctor recommended it and then, snip, snip. A little pain, but no big deal. And her mother told her she likes it much better now. "Very nice," she said to Lucinda.'

He shuddered. 'Yecchh.'

I rested my head on my hand. 'Yeah, that's what she said. But she was more grossed out about the thought of her parents having sex than anything else.'

I considered as I looked at him. Women were usually not versed on the mechanics of the penis, and in particular that extra cowl of skin. Most of my women friends – Harriet, Jemma, and particularly Marie – had opined at one time or another that penises were ugly, abnormal and too infuriatingly connected to the male brain to be given much validation in the female psyche. But foreskin was different.

'In my country,' I began, as Aidan sat down and rearranged the bedclothes around his torso, 'couples have serious arguments about their little boys' penises. You'd think the men would be anti-cutting, feeling sympathy pains and all that, while the women would be pro-cutting, citing hygiene. Well, it's just the opposite.' I paused and patted his hand. 'Don't worry – it won't be on the citizenship test.'

He leaned against the wall and scratched his cheek. 'In my country, we don't discuss it.'

'My other friend Laura thinks uncircumcised penises are very unhygienic looking,' I said. 'Maybe it's all cultural. Let's call Jayne,' I reached for the phone. 'It's what, four in the afternoon in London? She should be home.'

Aidan looked disappointed. 'Now? Right now?'

'Don't worry. I'm putting it on my calling card.'

'No, go ahead and dial direct, but that's not—'

'Jayne?' I said as she picked up. 'It's me. Remember what you said about my Celt-o-Meter?'

'Hello, love,' she said. I could hear her stirring something. 'About the penises.'

'Not again,' I heard Trevor say in the background. 'It must be the Yank. Let me talk to her. Does she think this is the Foreskin Hotline?'

'Shush,' Jane said. 'We're making lunch,' she told me. 'Bangers and mash! No, not really. But what about it?'

'We never really talked about the female European view.' Aidan slumped down on his side and opened my book to Chapter One, preparing himself for the long haul. I petted his head sympathetically.

'Well, as a true Brit Girl, I found all that skin very normal,' Jayne said. I heard her taste something. 'What was that? Oh, right, Trevor says until Nick Jacobs. That was the first, um, Happy Helmet I ever saw. No, the second. I remember in Spain, lying on the beach, observing all the penises when a circumcised one walked by. I just thought, "Gosh, it looks so weird." So, so . . . bald, or revealed, or *humiliated*.'

I heard Trevor mumble in the background. 'Oh, right,' Jane said. 'Trevor said when he was a little boy he was afraid his willy would drop out if he pulled it back, and eventually he had to ask his Mum about it, who assured him that it would not. And my Mum, well, she always said that she thought uncut penises look really nice and clean because they're covered up, meaning that ugly scary thing called a willy is hidden.'

'The mothers really seem to be weighing in on this issue,' I said. Aidan shook his head.

I heard her slurp again. 'Well, is that it? Have I answered your questions? Remember, we come over in two months. November 23. I still hope your mum wants to have us.'

'I'm sure she does,' I said, thinking that in two months, the kitchen should surely be finished.

'I have to go run, my sweet,' Jayne said. 'The bolognese sauce is done, the pasta is al dente. Why don't you run down to the shops and pick up a packet of sausages, now?' she asked Trevor, giggling as we said our goodbyes and hung up.

Aidan had traveled underneath the comforter, and wrapped himself up like a mummy. 'Hello?' I called to the mound of comforter and sheets beside me. He'd bravely put up with enough analyses for one day. Now it was time for research. I reached underneath and groped around. 'You know, despite what Jayne says, it's all the same to me when it's up and running.' I nuzzled my head between his legs and kissed him. 'You see, the turtleneck has been shed.'

That had been bad of me, I thought now. I was practically . . . *using him* for sex, although I had many other reasons and excuses and other explanations as to why we were still enmeshed in this limbo. Plus, I'd never lied to him, right? I'd never said I wanted or expected more, yes? I enjoyed what we had, and if he was dissatisfied . . . well, he was a big boy. He could take a walk.

But it was all starting to make me feel very uncomfortable. And so, the entrance of Little Missy was probably a good thing – although it was two days in a row now that I had woken up in a blazing argument with him, and had a whole logical argument worked out in my dream state about why he

was at fault for dating someone else, which of course immediately evaporated the second I got out of bed. I hadn't
discussed this with Harriet – she had her own travails – and
three weeks after her operation, right after she packed her
mother off on the plane, she and Jerry were due to go to a
friend's house in Connecticut for a few days to celebrate her
thirty-ninth birthday. And so, it could only be described as
unsisterly if I were to unload my dark little clouds on her
parade. But without our daily phone calls, I felt unconnected
and unbalanced. I even considered calling Clark, just to
commiserate, before coming to my senses and realizing that,
given his history, Harriet might not be so understanding no
matter how innocent the phone call.

Deep down, there was a karmic transaction being played
out with Aidan. And unfortunately, he had walked in right
when I'd begun to look back at all the bad relationships and
recognize the underlying thread: how stupid I'd been. It was
the definition of Defining Moments: all the signs would be
there if I knew where to look – I simply refused to see them,
like most people who were to be imminently dumped. It was
true that now my anger was directed mostly at myself, but I
was naturally enough fairly pissed off that all the Sean-types
had not made themselves a little more clearer, a little less
enigmatic and a whole lot more loving.

Had I been doing the same thing to Aidan? It seemed clear
that I was. It also seemed clear that not only was I no better
than the Seans of the world, I was a whole lot *worse* – because
I liked and respected Aidan, a man who had never done
anything apart from arriving at the wrong place with the
wrong woman at the wrong time.

'What is this funny little box?' Jayne wanted to know the
next morning, picking up the Caller ID, eating her organic
cereal with organic yogurt and soy milk.

I yawned and stretched out on the sofa. 'It's a device to
make you neurotic. Hundred percent satisfaction guaranteed,

or your money back.' At this point, I rarely looked at the Caller ID, but to demonstrate its capabilities, I held out my hand and she dropped it down. I pushed the button a few times. 'See? Eight calls last night: Unavailable, Unavailable, Anonymous, and – oh, okay. Well, here Lizzie called me, but we knew that since she left a message. Now who is this?' I read the last name: *Mallon, J.* The name sounded familiar, but I couldn't place it. I squinted at the phone number. 'Oh, so my friend Jemma called me.' And called again, and again. I wondered why she hadn't left a message. I blinked up at Jayne. 'How did you sleep?'

'Terribly,' she said with that certain passive-aggressive cheer donned in the face of adversity, for which her countrypeople were famous. 'It's the strangest thing! I haven't been allergic to a cat in years, but yours seems to really get to me. I was up all night sneezing and pacing. Trevor was ready to kill me.'

'I could put her in the closet.' I pulled my comforter closer to my chest.

She sat down next to me and I moved over closer to the pillows, giving her room. 'Will you ring your Irish lad and see if we can all go out for a coffee?' she asked.

'I don't think so,' I said peevishly. 'He's um – I don't know what's going on. I think he's seeing someone.'

Jayne stirred her cereal. 'Is that a problem? I thought you weren't an item.'

'We're not,' I said. I had tossed and turned about this all night. How dare he sleep with someone else? What was wrong with our little arrangement? The more I thought about it, the angrier I got. Around three, I had looked at my sportswatch in the dark and felt horribly and utterly alone. I turned over again and again, trying to find a comfortable fetal position, as the cat, slumbering across my legs, rolled around like a rowboat on the open seas. The truth was, no matter how you looked at it, that I wanted him all to myself but wasn't willing to give much in return. How did I turn out to be such a brat,

I wondered. Some tears of self-pity had slid out of my eyes, wetting the pillow and giving off a sweetish smell, like an overripe pineapple. Then I fell asleep and had a dream about carrying around a bag of corned beef, trying to find its owner.

'Do you know this for certain? That he's dating someone else?' Jayne asked.

'Yes. Well, no. Not really. It's just a sense I get.'

'You're probably right, then—' She broke off as Trevor came into the room and flopped down in the arm chair opposite me. 'Hullo, darling! Are you frightfully cross with me for keeping you awake last night?'

'No,' Trevor yawned. I wondered if Trevor had even noticed Jayne's alleged allergy attack. I was starting to realize that he tuned her out quite as much as he appeared to listen to her. Maybe this was how couples stayed together past the three-month point. 'We have to get on the road by midday, Jayne. I'm going to take a taxi to the car hire. Can I get one on the street or do I have to ring?' He directed this at me through a yawn.

'You have to ring,' I said. Jayne offered a spoonful of dripping cereal in my direction and I shook my head.

'All right,' Trevor said, heaving himself up, all business. 'I'm heading for a shower. Do you have to turn on the immersion heater—'

'No. We have hot water in our country twenty-four hours a day. It's just one of the little perks of being an American.'

'Oooh, I'll come join you,' squealed Jayne to him, and put down her bowl.

'Speaking of bathrooms,' I said, 'what was Anna's take on the whole Nigel thing?'

'Anna the Man,' Trevor commented, and headed off in the direction of the shower.

'You're . . . you're like a bloke,' Nigel said. She'd grabbed him in the hallway, placed his hands on her enormous tits (she assumed, rightly,

that Nigel was a breast man) and led him into the cavernous bathroom, unzipping his trousers along the way. Now Anna was propped up on the edge of the sink, legs flailing about at absurd angles around Nigel's shoulders. Despite herself, she laughed loudly – her signature laugh, a cross between a bark and a neigh.

He clapped a hand over her mouth. 'For fuck's sake. People are right outside.'

'Like I give a toss.' That seemed to excite him even more, and he moved faster. She braced herself more firmly, arching her back, and then he let out a groan. She'd come a long time ago, and after a minute she sat up, unceremoniously sliding herself away from Nigel and his limpness. She jumped off the sink, wiped herself quickly, pulled on her tights which Nigel had thrown in the direction of the bathtub, and struggled to pull down her bunched-up skirt over her ample hips.

Nigel was still panting, one arm leaning against the sink, his trousers around his ankles. His white starched shirt was wrinkled and his face was red, as if he might have a heart attack. 'You look ludicrous,' she said, and laughed again. 'Get yourself to the gym.' She leaned around him to look in the huge circular mirror, and when he tried to kiss her neck, she turned and gave him a huge wet kiss on the mouth.

Candlelight from the votives flickered across the walls, reminding her of church. The church of sex, she thought, and laughed again. Nigel smiled. 'You're one to talk about getting to the gym.' He tried to grab the cheeks of her ass, but she skirted around him. 'See you in the kitchen,' she said, opening the door as the sounds of the party flooded into the bathroom.

At the bar, Anna poured herself a glass of tonic water and lit a cigarette. Everyone at this point was completely gone, blitzed, as she herself might be if she hadn't decided early on to take Nigel into the loo and fuck his brains out. She laughed again and blew smoke toward the ceiling. Men – they were so funny. All it took was a bit of confidence and there they were, limp (so to speak), in your hand.

It was much better to be the seducer than the seduced, Anna thought. You knew exactly where you were and where it would go. Jayne would say that she worried about Anna – was she happy, living in New

York? Having these men lurking around whom she never called her 'boyfriend' (Anna hated that word – refused to let any man say it in relation to her) but never living with anyone? It rather infuriated Anna that Jayne didn't seem to take into account that Anna loved her job at the ad agency and was remarkably successful at it. She loved every high pressure minute – furthermore, it was one of those American jobs which truthfully did not leave any time whatsoever for a committed relationship. Anna didn't want children, she didn't want to give up her apartment or her space to accommodate some man who would invariably want more than she could give. She loved Jayne, but for God's sakes – would she be expressing so much worry and concern if Anna were a man in the same set of circumstances?

Jayne now came weaving over to her at the bar. She'd seen Anna lead Nigel into the bathroom and despite her concerns about Anna, couldn't help but think it might teach Nigel a thing or two. 'Mission accomplished?' she said, and Anna bared her teeth in mock ferocity. They laughed and Anna, feeling triumphant and flushed, added a generous splash of vodka to her tonic water. Jayne was a great friend, Anna thought, and not for the first time that night, she felt that she wanted to kiss her in gratitude. She didn't have this many good girl friends in New York, where she lived. Lots of men friends, yes – Anna always had plenty of male friends, all around Europe and parts of the United States – but women, they were always so much harder to get to know in America. You almost had to court them, so cliquey and neurotic were they.

'How's Trevor feeling?' Anna asked.

'Blitzed. Out of his head. I think it was the coke. Did you get that here in London, by the way?'

'Good Lord, no. I brought it from New York.' Anna smiled, and Jayne closed her eyes in humorous disbelief, saying 'Don't tell me anymore.'

Jayne of course knew all along what Anna had been planning that night with Nigel. At the start of the party, they'd barred themselves in one of the bedrooms with Trevor. 'Should we invite Caroline?' Trevor asked, mindful of the hostess's feelings. 'She might feel a little left out, seeing us lot tramp off for mysterious activities.'

'Fine,' said Anna. She was tapping out the coke on a gilded hand mirror. These Chelsea homes – whoever used hand mirrors anymore? For that matter, who did cocaine anymore – which she only brought when she came back to London, just to help her along with the pressures of being back on home turf. Sometimes she couldn't believe she used to live here; what with all these couples, couples, couples. Much as she insisted upon her single status, after only a week of being in London she would start to feel tense and lonely. It was much better in New York, where there were plenty of women and men swanning about, happily uncommitted. The couples were considered to be more of the exception than the rule.

But Trevor fell silent, watching her cut and crosshatch the white powder. 'So what are you planning, Anna?' he asked. 'What are you plotting and scheming about?' The three of them had been friends forever, and Anna shook her head in innocence.

'Anna doesn't plot and scheme,' Jayne said. She was stretched out on the damask-covered bed, sipping a Pernod. 'That would be far too female of her.'

'That's right, I forgot,' Trevor said. 'Anna is really a man in sheep's clothing.'

Anna had heard all this from Trevor, many times. 'The problem with you, Trevor, is that you didn't get all the gratuitous sex out of your system before you paired off,' she said, nodding at Jayne and expertly drawing out six lines. ' "She's just like a man. She thinks like a man." All because I like sex.' Anna smiled to herself. 'And because I'm fat and I don't care about it. And because I fuck a guy and don't necessarily want to be his little girlfriend.'

'Well, don't hold back from what you really think,' Trevor said, stroking Jayne's calf. Trevor liked Anna and loved hearing her stories – 'vicarious fucks,' as Jayne called them. Trevor was one of those blokes that, in his single days, would have loved to have slept with Anna but never would bring her home to meet mum.

'You men certainly think you hold all the cards,' Anna said.

'Absolutely not. It's you birds who do. We just sit here like fools, hoping you'll give us the privilege of a shag now and again.' The three laughed again, and Trevor kissed Jayne affectionately. 'How 'bout it, luv? Fancy a shag?' he asked in broad Cockney.

Anna sniffed quickly and looked to the ceiling, eyes watering. 'Right then. I hear that Nigel's coming tonight. What's going on with him?'

Jayne wrinkled her nose. 'He's with this little twit, Kath. I heard they broke up, but she's got wedding bells on her mind and I'm sure she wants him back. She's nice enough I suppose, but seems really wrapped up in this idea of what's expected of her and all that.'

'She must be young,' Anna commented.

'She is,' Jayne said, obviously feeling as if she had Nigel and Kath's relationship all figured out, all of a sudden. 'And she's remarkably self-centered! Really, love to her is only a charm bracelet that you wear to show your girlfriends.'

'Stupid cow.' Anna passed the mirror to Trevor. 'Well, all the better that Nigel's with someone. As long as he doesn't bring her tonight. Actually, maybe that will make it even more interesting.'

Trevor sniffed now and coughed. 'If you shag Nigel,' he said, and they started to dissolve in giggles again, 'well, I'll eat my shirt. It's not fair. It's just not fair.' He kissed Jayne's behind, glad that all these machinations were a distant memory for the two of them.

They emerged from the bedroom looking slightly guilty, that drug-induced heightening that reddened the tips of their ears and gave a glint to their eyes. Anna and Jayne were sitting in the kitchen, eating Greek olives and smoking, when Anna thought she caught sight of Nigel in the foyer. He'd just arrived and was looking around, excited, shouting 'Hallo' across the room to Caroline, the hostess.

But he'd gained so much weight that Anna couldn't really be sure it was him. It had been five years, and while Anna had always been a big woman – and emphasized it with her mini skirts and tights – Nigel had been a rugby player, lean and ruddy. Now he looked like a beached whale. Ugh she thought. What had happened to him? She smoked some more, drank a glass of champagne, and watched as he galumphed around the room. Of course he didn't even look her way, but then men rarely did. At first.

Fuck it. 'Hallo, Nigel,' she said loudly. He looked pleased but confused – he obviously didn't remember her. She handed him a glass of champagne. 'Has Caroline given you a tour of the house? I'll show you where to lay your coat.' Smiling, she moved her head almost imperceptibly in the direction of the hallway.

'Well, I, em, just–' he began, but Anna had turned and walked away. She heard his footsteps following her, as she thought she might. 'You know, she just had the bathroom completely re-done,' she called over her shoulder.

Kath was eighteen when she lost her virginity. Her boyfriend, Rory, had been pressuring her steadily for a year and, though they'd been going out since they were fifteen, she knew she did not want to do it with him. It wasn't that she was a good Catholic girl – she couldn't give a toss about the Pope or the Church. It was just that sex sounded not very interesting, and not very nice.

And so she surprised even herself when she found herself at a party in the wee hours of the morning groping, kissing and ultimately having sex in the laundry room of her best friend Bridget's house. Bridget's family had gone home to Ireland for a funeral, and the whole gang was there – by midnight some of the boys were throwing up outside, and many of the couples had slunk away to various rooms in the spacious Glasgow home. But Rory had been felled that week with a cold, and so it was that suddenly she wound up going to the party with his best friend Blackie, and ultimately . . . well, yes, flat on her back, on the cold tile floor.

And it wasn't that it was bad. She liked kissing Blackie, and she liked his hands up her thin shirt, the way he slipped his fingers underneath her nylon Marks & Spencer bra, fondling her pert nipples. But suddenly his trousers were down around his ankles, and her skirt was bunched up around her waist, with her tights and knickers locking her feet together. They were kissing as he clumsily tried to find her hole with his fingers, and suddenly his penis was inside her. But it wasn't that bad. And after a quick stab of pain, she began to feel herself relax a little, knowing how excited he must be. Then Blackie

214

suddenly came (all over her stomach, even getting some goo on her skirt) and it was over. Just like that. It wasn't terrible, and it wasn't painful. It was just . . . nothing. Maybe this was what happened when you had sex with people you weren't supposed to have sex with. Maybe you had to love someone the way her parents did to find it really wonderful.

Rory never found out and she and Blackie never did it again. No one knew. It was as if it hadn't happened at all. When she at last had sex with Rory, it was the same thing: pleasant, a little damp, then nothing. Obviously she didn't love Rory either.

It was three years later that she met Nigel, at a drinks party in London sponsored by her magazine where she worked as an editorial assistant. Rory had long since fallen by the wayside, and Blackie, well, who knows? She'd snogged a few men in London when she was drunk, even slept with two of them. Kath knew she was pretty and lively and that men liked her. She discovered it didn't take much to make them want her in that way. She had only to sit back, laugh, and be silent and they all chased her, panting like overexcited dogs.

Nigel was no exception. Initially, she hadn't the slightest interest in him: he looked like an overfed schoolboy, with his blond curls and jumpers that stretched over his protruding tummy. And he was old: in his middle thirties, at least. But there was something sweet about him, and the way he looked at her incredulously, like he couldn't believe his luck. He reminded her, actually, of her father, who was the kindest and most decent man in the world, and who loved her mother to pieces. Even now, her father waited on her mum hand and foot, while she gently shooed him away and told him not to be so silly. Dad adored Mum. It was the best marriage ever – everyone said so – and Kath was determined to have the same.

So when Nigel began to pursue her, sending her flowers every week, she knew to just wait. She let him think she was dating other men (she wasn't), she never phoned him, she even stood him up a few times, just to let him know who was boss. Nigel was so used to having his own way that she could tell this really confused him. Later, when they were together, the trick would be to let him think he was having his own way when in actuality it would be Kath who was controlling the relationship. But that was later.

Then one night, she was supposed to meet him in the West End at Mezzo with their little group (Kath had become quite friendly with the girlfriends of Nigel's friends), and Nigel simply didn't turn up. She rang him on his mobile, she phoned his flat, his office – he was nowhere to be found. Nobody knew where he was. She began to grow panicked. Throughout the evening she kept ringing, ringing, ringing from her mobile. Had something happened?

Finally, the next morning at 7 a.m. Nigel answered his phone. After determining that he hadn't been in an accident, Kath let him have it. How dare he? How dare he just come home and go to sleep, without a word to her? At that point, having been up all night, she'd worked herself into a frenzy and was bawling down the phone, pleading with him that she wanted to skip work and just come to the flat, just to see him. Gently, Nigel said that was ridiculous. He'd fallen asleep after work, he was sorry, and he'd see her later. He seemed genuinely bewildered by her reaction.

But nothing seemed right after that incident. Somehow, the balance had shifted, and Nigel grew more distant, more unavailable. Why did he not like her anymore? She began to phone him more often, and decided that her tactics had been all wrong. It was that Yank book **The Rules** she decided: she should have known it would work for those brutish American men, but not her Nigel. No, now she'd shower him with love and affection. That's what he needed, that's what most men liked anyway. She'd kiss him more, be nicer to him, maybe make love with the lights on or in the morning. But Nigel had never really seemed that interested in that part of the relationship – Kath thought maybe he was one of those sexless men, which was fine with her anyway.

When they had sex, Nigel would have this funny look on his face, like he was somewhere else or thinking about something else – a book he'd read, a movie they'd seen. But he was gentle with her, and their lovemaking was soft and nice. She felt cuddly in his arms, and magnanimous, like she was giving him a little present, a treat that she knew he liked. This must be what it means to have really wonderful *sex she thought, and when asked by her girlfriends, she always said how lovely it was. Though she'd never had an orgasm, she lied and told her friends in serious tones that she always had many with Nigel. They all looked at her with what seemed like envy: silent, wide-eyed nods.*

A week after the oversleeping incident, Nigel suddenly broke it off with Kath. Kath knew it was coming, but she nevertheless lost control completely when he told her at his flat that evening. He handed her a box of her things that he'd packed up, and said rather coldly that he was sorry, that sometimes these things happened and there was no reason for it.

Weeping uncontrollably, Kath fled in a black cab back to her south London flat that she shared with three girlfriends from Glasgow. That night, they sat up the rest of the night around the kitchen table, smoking and drinking tea, plotting. Because Kath had to get Nigel back. She had to. He was the one. She would get him back and she would marry him, because he was the right one. And then they would have a marriage as good as Mum and Dad, who were, after all, the envy of all their friends in Glasgow.

And then suddenly the breakup was over, as quickly as it began. Kath knew in her heart of hearts they were meant to be together, it was just a matter of time. Now, two months later, it all seemed like a bad dream, that horrible little short time they'd been apart. Flipping back through her journal that she kept under her bed in a shoebox, she was startled to see they'd actually only been broken up eleven days. During that time, every single minute of the day had been felt – no, every second. Her heart banged when the phone rang at the office or at the flat: was it Nigel? Would he come back to her now? Why had this happened? She looked forward to crawling into her single bed at night, trying to put out of her mind the last time she'd seen him, when he had handed her a box of her books, CDs and knickers. But of course when she closed her eyes all she did was dream about him.

But now they were back and things were almost the way they used to be. Almost, because Nigel still seemed a bit on edge. It was probably his job, which he told her was 'very stressful' lately, everyone pushing and pulling on him, wanting more and more. He was drinking a lot, even for Nigel, who could drink everyone under the table. They never talked about why they had broken up, and Kath didn't ask.

Mum said maybe they needed to get used to each other again. It was strange for Mum to make a comment like this, since she'd always seemed to be against Nigel. But this time, Kath wanted to be smarter. She'd never thought much of Nigel's friends – they were always loud and laddish, talking about this bird's tits and that one's bum – and so this time around, she'd try to manage it that they didn't spend as much time with them. Nigel was so distracted nowadays that she doubted he even noticed. When she said sweetly that she'd rather stay in with him and watch telly instead of meeting the group down at the pub, he nodded blankly. They'd get an Indian takeaway (always mild, since Nigel had stomach problems) and drink some of his cellared wine, sometimes get a video. It was comfy and pleasant, and they didn't fight as much as they used to.

One Friday evening, about three months after they'd gotten back together, Nigel picked her up after work as he usually did. 'There's a party at Trevor and Jayne's,' he said casually, drumming his hand on the steering wheel, his face red from the reflections of the brake lights in the rush hour London traffic. 'I want to go to it.'

Kath hesitated. She didn't like Trevor, or even Jayne for that matter; they were older, flashier, and liked to talk about politics, a subject Kath had absolutely no interest in. (She also got the impression they didn't like her as well.) But Nigel had gone to university with them, and, put on the spot, she couldn't think of a good reason not to attend. 'Well, all right,' she said slowly, with just a little drag in her voice. She put her hand on her stomach and grimaced slightly.

Nigel looked at her curiously. 'All right? Got your period, then?'

'Yes,' Kath said. 'But let's go to Trevor's.'

'You don't have to go,' Nigel said, accelerating through the cars, weaving in and out as they buzzed along Charing Cross Road. 'Don't come if you don't feel well.'

'I'll be fine,' she said. She leaned over and gave Nigel a kiss on the fold of skin above his tight shirt collar. 'Thank you for worrying about me.' Nigel, concentrating on the road, patted her knee.

They got there about ten o'clock, having downed two bottles of wine and eaten some old chips left over from the night before. She did feel a bit poorly, actually, and hurriedly drank a glass of gin in Trevor and Jayne's fashionable Conran bathroom, painted in bright yellow and royal blue. As it turned out, it wasn't even really a party at all, just ten of the gang, all university chums, and their girlfriends and boyfriends. And some woman with fat legs and too short a skirt, who'd just flown in from America and was drinking champagne and eating crisps, one after another. Gales of laughter erupted from the kitchen, where they were all planted, and Kath leaned against the sink, taking a deep breath. She put on more MAC lipstick that Nigel had bought her and again thought of Mum, telling her to smile since she looked so much prettier that way.

In the kitchen, the woman who lived in America was telling a joke. All the men were standing around her, silently, some staring at her huge chest. The women were somewhat in the background, listening too; Jayne was laughing, pouring wine, and said, 'Oh Anna, this is not a true story!'

Kath sidled up to Nigel and laid her arm across the small of his back, resting her head on his shoulder. But Nigel was listening to Anna, and moved away slightly to extend his cup toward Jayne, who smiled brightly at Kath and filled Nigel's cup to the rim.

Later, Kath went out on the balcony overlooking the garden to get some air. She'd been talking to that Anna, who had come over to talk to her while she was standing next to the stove, trying to find a match to light her cigarette. 'Here you go, I have a light,' Anna had said, and extended her silver lighter in her direction. Anna watched her intently and lit a cigarette herself, blowing smoke toward the ceiling. She was friendly, Kath thought, even if she was rather fat. Not many women in Nigel's group ever seemed that interested in Kath, but Anna asked her many questions: How did she like London? Did she miss Scotland? How long had she known Nigel? Were they getting married? How old was Kath? At one point Anna raised her glass in a toast, rattling something off in Spanish. 'I learned that from a busboy in New York,' Anna said, smiling in a seductive manner. And then she moved away.

❊ ❊ ❊

Outside, in the cold autumn air, Kath shivered and was just about to head back inside when she heard voices from below, in the garden. If the truth be told, she knew Nigel was down there, and she was just slightly curious what he was talking about. He and Trevor were standing under the apple tree, smoking and laughing uproariously. She backed herself in a niche, wondering if Nigel was talking about her, hearing the men's slurred voices. Trevor punched Nigel in the arm and was saying 'you dog, you dog,' and laughed some more. 'But you're back with Kath. What is it that you like about Kath then? You love her? You must really fancy her sexually—'

She heard Nigel mumble, 'Uh, I guess so, yeah I guess so.'

'What is it? I want to know what it is you fancy so much.'

'I like it that Kath comes with just a flick of my wrist,' Nigel said in a stage whisper. 'She comes all the time. Just like that.' He snapped his fingers, and the two of them laughed. Kath felt her face flush in pride. She of course had never come in her life, but Nigel didn't need to know that. Trevor said something like 'worrrrhhhh—' and then dropped his voice. Kath couldn't hear what he said, but then Nigel sighed like an explosion of air was escaping.

'Can't even describe it,' Nigel said, slurring. 'Only wish one thing: that she'd lose a bit of weight in the old bum. But her tits—' Both the men were silent for a moment, then began laughing again.

Kath felt disgusted. Why did Nigel have to behave this way with his friends? It was all Trevor's doing, she was convinced of it. She'd just have to figure out some way to keep him away from this group. Nigel was never this much of a lad when he was alone. And what was all this about her bum? He'd never said a word about her being fat; if anything, he'd told her she should try to put on some weight in that area. But it was true that he always seemed to like her small breasts, or at least, he always stared at them with a serious look on his face, as if he were trying to understand some deep mystery about them. Men, she sighed. Pity she couldn't talk to Mum about this.

She backed into the house again, and turning to go into the party, she almost fell right into Anna who was standing in the doorway in the dark. 'Getting some air too, I see,' Anna said, and smiled at her in an *odd way, reminding Kath of some feline, one of those exotic animals featured on those nature programs that she'd watch with Mum. 'We must get together for coffee next time I come back to London. I'd love to have a chat with a new girlfriend.'*

Right after Jayne and Trevor donned their pointy sunglasses, packed up their convertible rental car and drove off into the sunset, looking more American than any Americans I knew, I ran back up the three flights to my apartment and called Aidan. I had been determined not to call him until he called me, but I couldn't take it anymore. I had to know what was going on. I would just leave a message, ask him nicely to give me a call since I thought we should have a little talk – or no, maybe I wouldn't put it that way, because even I agreed with Harriet that men never responded to that 'we need to have a little talk' crap, and then he would never return my call . . .

'Hello,' Aidan said, sounding tired.

'Oh, *hello*,' I said, flustered. 'What are you doing home? I thought you had to be at work at four.'

'I work days on Wednesdays. Remember?'

'Oh, right,' I said. Now that I had him on the phone, I didn't know what to say.

'Besides, if you knew I was at work, why are you calling me here?'

'I was going to leave a message,' I said stiffly. 'I didn't want to bother you, since you seem so busy nowadays.' Aidan didn't answer, and so I continued, 'Well, how are you? What's going on?'

'Okay,' he said, but he didn't sound okay. He sounded a little off-hand, or tired, or distracted. 'We lost another sous chef, so it's been hectic at work. Last night I didn't get out of there until 12:30, and then I had to turn around and come right back this morning—'

'Aidan, are you seeing somebody?' I suddenly burst in.

'What?' he asked, even though I knew damn well he'd

heard me. I waited, and he cleared his throat. Then, 'No, no I'm not. Why are you asking me that?'

'It's just a feeling I have.'

'No, I'm not. And if I were, I don't think it would be any of your business.'

'Oh, really? I think it is.'

'And why would that be?'

'Because I don't want to get a disease from some little filly that you're frolicking with,' I said. I hadn't even thought of that aspect, actually, until just this minute. But now that I said it, I was surprised by how legitimate it made me sound. *No, I'm not jealous, I'm just concerned about a public health risk!* Aidan hesitated, which served to only shore up my claim. 'That was the deal, remember?' He was still quiet and I started to seethe. 'Hello? I think I have a right to know.'

'You're not going to get a disease,' he said.

'So you're using condoms with her? *We* haven't been using condoms, remember?' Like most heterosexual couples I knew, he and I had a hate/hate reaction to condoms, using them when we first began to have sex, until we both trundled off to get an AIDS test, more for posterity than anything else. We'd relied half-heartedly on my diaphragm since then, when we weren't using a crazy version of the rhythm method. For someone as anti-kid as Aidan and I professed to be, at this stage in our life, we did take an inordinately irresponsible attitude to birth control – but again, no different from my straight friends. 'Aren't you afraid you might give *her* something? When was the last time you got an AIDS test?' I demanded.

'Probably the same time that *you* got one,' he said.

'No, because I just got one last month. When I gave blood.' Ha! Now he had virtually admitted that he *was* sleeping with someone. I felt triumphant, until I remembered the source of my triumph. Aidan didn't answer and I said, 'Well, fine. Have a good time with Little Missy, whoever she is. Because our arrangement is now officially over.'

'I thought we were friends,' Aidan said, pissed off now. 'This has been playing with my head too much and it's too difficult. If we're friends then I think whatever I do with other women shouldn't matter—'

'You lied to me!' I said. 'And you put me at risk, if you're sleeping with someone else while sleeping with me and not using condoms!'

'I didn't lie to you! And you never asked, until just now!'

'I have to ask you? What, every day? "Aidan, are you sleeping with someone else?" And then the next day, "Aidan, are you still not sleeping with someone else?" ' Aidan groaned which I took to mean as yet another admittance of guilt. 'How much crossover has there been? Are you using condoms? You better, because if you've given me something, I'm going to have your head on a platter!'

'Not that it matters, but we have never made a deal to be monogamous during this *arrangement*, as you call it! And I have never liked this arrangement anyway! It's crazy!'

'Did you use condoms with her?' I persisted.

'You have no reason to worry,' he said, sounding like a robot. 'It isn't possible, because—'

But I didn't hear the rest because I had decided within the last five seconds that I couldn't talk about it anymore. In the olden days when I got angry, I would hang up the phone loudly, obviously, with a satisfying *clunk*. But that was in the time when the Princess Phone reigned supreme – now, in the cordless age, somehow hanging up on someone had lost all its fun. Nowadays, you could break your phone by punching the 'Talk' button too violently.

So I put the phone down on the sofa, between the cushions, and sat there looking out the window. Aidan, oblivious, was still going on, his voice floating up to me like little electric bees. It was four o'clock and already the sun hung low in the sky, ready to dip down into the ocean which lay westward. An old man and woman – they were perhaps in their eighties, judging from their shrunken apple doll faces which I could see even from my third story perch – were tottering up the hill, holding hands. In her free hand, the woman was holding a leash to which a tired, stumpy-legged basset was tethered. The couple were silent as they made their way up the steep street, and when I opened the window and leaned out, they both looked up at me. The man lifted a hand straight in the air as if in a salute, and I saluted back. Then I shut the window.

CHAPTER 9

'It's a Manhattan tonight,' Harriet was saying, after taking another sip. 'Delicious.'

'I'm glad your convalescence isn't getting in the way of the really important rituals,' I said. 'Do you know that I can make pesto, but I don't have the foggiest idea of how to make a Manhattan?'

'There's a whole cookbook industry geared toward you,' Harriet said. 'You're the generation who knows what balsamic vinegar is, but couldn't make a white sauce to save your life.'

'Yeah, that's me.' That made me think of Aidan, who had once talked me through a white sauce on the phone. 'Now add the flour, little by little,' he'd said, relishing his rare role as advisor and teacher. 'Don't forget to keep whisking! Are you whisking? I don't hear whisking sounds.' We hadn't talked since that Wednesday on the phone, nearly three weeks ago. I was doing a series of activities to distract myself – crosswords galore, naps, and actually working. Every day I'd check my Caller ID, just to see if he'd phoned and not left a message, but he hadn't. A part of me was curious to see how long we would hold out, and another part of me wanted not to talk to him ever again. Still another missed him terribly, particularly when I went running, which I had taken up again, puffing my way up and down the hills of San Francisco, wondering if the cave women ever thought about thinner thighs.

In the meantime, Harriet was due to arrive in two weeks. Her operation had been a success, of sorts, since they got out all of the fruit bowl, including the tangerine which had since graduated to a potato. 'What kind of potato?' I wanted to know. 'New potato? Ruby red? Yukon gold? Fingerling? What?'

'An ordinary Idaho Russet,' Harriet had said weakly from her hospital bed. She'd had to stay there for four nights, not two, because they couldn't get her fever down – causing a massive wave of panic and phone calls across the country among her mother, me and the New York Network. Jerry had been coming to her apartment daily, after work, bringing her dinner and newspapers, but Harriet was unusually quiet about this. I wondered if he had failed some *Rules* chapter about convalescing – 'If he brings you flowers when you're sick, then you may return his calls the following week, but only if they are not daisies . . .'

'I'm going to start running,' she said, as I heard her set down her cocktail. 'I started doing that Cindy Crawford video a few months before the surgery, and I'm convinced that's why my recovery wasn't so long. I don't even think I needed my mom to stay here as long as she did.'

'Great!' I said. 'I hate running. We can do it together while you're here.'

'Absolutely!' she said, matching my shout. Harriet certainly seemed energetic since getting rid of her fruitbowl. She said she'd had an 'interesting' time in Connecticut with Jerry, and when I pressed her, she said she'd tell me more about it when she got to California. Apart from the daily visits, I sensed that something was shifting between them.

'How *are* you feeling, in general? And what's Jerry doing for your birthday?' I asked.

'Oh, thanks for your card,' she said automatically. 'I got it today.'

'You're welcome. We'll do something while you're here too.' Hopefully there would be some sort of detente between Aidan and me, but it certainly wasn't looking good. 'What did Jerry do?' I persisted.

'Oh, well. Tonight he's taking me out for my birthday dinner,' she said neutrally.

'Uh huh,' I said, waiting for more. 'Is that all you're going to say? I mean, where? Are you excited? You don't sound very excited.'

'We're going to First,' she said. 'I like First. I picked it. I made the reservation. Did I tell you what he gave me for my birthday?'

'Uh, no.'

'It was a very elaborately wrapped gift,' she said. 'He gave it to me the night before last, right before we were settling in to watch a video. And do you know what it was?'

'A ring?' I asked hopefully.

'Nope. A professional cheese grater.'

'Oh,' I said. 'That was a joke, right?'

'No. He really gave that to me. And he really meant it. He looked all happy when I opened it, and said, "See? Now we don't have to use your little cheap grater when we eat pasta at your house." I tried to act happy, but I was so disappointed.'

'God,' I said. 'That wasn't *the* present, was it? After all you've been through? He can't be that heartless.' More and more, Jerry was starting to remind me of Fred Mertz.

'No, I'm sure there's going to be something else. It's not a big deal.' I heard water running, and she said, 'I'm just going to put on my makeup now.' She began brushing her teeth and said, 'Kee' talking.'

I considered for a moment. 'It isn't a big deal? I don't believe that for a minute. And isn't there some Rule about gift giving?' I asked. Oh, no. Now they were starting to come to me without even having to think about it.

'There certainly is,' Harriet said, after spitting out her toothpaste. 'Number 12. Move on if he doesn't give you romantic gifts for your birthday or Valentine's Day. So, this year there were no flowers on Valentine's Day and a cheese grater for my birthday. That's two for two, I'd say – no, worse, because when he came back from a business trip to Italy, he brought me a coffee mug. It was a very nice coffee mug, a nice Florentine blue with gold letters on it, but how romantic can a cup be? I'm *sure* I told you about that.'

'No, you didn't,' I said. 'Well, Aidan gave me martini glasses for my birthday, last year, if that's any consolation.'

'Yes, but you don't care about Aidan that way,' Harriet said. 'So it doesn't matter. I'll bet you didn't even think twice about it.'

'I remember thinking that it was a good excuse to learn how to make a cocktail. I mean, a *real* cocktail – the kind that you drink. But I never followed through.'

I heard some more water running, and Harriet said, pausing between words as she did when she was putting on her mascara, 'When I got that coffee cup . . . it really threw me into a panic. *The Rules* absolutely says . . . that the man is not in love with you . . . if he gives you unromantic gifts.'

'Now come on. Isn't that a bit of a generalization?'

'It does seem a little heavy-handed, I know. That's probably why I didn't tell you until now.'

Harriet, I'd noticed, had been a whole lot more open as of late. 'Try to have a good time tonight,' I said, and asked lightly, 'Have you talked to Clark at all recently?'

'Not at all,' she said, to my surprise. 'Truthfully. I think Clark has left my system – just flown out, after five years. I feel completely done with him.' She shuffled the phone around, and added 'I tell you, this operation put a whole lot of things in perspective.'

I thought about that – it reminded me of a conversation I'd had with Harriet about the love-of-my-life boyfriend five years ago. Michael and I had had just about the most passionate and intense relationship a couple could have, one of those for which your friends hate you and whose insufferable outbursts of public passion make it impossible for anyone to else to stomach. 'I would have walked to the ends of the earth for

Michael,' I'd said to Harriet wistfully, abandoning myself to the cliché. We'd calculated that I hadn't been that in love – not even with the Irish George Costanza – since him. 'Five years is way too long,' Harriet said authoritatively, and I had agreed. But that passion – where was it now? Where did it go? Little by little things had gone wrong with Michael, until we tried out a trial breakup, and then time passed and it really was done and over with. Now here we were, five years later, and Michael was married to someone else and that feeling like I'd walk to the ends of the earth for him was a distant memory, like the way you remembered a bad case of stomach flu. You knew it was intense, you knew you had felt it with the entire core of your being at the time, but you couldn't call it up, not even the tiniest part of the feeling.

And what if I'd gotten *married* to Michael? What if that love had just floated away as obscurely as it had come? Then what? No married people seemed to be able to assure me that this would not happen.

'Have a good time tonight, Harriet,' I said to her now. 'I'll be thinking of you.'

Talking about all these hunter-gatherer issues made me think of Jemma. I wondered if I had a moral obligation to go back to the Power Exchange. One morning soon after the cheese-grater conversation, I sat in my kitchen poring over the crossword puzzle, in between eating a bagel, listening to AM talk radio and composing a 'Things To Do' list on the back of an envelope. I caught the tail end of a news bulletin: in a town about 200 miles north of San Francisco, a man had marched into the local police station and announced that something was 'weighin' on my conscience.' Saying that he had a 'problem' with the 'ladies,' he proceeded to tell in graphic detail about all the women he'd killed over the past few years, and then pulled a severed breast out of his pocket – proof, I guess.

The man had all the stereotypical qualities of a serial killer: polite, kept to himself, wouldn't hurt a fly, kept his cab clean (he was a trucker who was on the road most of the year), etc., etc. All of a sudden, as I listened to this, my bagel held mid-air, I began thinking of Sir and Jemma. Sir traveled a lot in his job too, Jemma had told me, but that wasn't the prick of recognition. It was a huge leap, certainly, from a consensual arrangement to a serial killing, but there were certain disturbing (to put it mildly) similarities that anyone could see: sexualized violence, an obsessive need for dominance and control, and how about that severed breast?

ME: *What do you think about that theory in the article I gave you that S/M is a substitute for acting it out in real life?*

JEMMA: *Acting what out in real life?*

ME: *Well, say you're a really aggressive guy, and it's a way of acting out your aggression. Instead of acting that way all the time, you get it out in this way.*

JEMMA: *I'm not sure I've ever come across that. Most of the guys that I've come across who are dominant in their non-vanilla life are dominant in their vanilla life. It's whether they have the . . . it's whether they can back it up or not. But here's more of what you probably mean: some guys, you know . . . you get these weeny, ugly little toads or turds that no one would take a second glance at in real life, but they have got a slave, and she will kneel down, and she will do all these things for whatever reason she chooses to do it with him, and then he's a big tough guy in the dungeon. But in real life he might be a nobody.*

ME: *A loser, you mean.*

JEMMA: *Yeah, you can certainly get that. Or someone not particularly important, not necessarily a loser but just not a big cheese. Whereas in the S/M world he can be a large Gouda.*

ME: *Tell me again the things that you won't do?*

JEMMA: *I won't do wee-wees. I won't do shit. I don't want to do other guys, but if Sir really wanted me to, I would, but I wouldn't do just anyone. Let's see, what else won't I do?*

ME: *Children?*

JEMMA: *Children. Nope.*

ME: *Guns?*

JEMMA: *Done guns.*

ME: *What?*

JEMMA: *Done guns. I mean, I have done.*

ME: *What do you mean? What have you done?*

JEMMA: *Oh, things at gunpoint, that sort of thing.*

ME: *Loaded? Are you serious?*

JEMMA: *'An unloaded gun is a hammer.'*

ME: *You really believe that?*

JEMMA: *Yeah. It is. It's pretty much no use to you.*

ME: *How did you know it was loaded?*

JEMMA: *He told me afterwards.*

ME: *Sir told you? What did you say?*

JEMMA: *I went, 'Oh.'*

Right before we stopped speaking, Aidan and I had sat at the bar in an empty, brightly colored Mexican restaurant on Haight Street, watching the army of homeless, scruffy teenagers roam up and down the sidewalk, scratching their dogs' bellies in between plaintive pleas for spare change. In high school, my friend Kaitlin and I would come to the Haight Ashbury to buy the special imported hair dye from England, which came in such colors as candy floss pink, vermillion, scarlet and azure. But even then, some fifteen years after the Summer of Love, the Haight scared me. It still represented complete abandon, where dirty barefoot people could get right in your face and scream things at you, where begging for money and drugs was not just accepted but a practical way of life. When I was four, my mom and I would get into her Volkswagen Beetle and drive over to the Haight to buy the special piroshkis that she liked. I remember it disturbing me even then that there were so many spacey, blissful grown-ups who wore no shoes.

Aidan, who used to be a track star in Ireland, was talking about a new pair of spikes he'd just bought, and his voice was drifting in and out of my head like the AM radio programs. It was a rainy Monday night, and we were drinking frozen tamarind-flavored margaritas. I was watching a blond-haired girl who was leaning against a tree, laughing. She looked to be about fourteen, and a man in his fifties or so wearing combat fatigues was showing her something in the palm of his hand. She was leaning back, pressing the rear peaks of her mohawk against the slender trunk of the tree, so that when she leaned forward again they stuck out at right angles to her head. I lifted my glass, viewing them through the frosty residue of the drink. A woman wearing a tie-dyed cape and a hat with a crown of plastic daisies shuffled up and joined them. Then they all drifted up the street, out of sight.

'—because they don't have New Balance in Ireland, although that's the brand of running shoe over here that seems really popular. I've always liked Adidas though, because they just feel better, but in Artane, where I grew up, we didn't—'

'Another margarita?' The woman behind the bar asked. She was wearing a t-shirt that had a line drawing of James Joyce on the front, and some scripted verse on the back side.

'Yes,' I said. I looked at Aidan. 'How did your parents teach you to find a mate?'

'Huh?' He turned around to see what I had been watching through the large plate glass windows, but only a medium-sized brown-and-black dog remained, tied to the tree with a short length of unraveling rope. He was barking and straining, trying to chew his way through the cord so as to join his dog friends who were lying, untethered, across the street in front of a drugstore.

'Poor dog,' I said, and Aidan sniffed. Aidan didn't like dogs – or rather, he didn't trust them, particularly dogs in packs. He said he'd been chased by too many of them in his running days.

'Does that dog make you want a dog?' he asked. 'Maybe you don't have to settle for just a cat.'

'I'm not settling,' I said, thinking again how weird it was to know someone who had absolutely no affinity whatsoever with animals, never mind dogs or cats. Aidan thought it completely absurd whenever he heard me attributing human characteristics to my cat: boredom, loneliness, temptation. 'This is what I think you'd call *projection*,' he'd say, and I would invariably reply, 'Thank you, Dr Aidan.'

Now I said, 'I wonder when I turned the corner and became the kind of person I used to laugh at. The kind that worries more about pets than people. That wears a sportswatch, and what's more, loves using all its functions. Who wears sweats and Tevas to the coffee shop. Who buys Maybelline instead of Bobbie Brown, and who does comparison shopping. The other day, I went into the grocery store armed with a fistful of coupons.' The bartender set another earthy-brown colored margarita in front of me and clucked sympathetically. 'What *is* a tamarind?' I asked her.

'Beats me,' she said, and retreated to the far side of the bar to continue eating a plate of cheesy tortilla things.

'Don't you worry about that stuff?' I asked Aidan.

'Like, what a tamarind is?' he said confusedly.

'Well, yes. I mean – I used to make a point of finding out about things like that. Now I just accept that I don't and won't know. I won't go home and look it up in the dictionary, like I would have at one time.'

'I have a dictionary at home,' he said. 'It's only a paperback, though.'

'You see, that's just it,' I said. 'When did you become the person that settles? Why is that good enough for you? Wasn't there a time where having a good, hardback dictionary meant something to you?'

Aidan thought for a moment. 'No. Never.'

I sighed. 'I just remember that when I used to buy pink

hair dye in the Haight, much as the place kind of frightened me, I was sure I would never become the kind of person who sits in a bar and looks out at all the so-called alternative types with a look of horror and non-comprehension. And pay for my margaritas with my American Express.' I took a swallow of my frozen drink, and immediately a stab of pain bore into my temples. 'Ouch,' I said. 'Do you know what I'm saying?'

'No. I have no idea what you're going on about.' Aidan's brows were furrowed together. Actually, of all my friends, Aidan was probably the most contented with his life, living in his big rent-controlled apartment in the Haight by himself after his fiancée moved out on him some two years ago. And from what I could tell, the things that had made him happy ten years ago still made him happy: running on the track in brand new spikes, making an average but not obscene amount of money, drinking beer with his guy friends over some televised sporting event or episode of *Star Trek*, having sex every so often with someone he trusted.

'Did you always think you were going to get married?' I asked him suddenly. He'd finished his margarita and was now eyeing mine covetously. I pushed it toward him.

'Well,' he said, and stopped. Aidan wasn't one of those kinds of men that got lily-livered and pale at the mere mention of the M word – probably because he'd been engaged for a time, until his fiancée got cold feet and moved out of their apartment into the abode of her former boyfriend. 'I think that was the reason I got engaged that time,' he said thoughtfully. 'In Ireland, it's pretty much expected that by age thirty, you'd be settled down with a kid and a house. I mean, this is the pressure I put on myself – I don't think my parents ever said this to me.'

'How *did* you propose?' I asked. 'Tell me.'

'No.' Aidan said this with some strength, and I could see he felt something akin to embarrassment. I was touched by this, and shoved him gently.

'Okay,' I said. 'But *why* did you propose? Were you crazy in love?'

He cleared his throat and looked out on the sidewalk, shining with rain. 'I think,' he said slowly, 'that it was all fear. I was just so afraid that I would get older all alone, and die alone. My thirtieth birthday was right around the corner, and I – I – *panicked*, to tell you the truth.'

I looked at him with newfound respect. 'Really?' Aidan could be so refreshingly honest it was hard sometimes to equate with him the kind of species that fell for the Rules games played by gamine females. He shook his head, embarrassed again, and finished the drink. 'You're a pretty straight kinda guy,' I observed. 'I don't mean that in a *bad* way,' I added when Aidan looked at me through narrowed eyes. 'Maybe it's just Ireland. I didn't know there was a bio clock ticking for men, too.'

He rolled his eyes, and took a slug of my margarita. 'Well, why do you think I got out?' he parried, pronouncing 'think' in a broad Dublin *tink*. 'But you know, even when I was growing up in Artane, I never liked the music I heard when I was a teenager. I liked listening to music from the 70s.'

A vision of an acne-faced, teenage Aidan lying on a chenille-covered twin bed, surrounded by Neil Young posters, listening to Yes on giant headphones popped in my mind. 'Did you want to be like your parents?' I asked. 'Or any of the other old people that were around you that were unhappily trundling toward the grave? What lifestyle did you think was going to make you happy?'

'My parents aren't unhappy.' Aidan looked in the glass guiltily. He was always afraid that talking about his content, united family in Dublin would make me feel bad about my splintered, modern American upbringing. Now he had his nose in the glass, sniffing. He hadn't shaved that day and had big bags under his eyes, looking older than his thirty-one years. 'Isn't tamarind a root?' he asked.

'I don't know,' I said, regarding him closely. It was out of character, now that I thought about it, for Aidan to have left his native land five years ago and chance it in America. It was true: he liked a familiar, steady life – a regular paycheck, *Deep Space Nine* on Wednesday nights, cheese sandwiches and canned tomato soup. He *was*, in the best sense of the word, a straight arrow. Once, I had played a trip-hop CD at his apartment, and he confessed that he didn't like it because 'there were too many things going on at once.' I suddenly said, 'I'm going to watch Jemma again this Friday.'

'Oh.' He sat up. 'Can I come?'

'No,' I said.

'Why not?' he asked immediately.

'Because you can't.' I had already thought this part through. 'I need to be anthropologically curious, and it'll be too disruptive if there's a man in the mix.' The idea of Sir and Aidan shaking hands, trading conversational bits like 'how 'bout those Niners' or whatever it was that men said when they didn't know each other that well, was off-putting.

'I can be anthropological,' he whined.

'No.' Absurdly – after all this talk of taking chances and marginalized groups and not being like one's parents – I just didn't want Aidan, my pillar, my rock of Gibraltar, to be brought into that crazy atmosphere of domination and submission. Plus, what if he wanted to try out some role-playing in our own sex life? I'd always felt I was the open-minded sort, but the thought of *him* telling me what to do or being particularly aggressive did not turn me on in the slightest. It would be downright creepy.

'Why are you going again anyway?' he sighed.

'Because I don't get it,' I said. 'In a way, it's to be supportive of Jemma. In another way, I'm trying to get into a place where I can feel that what she's doing isn't sick or odd. And I haven't reached that place yet.'

❀   ❀   ❀

I did go one more time, about a month later. By this point, Aidan and I weren't speaking, and I decided at the last minute to take a cab down to Otis and Gough. It was obscenely crowded this time, and Jemma and Sir and Ellen had been demoted to a tiny cell-like room with a medico-dental theme in the basement. A wheelchair blocked the entrance, and I stood leaning against the door frame, watching. It was more of the same – elaborate knot work, some paddling on Jemma's thong-donned butt with an instrument that looked like a giant lollypop, but no single tail whip (no room) and no States and Capitals game (too loud). The crowd was milling around the basement, poking their heads around here and there, but they had a much shorter attention span this time. If there wasn't any overt nudity or outrageous sexual act, then off they went, ready to look at the next exhibit, like patrons at the zoo.

In the center of the basement space, a huge group was watching a shirtless red-haired man going down on a naked Asian woman who was tied on what looked a Medieval stretching rack. I pushed my way through, wanting to see what all the fuss was about, watched for a minute, and threaded my way back to the little partitioned area where Sir was 'working' on Ellen, tying and fastening knots up the length of her corset-clad torso. Jemma was lying face down on a doctor's examining table – waiting, I guessed.

It was a small area, this little spectator's gangway, and a tall man with glasses on the left of me was crunching something. I glanced in his direction.

He held out a metal box. 'Would you like an Altoid?'

I regarded the little white mints, all nestled cosily in their white paper as if they were tucked in for the night. 'No, thank you,' I said.

'Would you like to take a walk with me?' the man asked politely.

'No, thank you,' I said, just as politely. That transaction settled, we turned back to the knot scene.

I left soon after that, hoping that my departure wouldn't distract Jemma or make her feel that I wasn't interested in her performance. But it was a little difficult to convey my intended actions to her, lying as she was, on that examining table, waiting for Sir and her turn to be whipped or knotted or whatever. Since that night we'd exchanged long telephone messages, and only spoke quickly if we actually got a hold of one another.

So when she answered her temp job in a sing-song voice, ('Hello, Customer Service, this is Jemma!') I wasn't prepared to actually talk to a human voice.

'Hi.' I tried to think up some question I could pose in a nasal voice about hard drives, couldn't up with one, and said, 'I don't think I've ever heard you sound so upbeat.'

'It's all part of the Customer Service, darling,' she answered, and her voice returned to its normal monotone. 'How are you?'

'Oh, fine,' I said. 'My friend Harriet is coming from New York and I'm going to throw a party. Can you come?'

'Certainly,' she said, sounding official. 'We would love to come. When?'

'I'm not sure yet,' I hesitated, wondering which 'we' she might be referring to. The royal 'we,' meaning just her? Hopefully, but not likely. Or just her and Sir? Or all three of them? Whichever way, their attendance would certainly add an extra 'oomph' to the party that I hadn't been expecting. I wondered how I would explain all this to my mother, if she decided to drop by as well. 'I just wanted to get a sense of what times were best for people. What nights are you nannying nowadays?'

'I'm not nannying anymore,' Jemma said in a low voice.

'Oh, really?' I stopped scribbling on my legal pad. 'Did something happen?'

'No. I just can't make enough money doing it, and the family I was working for needs more time. The little one is going into kindergarten this year, and she's having separation anxiety from her mother, from me, her other sisters – and it was just getting too complicated. Being so mommy-like with them, and being so unmommy-like in other parts of my life —'
The other line started ringing, and Jemma said immediately, 'Hold on a moment.'

'So any night is good?' I asked when she came back on.

'Yes,' she said. 'Except Wednesday nights and usually Saturday night, late.'

'Okay,' I said, writing that down. 'Thank you for letting me, uh, view you last month. I can't believe we haven't really seen each other since then.'

'Nor can I. That was a crap night. Much too crowded, and Sir was in a bad mood. He got very angry at my driving on the way there, and it put a little pallor on the evening for me.'

'Oh,' I said. 'Um, well, I'm sorry to hear that.'

'Oh, it's fine,' she said quickly. 'Hold on a minute.' Then, 'I'm back.'

'What have you been up to lately?' I said. 'Still going to every party and fetish festival in the city?'

'Oh, my God,' Jemma said. 'I am so tired. I don't know what's wrong with me. Actually, I was going to ask if you wanted to go to this Dark Nights party with the three of us, but now I'm glad that you weren't there. It was – hold on a moment.'

A minute later, she said, 'Now where was I?'

'A party you didn't want me to go to.'

'Oh. Oh, yes. It was just sort of awful,' she said, and then laughed. 'Ellen started getting really freaked out, actually. We had to leave early.'

'How come? By the way,' I paused. 'Do you even know Ellen's real name?'

'Nope. But that's not so strange. The first couple that I met over the Internet – you know, the ones that took me on to

239

teach me about submission – I had no idea who they were, nor where they lived. And that went on for almost a year.' I heard her close a door, and she continued. 'Have you ever played that Porn Star Name Game?'

'Work is really keeping the brain occupied today, I see.'

'Take your mother's maiden name. That's your last name. Now, take the name of your first pet. That's your first name. So, I'm Misty Mallon. What's your name?'

I thought for a moment. 'Lazy Bones Smith.'

Jemma sighed. 'Oh, dear.'

'You were saying about the Dark Nights party,' I prodded.

'Oh, yes,' she said. 'Good God. I think there must have been some sort of weight requirement on the door, which Ellen and I qualified for if we stood on the scale together. It was awful. I mean, I'm not really a look-ist, but these were some of the ugliest people I'd ever seen in my life. Really, truly awful. And wearing fetish gear! You know how you can kind of get away with being very bad-looking if you dress a certain way – as in, lots of dress? Some weren't wearing anything at all. Hold on a minute.'

'Why was Ellen getting freaked out?' I asked when she returned.

'Oh. Sir was playing with her, and she had a blindfold on. She couldn't see what was going on around her. I was tied to a pillar actually, so I could see everything, and I tell you, at one point I almost asked for a blindfold, there were so many uglies walking around. And there was this really fat woman who was getting flogged with a single tail. And it was making a *lot* of noise. At one point, she was being whipped solely on her vagina, and after a few minutes her whole genital area just looked like hamburger meat. It was pretty gross.'

'Gee,' I said, after a minute.

'The sound of the woman getting flogged was incredibly loud. And it just really started to freak Ellen out, so Sir and she had to stop. She was lying next to me at one point and I said to her, trust me you don't want that blindfold off. It's really awful in here. I myself started getting creeped out by the fat woman – me, who's been in the scene for two years! I had to keep saying to myself, this is consensual, this is consensual, she has free will, she can stop it at any time.'

'Huh.' I drew a doodle of a bubble-bodied woman with curly hair, saying OUCH, THAT HURT.

'Do you want to have lunch today?' Jemma asked suddenly. 'It would be nice to have a girl chat.'

'Great,' I said. Any excuse to close this laptop and do something much more interesting, like eat and talk. I pushed my crossword puzzle to one side and happily put the computer on 'Suspend.' But Jemma's voice had dropped and I paused. 'Is everything okay?'

'Oh, sure,' she said, but with a catch in her voice. 'See you in two hours? At Sallie's? We can get that vegetarian blue plate special that you like so much.'

Maybe this would be my official debriefing to the whole Power Exchange adventure. I had gone back and forth about going back that second time to watch them play, to see if there was something that I'd missed the first time – some real reason to be involved in the S/M scene, some subtle answer to why any woman would want to be a whipped and poked and prodded while half-naked. There was, of course, the performance element to it – maybe Jemma was a frustrated actress, or one of those women that needed be the constant center of attention when men were around. But going back to see the trio play didn't answer any of the other nagging questions, like that little matter of Jemma consensually giving over all her responsibilities to an older man, leaving her virtually without any say-so.

But maybe that too was a relief for her. It could be tiring being a single woman nowadays; Harriet, Marie and I certainly could attest to that. ('How about being a single *person* nowadays?' I could hear a mini-Aidan and Marco intone.) Maybe what Jemma had was a different sort of freedom: freedom from decision-making, freedom from responsibility, and freedom from the guilt that you might be screwing up your life.

But lately I'd realized that exhaustion was never far from Jemma's voice. In the weeks that we'd volleyed messages back and forth, she sounded terribly busy with the autumn social events. A Halloween fetish ball, trips up and down California on the back of Sir's motorcycle to attend the all-day Renaissance Faire – which to my surprise had a heavy S/M theme – Power Exchange every Saturday night, Bondage a Go Go every Wednesday. Just listening to her litany made me yawn.

'I don't know how you do it,' I had said to her on the phone. 'I can barely drag myself out the house for *one* weekend event.'

'Well, I *am* rather tired,' she admitted. 'But Sir and Antonia broke up. So things have been very up and very down lately. There have been a few times I've just told him to go to these things by himself, because I am literally so exhausted by the time the weekend comes, that I just need to fall into bed for two days.'

'Broke up?' Now what did this mean? Jemma had hinted around that monogamy – or rather Sir's lack thereof – was a consistent source of conflict between them. 'So – that's a good thing. She was his other submissive that he had sex with, right?'

'Ye–es,' Jemma said carefully. 'But all that really means is that now Ellen's going to come more in the focal point. I mean, she's not his number one, and he isn't in love with her or anything, but I know this is going to happen.'

'Why?'

'Because Sir is not a fan of monogamy,' she said, not for the first time. I thought: Neither was I when I was going out with Aidan. And neither is Aidan when he's not going out with me.

It was a crisp, sunny, beautiful autumn day when I walked down the hill to meet Jemma. White light filtered through the scrubby trees planted along Hyde Street, throwing mosaic shadows along the dirty sidewalk. I wondered if Jemma was ever zapped with that sappy, it's-great-to-be-alive feeling on days like this. It was hard to tell with her.

As usual, she was engrossed in a novel when I came upon her, sitting outside of the restaurant at the foot of Potrero Hill. She had her glasses on, and a fuzzy aqua-blue sweater zipped up to the neck. Her hair was sticking up in parts, as if she'd slept on it wrong – all in all, she reminded me of a bookish little girl, or an intelligent furry animal, maybe a baby owl.

I watched her for a moment. She was completely absorbed in her Penguin Classic, oblivious to the chattering office workers around her, standing in line. She'd told me that, as a child, all she ever did was read – 'at the dinner table, in the bath, on the toilet, in the car. So, when my parents announced to me when I was eleven that they were getting a divorce, I was completely taken aback. I'd had no idea that there was something wrong – I was so involved in my books. Whereas, my brother – he knew *everything*.'

I turned my head upside down to try to get a glimpse of the title. Still on her Dickens kick. She jumped up and gave me a big hug.

'Hullo, darling,' she said, unzipping her sweater revealing a black, Jenny Holzer T-shirt that had fifty little aphorisms written on the front – things like 'romantic love was invented in order to make women feel bad about themselves' and 'really bad people will get a really bad punishment someday.' It was going to be hard to talk to her with a distracting t-shirt like that – I'd want to sit there and read it. And would I ever be able to look at her without the S/M filter coloring my every assumption, whether it be her choice in earrings (silver – better to conduct electricity?) or little black tied-up booties or blue jeans (a little mundane for a player in the S/M scene, no?)

'Which one are you reading?' I asked.

'*Hard Times*,' she said matter-of-factly. Obviously her irony meter was on the blink. 'I'm doing fairly well in the Dickens venture, I'd say. I just have to finish *Bleak House* then I'll have accomplished my goal of reading all of him by the end of the year.'

'That is quite a scholastic goal,' I said. 'Give me *The Mill on the Floss* any day over Dickens. I couldn't stand *Oliver*.'

'*Oliver* is not too terribly interesting.' She folded over the page and stuck the book in her large leather backpack. 'Try *A Tale of Two Cities*.'

We ordered from the counter and soon began searching for a clean table. 'Sir is dying to tell you what happened on that Saturday night after you left,' she began, as we carried our brown rice with black beans toward the back of the crowded restaurant. 'The first Saturday. Not the crowded Friday.'

'Why?' I said lightly, but immediately suspicious.

'Well, just to tell you what happened chronologically,' she said.

'Okay,' I said. Was this all to shock me? Sometimes I wondered.

'So, um . . . after you left, I went back to the Medieval Room. And he was playing with Ellen. There were a lot of people watching. And I did some things . . . touching her and stroking her—'

'And getting all the guys hot and bothered.' I sat down and arranged my silverware.

'Yeah, probably. And then he played the States and Capitals game. Again.'

244

I sprinkled some salt and pepper on my rice. Then I added Tabasco. 'You must like that game.'

'Yeah. Only this time, he asked the questions and if I got them wrong, she got hit. And I got so many of them right, it was unbelievable. *I* couldn't believe it. People from the audience were yelling out the answer, it was very funny. It was a big audience participation game.'

'Just like TV,' I said brightly. She looked amused at the thought, and was clearly oblivious to my ambivalence. She began to plow into the beans.

'So every time I got it wrong, I was like, "sorry, Ellen!" and she goes, "it's okay!" '

I put my fork down. 'What's the capital of South Dakota?'

Jemma paused, fork mid-air. 'I don't know.'

'That's what I got tripped up on that first time,' I said to her. 'That's why you got —'

'That's why I got the bruises!'

I kept eating, looking at her. 'Do you play that game every time?'

'No, only sometimes. We used to do capitals of Europe, but I knew all those, so it wasn't any fun.'

'Uh huh,' I said. 'Is this what you wanted to talk to me about?'

'No,' she said. 'I'm getting to that. In a roundabout way. Is this boring you?'

I put down my fork and looked at her with exaggerated patience. 'I think you know that hearing this is a lot of things to me, but boring is not one of them.' I continued to eat my rice and beans, making a little moat around which the carrots and broccoli sat. Jemma looked so lively in her descriptions – that is, as lively as an exhausted person can look – that it didn't feel right to rain on her parade. I wondered how much different this was from my college-age sister telling me pridefully about the Sartre play she and her boyfriend had just starred in.

'And then a friend of ours turned up called Allison and she had a woman with her and then—'

'What time was that?'

'Oh, I don't know,' Jemma said carelessly. 'None of us wear watches. Probably about one?'

'Go on,' I said.

'And then two other friends turned up, called Brenda and Susie. Let's see, and who else was there? Anyway, to cut a long story short, what ended up happening was me lying on the table, Brenda holding my hand, Susie and Sir going down on me at the same time—'

'Susie *and* Sir? At the same time?'

'Yes.'

'Wow,' I said, trying to picture this. It seemed a bit of a logistical nightmare. 'On the long oak table?'

'Uh huh,' Jemma said.

'With the, the —' I tried to remember what else was on the table – there was some sort of faux centerpiece. 'The, um, turkey?'

'It's a fake wild boar,' Jemma said, as if she were a kid recounting a wild and crazy Halloween party in which everyone ended up bobbing for apples at once. 'They were going to insert the pig into me. Brenda kept threatening me with vegetables. It was very scary.'

I chased an errant bean around the plate with my fork. 'Are those vegetables plastic?'

'Yes. As far as I know. So I had Brenda, Susie, Allison, Ellen and Sir on me. It was very nice.'

'Sounds very tactile,' I said. 'How many people were watching?'

Jemma had stopped eating. I read another aphorism on her shirt: 'I think therefore I shop.' 'Lots,' she said. 'Don't know. But also, at that point – oh this is really weird. Remember that guy who was there, Howard? The creepy guy?'

'Now which one would that be?' I asked brightly. Jemma

glanced at me, trying to see if I was being sarcastic. A mini-Harriet reappeared on my shoulder, about to shake her finger and give me some guidance, but for once she opened her mouth, and was speechless. 'No, I mean – Paul Bunyan? The other guy in the room with you?'

'That's the one,' said Jemma. 'At one point when Sir was working on Ellen, Howard beckoned him over and said "When are you going to be done?" Sir responds, "When I'm finished." We were using exactly half of the room. In fact, less than half the room, and he wants to know when were going to be done? So Howard got really pissed off and packed all of his stuff away and he left, which means he took his rope away, because that's his rope. We have our own rope, and we could have put ours up, but we didn't. So it meant that the audience got further and further and further into the room so everyone had to be quite aware of where people were, and Sir was telling people to back up quite a lot, stuff like that. But we're very glad that we pissed Howard off. Perhaps he won't be back.'

'Uh huh,' I commented. 'Have you really finished your lunch?'

'Do you want the rest of it?' Jemma asked. 'I'm just not so hungry lately.'

'Sure,' I said, and we exchanged plates. 'What else?'

'Well, I was talking to Gray the doorman about it later, and Howard and this woman usually play in that room. And because they have no life, they get there at nine o'clock in the evening. Now I know we were there at nine but we don't usually do that, it was a different situation. Um, so they get there at nine o'clock, and they play with each other, but they get bored. So what Howard does is he trawls around the place, looking for other women to play with. He wears those finger things with nails on them, silver finger cuffs, that have these long spikes, and he'll go up to a woman and she'll admire them and he'll say "this is what they feel like." Stuff like that, just come-on lines.'

'Ick,' I said.

'I know. That's why I dragged you away from him. And they started putting these signs up: "Free Flogging!" "Come in and get a bunch of flowers for a spanking!" and all that kind of thing. Which is just *sad*, it really is – it's pathetic. It's like, it smacks of such – *desperation*, as far as I'm concerned.'

'It certainly had me wondering,' I said.

'Gray told me that Howard and Margaret were playing in there a couple of weeks ago and they finished. And Margaret was lying on the bed, probably half-clothed, and Howard left the room, for one reason or another. She knew he left, but she was lying on her front. And some guy walked into the room, picked up one of the floggers and hit her with it. Okay? Which is a total no-no. So she jumped up and screamed and freaked out, and Howard freaked out, and they blamed Gray and the other monitors. They said, "You weren't in the room checking that everything was okay!" And Gray was just like, "Bullshit. You have a responsibility. You should look out for where you are." They said they wanted to complain to the owner, and Gray said "Try it – he'll ask you not to come back." Because the monitors can't be everywhere all the time, it's a big place. You have to bear some responsibility.'

'Because those are the rules,' I added helpfully.

'What Gray *didn't* say to her – and he should have – was "You have a sign on the door that says *Free Flogging*. What do you expect? What do you think people think that means?" '

'Did the guy get thrown out?'

'Yeah. He broke the rules. It wasn't consensual.'

I added some more Tabasco to the rice and mixed it around on my plate. 'Just out of curiosity, what does this Margaret look like?' Apart from Jemma, I had yet to see any really beautiful or attractive people involved in the scene, which I surmised was one of main fears that kept 'vanilla' folk away from a public sex venue – that the patrons would all turn out to be like the bar crowd from *Star Wars*.

'Margaret looks like a guy. We wanted to do a DNA check on her. There's been a long-standing rumor going around that she's a sex-change. She's a perfectly nice woman but my God! The two of them together is just irritating.' Jemma ate a stalk of broccoli and stared at her plate.

'Jemma,' I said, and put down my fork. I'd noticed lately that this no-talking-with-Aidan situation had gotten me a lot more confrontational. Just the week before, my mother and I had finally had a knock-down, drag-out telephone fight concerning Zippy's alleged loneliness. I'd told her, 'You know Mom, you can't mess with people's lives this way. You can't pluck them out of their existence and plop them down just because you feel like it, give them attention when you have time and ignore them when you don't.' My mother said, 'Courtney, we're talking about a *cockatiel* here,' but I was already wondering that I'd just described my own interaction with Jemma. Which was a little absurd, when you thought about it, because Jemma had more than enough activities and acquaintances that she could possibly squeeze into her life as it was – she certainly wasn't waiting around for me to take an interest in her. Still, I thought about Zippy in his cage with his little pink-edged mirror and his half-gnawed cuttlebone, doing his anxiety dance while all these giant eyes were looking in and it made me want to cry.

'I know this is consensual,' I said now, 'and uh, I know you get a lot things from Sir that you want – physically, emotionally, otherwise. You're in love with him, I know. And you say you're his number one . . .' I paused for a moment, trying to collect my thoughts. What was this 'number one' stuff that Jemma seemed to put such store in, anyway? She repeated that phrase all the time. 'But there's a couple of things – uh, okay.'

She looked at me expectantly – certainly not with any anger or defensiveness. Most likely, she'd gotten this speech from her other friends, and was by now used to the vanilla response to her lifestyle. If anything, she looked slightly pitying of me, which she was gamely trying to conceal under a veneer of interest: leaning forward, her chin resting on her hands.

'I'm not judging you,' I added hastily. Once upon a time, Jemma used to remind me so much of myself in certain ways – her strength, coupled with her insecurity, her sense of humor, her separateness. Where was that person now? 'I think women do a lot of things for men if they're in love with them. Well, strike that – I mean, people do a lot of things for people if they're in love. Very trivial example, but: I hate house painting. *Really* hate it. And I've painted an entire apartment for my boyfriend because he asked me to help him.' I didn't add that that was one of the dumber things I'd done in my life – that when I met this guy in heaven or hell, I would demand those three days of my life back.

'Uh huh,' Jemma said.

'But you don't seem that happy with this,' I said. 'You tell me all these things, but somehow I can't sense that it makes you really – content with your life.'

'I'm not a very happy person in general,' Jemma said. 'I never have been. I think I used it all up with James, in my marriage.'

'You don't really believe that,' I said.

'Well, I don't know. But going back to what you said – Sir provides me with a certain life and he has certain responsibilities to uphold by being the dominant one. He doesn't use me emotionally, although he could. And I have certain responsibilities too, as a submissive. And it's completely—'

'—consensual,' we said in unison.

'Right,' Jemma said.

'He's awfully – paternal with you,' I said, after a moment of silence. 'Besides the fact that he could be your father, age-wise.'

'I don't like to go there,' she said. She drank some water and added, 'It's funny, because we talked about that last week, and we had a really good conversation. And this is what I wanted to talk to you about, because of what you said at the Power Exchange – you know, about where my responsibilities lie.'

'Go on,' I said, curious now.

'Sir and I talked about – again, responsibilities and – you're right, it *is* like a father or a mother/child relationship, when you think about it. You teach a child discipline. And discipline has to do with teaching the child about the way you want that child to behave. Um – and that child gives you love and adoration. And she doesn't always get it right.' I looked at her, expecting more, but she seemed to be finished. I heard a collective scream from feminists around the world, and I pushed my plate to one side. Jemma looked at her watch.

I paused. 'That's what you wanted to talk about?'

'Well, that and – well, maybe we'll save it for another time.' She looked at her watch again.

'How come you called me a bunch of times last month without leaving a message?' I'd been meaning to confront her about this, but I was embarrassed about owning such a neurotic, wasteful piece of technology as Caller ID. But Jemma looked out the window and was silent.

'I think,' she said slowly, 'I think I was going through a bad time. It's hard for me to remember.'

'Why didn't you leave a message? I would have called you back.'

'I didn't want to bother you,' she said, and looked at her watch again.

I passed a hand over my eyes. How could Jemma and I ever *really* be close friends? Clearly it was impossible – for all her candid talk, she was still unwilling to open herself on a very simple, emotional level. Sir, it appeared, was to be the only recipient of her intimacy, and I had my doubts about that as well. Ironically, for someone so concerned with needs being met, she was pathologically *un*needy. 'I know you have to go,'

I said. 'But, just one more thing. What you were saying about discipline – you teach a kid that because the end result is that you want the child to be an independent person.'

'Yes, but I am an independent person,' she said.

'No,' I grappled. 'What I mean is you teach a child these sorts of things so they have the tools to be independent of you.'

Jemma let that hang in the air for moment. I added, 'Do you ever think of leaving him?'

'No,' she said. 'I think that someday, he might leave me. Because I know the rules, we have the discussions again and again about how I'm the most important person, but I still can't get it into my head. I mean, it must be terribly frustrating for him, because it's the same discussion, and basically if I don't like the way things are, I have free will to change it.'

'Meaning – walk away,' I said, thinking she'd sooner run a 10K across hot coals from the way she was talking.

'Uh huh. I tell myself again and again what he says – that I'm number one, that we've been together for two whole years now, but I get so insecure. Like the other night: he had Ellen kneel in front of him the other night at the Power Exchange before he started playing with her. And he didn't ask me when he played with me. And I started getting really upset, thinking about it, getting myself in a state.'

We sat quietly for a moment. I said, 'Is this the thing that you wanted to save for another day?' and Jemma mumbled 'sort of,' and looked weary.

'This all just sounds so *tiring* to me,' I said, as Jemma nodded again. As well as vaguely familiar. I remember coming down with a series of colds and flu in the final weeks before Sean and I broke up, trying to make sense of the chasm between what I *sensed* (indifference) versus what I was being *told* (it's all in your head).

'How's Aidan?' Jemma asked suddenly.

I sighed. 'Oh, it's funny you should ask. We're not speaking, and it's starting to get to the point that if we don't resolve it soon, we won't be able to put it back together.'

'What happened?'

'He's sleeping with someone else,' I said.

Jemma said quietly, 'That's upsetting to you.'

'Yes,' I said, and looked out the window. Now who was feeling needy? 'Not that I have any right to be. As my haircutter says, we should just shit or get off the pot – but we don't seem to be able to make that kind of decision.'

''90s couple that you are,' Jemma put in – ironic, I thought, coming from her.

I shifted around. 'And we had an agreement that if we were to do that, we were supposed to tell the other. But he didn't tell me, and I'm pissed off. Don't you think I have the right to know if he's going to give me a disease?'

Jemma examined her hands, which were spread across the table in front of her. 'Is that the rule?'

'I thought it was the rule. But it was a little, um, unclear. We didn't really talk about it. But one would *assume* . . .' I trailed off.

'Maybe you should have made the rule clearer.'

'I know,' I said, and sighed. 'I don't know what my problem is. I don't want to go out with him like a girlfriend/boyfriend thing, but I don't want him interested in anybody else either.'

'Is there someone that you're interested in? Maybe it could get resolved that way.'

'No,' I said. 'It's a problem every way you look at it.'

Jemma was looking at me, and I could see what was running through her head as clearly as if they were stock prices on the electronic bulletin board at Times Square: *Now, if you two had rules and parameters like Sir and I have, you'd know exactly when and what to feel bad about. And because you consented to the rules from the very start, you wouldn't really have a right to feel bad about anything.* 'Humph,' I said, as if she had said as much. Maybe she had a point.

'I *am* tired,' she admitted, out of nowhere. 'I went to the doctor last week, because I have been so incredibly exhausted. He ran some tests – nothing. And lately . . .' She gazed out the window at the office drones, frowning. 'I really think I have the Yuppie Flu. Which is not fair, because I don't have any of the good things that yuppies have, like a Land Rover or a cell phone or a condominium. All I have is the chronic fatigue.'

'Yes, I feel tired too,' I said. 'And suddenly, really incredibly horny. And not just thinking about Aidan. I sit on the bus and think, *Now what would you be like in bed? Would you tie me up to your four-poster bed, would you spank me?* And I have never in my life wanted to be spanked.'

Jemma took a sip of water. 'I'll take that as a compliment.' She checked her watch again and we were both about to stand up, but she said, 'Lately, I sometimes feel like giving up with this.'

'Oh,' I said, hoping my expression read 'empathetic' and not 'overjoyed' at her declaration.

'Like, I feel – "Okay, Sir, do what you want to do, because I can't win." Like if he criticizes my driving, or wants to go out that night without me, or have sex with Ellen and I don't feel like it – in the past I would feel . . . chagrined, or chastised or left out. I mean, I still feel left out and jealous. But lately, I've been feeling sort of *nothing* about it, maybe because I *am* so tired. And that scares me more than anything else. If we get into the place where I don't care, then we're really in trouble.' She picked up her plate, looking around for somewhere to deposit it. 'We've talked about this.'

'What did he say? Is he worried?'

'Umm,' she paused. 'I would say "concerned" is a better word.'

I'll bet he's concerned, I thought. But I felt heartened at her words, these first baby steps. I looked out the window in an attempt to hide my face.

'But I won't leave him, because I don't do that,' Jemma

continued, and I sighed silently. 'People have to make the first move when they leave, even if I want it too. It's just the way I am.'

'That sounds very *fait accompli*,' I said, feeling like we'd taken five steps forward and then ten steps back. 'Is it the lack of monogamy that's the worst thing with your relationship?'

'That's putting it awfully strongly,' she said.

'Well, what I mean is: if he were monogamous, would it make the relationship much better for you?'

'I can't ever imagine that, but yes, it would. When they passed out libido, Sir got three times the normal dose.'

A likely story! Mini-Harriet and I snapped in internal unison. But unlike Harriet, I had never believed that men had more sexual drive than women. In fact, with most men, it seemed that I was usually the one to place the tentative hand on the hip, and start the preliminary grope. ('That's because you go out with Mickey Mice, not men,' Marie intoned.)

In fact, the problem now was that I really felt like I understood Sir's position. He wouldn't limit himself to one sex partner for the same reason that I hadn't with Aidan – *he plain did not want to and what's more, he didn't have to.* But when Aidan and I had gone through that phase, early in our dating career, it had ended up driving the both of us crazy – knowing that I was dating and sleeping with other people. *And of course, this new arrangement is so much better and spiritually fulfilling!* I wondered if Aidan felt like Sir now.

And here I was, knowing exactly what Jemma was going through as well. I closed my eyes briefly and tried to employ my usual tactic when presented with a moral or ethical dilemma: what would Jackie O do or say? Jackie O actually was a good person to invoke in this instance: a fellow-sufferer from the polygamous activities of an over-sexed, power-crazed partner. 'It seems that you have three options when your boyfriend is having sex with others,' I said. 'Option One is to do what Jackie O did in the JFK years: bury your head in the sand. Option Two is Jackie O in the Ari years: accept it. Option Three is to walk away. So, do you ever think about Option Three?' I asked.

'I've *thought* about it,' Jemma said slowly. Well, that was a start. 'But Sir and I would both like me to come to Option Two. I just don't know how to do it. I repeat and repeat things to myself, and I just end up feeling . . . well, tired.' She yawned suddenly.

'Think about all the extra energy you'd have to do other things if you got rid of the source of this tiredness,' I said. Everything was coming out more self-help-y than the rest. This was the sort of thing my mother would say to me during particularly bad moments of the Sean crisis. 'You could get a job you love.' She rolled her eyes at that. 'Well, what about exercising? How come you don't exercise anymore, by the way?' Jemma really was what Harriet would call an exercise freak – it occurred to me that I never heard about her karate classes or running or weight-lifting anymore.

'Too tired,' Jemma said, and laughed. We both stood up, and I picked up my plate. 'I have to go back to work,' she said.

'I know. I'll walk you some of the way.'

Her backpack was shoved under the table near my chair, and I reached down and handed it to her. It didn't matter that Jemma was involved in a non-vanilla world: she was still tripped up by all the vanilla angst and self-loathing issues that accompanied every bad vanilla relationship. And like every person caught up in the throes of Defining Moments galore, all the lectures and advice and support systems weren't going to do a bit of good until she was ready to move on. A mini-Mom now appeared on my shoulder to replace the censorious mini-Harriet, who suggested for Jemma a huge dose of Vitamin Self-Esteem, to be administered hourly in pill or liquid form.

❊   ❊   ❊

That lunch with Jemma did it. When I got home that day, after typing furiously and unceasingly for two hours, I picked up the phone and called Aidan.

'Hola,' I said to him when he answered. It was four o'clock and he was off that day. 'I'm sorry, Aidan. I miss you.'

'You're all right,' he said stiffly, the standard Irish response to an apology.

'No, you were right,' I said. 'I don't know what I want, but I know I'm not being clear and it's too absurd, this us not talking. Besides, Harriet is coming the day after tomorrow, and I really want us to hang out. Is that okay?'

'Um, all right,' he said. He sounded a little suspicious, and I added, 'You don't have to tell me if you're sleeping with anyone, or seeing anyone. But are you?'

'Courtney! I never was.'

'You weren't?' I asked.

'No, I wasn't,' he said. 'But I still don't think we should sleep together anymore. I don't understand it and it makes me upset and nervous all the time.'

'Okay,' I said, and felt that little dart of panic, fearing imminent abandonment. 'Never?' I said.

'Never what?'

'We can't ever sleep together?'

Aidan groaned. 'Let's just try it this way. Is that so hard?'

'Well, no.' *Well, yes.* 'What do you say we have a party for Harriet? Just to lift her spirits a little? She's had an operation and she's having a hard time with her boyfriend lately.'

'She should try a little honesty,' Aidan said shortly.

CHAPTER 10

When I saw Harriet's tall blond form floating along outside baggage claim, pushing her cart in the opposite direction from where I was standing, guarding my car from the hungry tow trucks and madly-scribbling meter maids, I jumped on top of the hood. 'Harriet! Harriet!' I yelled. 'Harriet!'

'Lady, you gotta move,' a helmeted officer was saying.

'Just one second,' I told him. 'My friend is physically incapacitated and – Harriet!' I bellowed. Harriet stopped and looked around. 'Over here!'

'Parking is allowed for the loading and unloading of passengers only,' Helmet continued. He waved his ticket booklet at me.

'HARRIET,' I screamed. She caught sight of me jumping up and down on the hood of my beat-up Honda and beamed, pushing her cart quickly toward me.

'You're here!' I jumped down and ran up to her cart, giving her a giant hug. She was smiling and looked pink and rosy, dewy almost. 'How was your flight? I'm so glad you're here!'

'Hel-lo!' she said. Her hair was sticking up on one side and she yawned, but she looked about as good as I'd ever seen her – certainly not the wounded cripple that I somehow imagined she might be.

'Are you okay? You look *great*. How's your scar? Did you eat?' I tried to commandeer her cart. Helmet Man was watching us, actually tapping his shiny boot. 'See?' I said to him. 'We're leaving right now. She's recovering! She had an operation!'

'No, I'm fine!' she said. We began a tug-of-war with her suitcase.

'Harriet, give that to me!' I yelled at her. 'You're infirm!'

'I am *not* infirm,' she said. 'God, you and Jerry! I feel better than ever!'

'Let's go, Miss Infirm,' the Nazi said. 'Move the car along.'

I threw her suitcase in the backseat, opened her door, shoved her in, ran around to the other side, hopped in and revved the engine. 'How *is* Jerry?' I said, as we settled in. 'Has he been helping you a lot?'

'Yee-ess,' she said carefully, fastening her seat belt with some delicacy. 'We went up to Connecticut two weekends ago. I told you about that, right?'

'You told me that he forgot to rent the car in time and that you had to take the bus,' I said. 'And that you were incredibly angry with him about it. And —' I swerved to avoid an errant trolley that had rolled out into the road, chased closely by a fat man with a wide hat on top of his head that made him look like a giant mushroom.

'We had a really good talk,' she said. 'I'll tell you about it.'

'What does *The Rules* say about fibroid surgery and fertility? I bet that's a real no-go area, huh?' I glanced over at her.

'What are those twinkling lights over there?' She pointed toward the hills. 'Do you know anyone who lives out here?'

'Do you know anyone who lives near JFK?' I asked.

'All the Rules do is protect you from getting hurt,' Harriet said after a moment, as if she were reading from a prepared text. 'I know it sounds ridiculous, but for people like my friend Love Lori, for example, who has always given way too much to her boyfriends, they need it.'

'I can't believe we're having this debate already. We're not even inside the city limits.' I merged into the highway traffic carefully, so as not to scare her. 'Anyway, you've never needed it.'

'The Rules give you confidence,' she said. 'And after a while, you start to believe that you're the confident, busy, successful and independent woman that you're trying to act like. It rubs off.'

'Let's not talk about this,' I begged. 'Besides, Harriet, you are confident, busy, successful and independent! If anyone needs the Rules, it's me.' I felt all aglow next to her. 'I'm so happy you're here!' I switched over two lanes, in the slow lane so I could drive and talk. 'Now tell me about your birthday dinner,' I commanded.

'Well, first I should tell you a little about Connecticut,' she said, with a funny look on her face.

'You were all angry at him, right?'

'Uh huh. Because I had to lug all this wine and cheese and food on the bus, because he'd forgotten to rent the car. And I was kind of giving him the silent treatment, with all our friends around, until finally I just exploded. I'd started thinking on the way up there: there aren't any concrete phrases coming from him, this relationship is the same as it was a year ago. And I just began thinking it would maybe be better to be alone – because it's always better to be alone than to be with a bad man.'

'Oh,' I said. 'Jerry's not a *bad* man, though.'

'No, not at all.' She reached in her purse and pulled out some chapstick.

'He'd said to me once that he'd broken up with his old girlfriend Linda because she really wanted to get married, but it didn't really seem to matter if it was to him or not. And I know that you've leveled that criticism at me, and I really had a good long think about it when I was in the hospital. I decided, No, that's not me, because I really love him and I want us to be together and not date anymore.'

'Uh huh,' I said, glancing over at her, feeling worried.

'So I was fuming up at Connecticut and I finally said, "Aren't you going to ask me what's going on?" And he said something typically Jerry, like, "I figured you would tell me eventually," which made me even angrier. I just burst out that I felt he wasn't really available during my surgery and I'd wanted him to be more around, and I started realizing that I hated becoming this person who was so full of rage all the time.'

'God,' I said, as I slowed down a little more. Where was all this detailed emotional openness coming from? 'I sure don't think of you like that. That sounds more like – well, me. Maybe not rage, but irritation. But go on.' We were approaching Candlestick Park.

Harriet smiled. 'And he started crying. I started crying. And he said "I thought you didn't want me around . . . you didn't ask . . . you had all your friends around, your mother . . ." Meanwhile, everyone was out on the porch under blankets and afghans, trying to leave us alone because they could see we were having this big fight.'

I envisioned this – the New York Network making teepees out of their blankets, their white oval faces barely visible from the fogged up windows, looking for all the world like multiple characters from 'The Scream'. 'I'm surprised you didn't break up after that,' I said finally.

'No, that's what did it.' Harriet capped the chapstick and asked me, 'How are *you* doing?'

'Wait, wait,' I said. 'That did *what*?'

'Well, after that, everything opened up between us,' she said. 'It could have ended right there. But suddenly it was like we'd been giving a new chapter, and . . . well, it all seemed to fall into place.'

'That's good, right?' I said cautiously. 'And . . . the cheese grater?' A station wagon full of red-faced, crying children roared past us.

'Uh huh,' she said. 'I was really terribly disappointed. It

seemed like all this push forward, then a slide backwards.'
She didn't *sound* disappointed though. I glanced over at her
again, to see if I could detect any bitterness, but she was
smiling to herself and I said, '*What*? Why are you looking like
the Cheshire cat?'

'I'm *not*,' she cried.

'Was it a nice birthday dinner?' I asked. She'd been
curiously silent about that night, which I attributed to her San
Francisco preparations and mixed feelings about Jerry. Could
Clark have made an appearance? She certainly looked . . .
something right now. Actually, if anything, she had that high,
slightly smug look that women take on after a particularly
great sexual encounter.

'It was,' Harriet said carefully. 'So over dinner, as we drank
champagne, I said, "Jerry, I really do love my professional
cheese grater. But are you going to get me anything else?" He
says, "Sure! What do you want?" "Jewelry," I said immediately, and we both laughed.'

'This doesn't sound very Rules to me,' I pointed out.

Harriet laughed again. 'And here you'll be proud of me. I
said, "Jerry, I really can't wait very much longer." '

'Really,' I said, impressed but then immediately felt worried.
What if all my advocacy of confrontation backfired? I didn't
want Harriet to feel that I'd steered her wrong. 'You honestly
said that to him? Gosh, that's downright . . . *upfront* of you,
Harriet.'

'I should have said it a long time ago,' she declared, turning
toward me and hugging her seat.

'Don't tell me you two broke up that night,' I said fearfully.

'No, we're getting married,' she told me, and then screamed
'*Aarrrgghhh*! Watch out for that station wagon!' as I floated
over to the other lane, my hands gripping the steering wheel,
as I tried to absorb what she had just said.

'Oh my God.' I jerked back into the slow lane. 'Are you
serious? I – I – can't believe it! How? What? Where?' I

slowed down even further and a car behind me beeped. I waved him past.

She laughed. 'It's true. Next year. And we decided to try to get pregnant right after the ceremony. So goodbye cervical cap.'

'I can't believe you've been sitting on that for two days!' I bellowed. I tried to hug her but she yelled again 'No, watch the road! I don't want to get killed before I get married!' I felt like I was watching a movie – floating over the two of us, watching our actions and reactions, curiously disassociated. And a wave of selfishness hit me, as I thought *Goodbye nightly phone calls*, and then I felt happy and sad and overjoyed and fearful all at once. 'Congratulations!' I said, now on automatic pilot. 'I really am happy for you.'

'I knew you would be,' Harriet said cryptically.

'How did it happen? Did he get down on one knee?' I kept trying to look over at her. She was hugging her legs now, looking like the birthday girl.

'Jerry said, "I know you can't wait much longer. So let's get married!" I said, "Are you serious?" And he said, "Sure! Let's do it." So I sat there for a minute, and then I said, "Well, do you think you could rephrase the question?" He said, "Harriet, will you marry me?" And I said, "I need two minutes to think about it." So I sat there and sipped my champagne and pretended to mull it over and finally I said, "I will." And then I asked him, "Were you nervous while I was thinking it over?"' Harriet laughed again.

'What did he say?'

'He said, "No."'

'I really am incredibly happy for you,' I said finally feeling truthful. 'You are my first female close friend to do this, and I know this is what you want and it's great.' A car honked again behind us and Harriet glanced at it.

She unfolded herself and said, 'Courtney, I have to tell you this. You know what's really great? I fell in love with him. I really and truly fell in love with him, just within these last two months. I don't know how or why it happened, but it did.'

'Then I'm *really* happy,' I told her. Another wave of selfish abandonment issues smacked me with full force. 'So – I guess the Rules work? You got the ring. Where *is* the ring, by the way?' I stared at her unadorned hands.

'Oh, I don't care about a ring,' she said happily. 'It's funny – that's all I used to think about, but now it seems so unimportant. We decided we'd rather spend our money on a wedding that all our friends can come to, with lots of booze and food. I was thinking that maybe while I was out here, maybe you and I could go look at wedding dresses? I'd really like your opinion. You always dress the right way.'

I looked down at my sweatpants and T-shirt and combat boots. 'Well, thank you, Harriet,' I said. 'I think you're nuts to put stock in my wedding dress sense, but I *am* flattered.'

'So tell me how the rest of the trip went. Mmmm hmm. Yes. Mmmm hmmm. Good. Good.' Harriet was sitting primly on my kitchen chair, talking to her friend Love Lori in Chicago. She'd called into her machine and listened to two semi-hysterical phone messages from Love Lori, back to back. 'You don't mind if I call her, do you? She sounds really desperate.'

'Go ahead,' I said, waving in the direction of the phone, curious as well. Love Lori was a relatively new friend of Harriet's – or rather, an old acquaintance. Like most Manhattan denizens, Harriet had scores of friends from her college, high school and elementary school years, who stayed in touch only intermittently – that is, unless they were coming to New York and needed a place to stay. In the past, Harriet had been, in my opinion, far too nice to these fair-accommodation friends, given the size of her closet-sized apartment and the fact that she worked out of this closet. 'How's the Concierge this season?' I'd say, around September. 'All booked up for the holidays yet?' But this year she'd had her surgery, and was feeling less accommodating to everyone and everything in general. This year, she was going to be much more choosy about who would be allowed to stay on her lumpy fold-out sofabed and crowd her handkerchief-sized sink with their toiletries and cosmetics. That eliminated all those from her hometown in Texas who only stayed in touch by 'sending me a Christmas card signed "Love, So-and-So" with no other personal information.' (Hence Lori's moniker.) Love Lori was one of the first unfortunates to be dropped from the short list, but on a recent trip to New York (where she stayed with a newly met boyfriend), she'd taken to calling Harriet and consulting her for Rules therapy.

'Does Love Lori know you're getting married?' I'd asked.

Harriet said, 'Why do you think she's so interested in my opinion, all of a sudden?'

'You should set up a 900 number,' I suggested. I was slowly getting used to this marriage news, telling even the boy at the corner store where we bought a bottle of celebratory wine, 'This is my friend Harriet – she just got engaged!' He solemnly put his hand out to her and said, 'I congratulate you.'

Now she was saying in to the phone, 'So all of this sounds good so far. Good. Good. Oh, I like that. So you didn't have to pay for anything while you were there? Uh huh. Not cheap places though – not just diners? Good. Was there sex? How did it happen? Yeah. Yeah. Mmm hmm. Oh!' Harriet shot me a look. 'Okay. Well, what did you say? What was the synonym? But you weren't putting the love word on it, were you? Good because that'll get them running away faster than anything.'

I was making a blue cheese dip to take to the cocktail party we were throwing at Aidan's the next night, and I paused to consult the recipe I'd torn out of a food magazine. I couldn't remember if I'd added in the heavy cream yet or not. It looked a little dry, with chunks of the expensive Iowan blue cheese that I'd bought specially, scattered around the sides of the bowl and not looking a bit like the whipped delicacy that I was now staring at, as if it would magically tell me if I'd missed a step. I poured a splash of cream in and began to work it in with my fingers.

'So tell me which Rules you screwed up and we'll see if we can fix them,' Harriet said. I groaned and she looked at me, whispering, 'Sssshhh.' She was finishing the glass of wine that I'd handed her, and I gestured with my elbow toward the bottle. 'Umm hmmm. Uh huh. Okay. Oh huh. Mmm hmm. So you felt that maybe you had sex too soon?' Clearly Harriet did, judging from her serious expression. 'Mmm hmm. It bothers you that he said his head is spinning? Because he's a little afraid, you mean? How long has he been divorced again? Hmm. Okay. Now what others? What other ways have you expressed your neediness?'

Now she was refilling her wine glass, watching me as I squeezed the cheese through my fingers. 'Oh!' she gasped into the phone, and gestured toward my empty glass. I nodded and she filled my glass slowly, listening to Love Lori's voice which I could hear in tiny squeaks. 'Lori – why? Why? You're supposed to call your *friends*. So you called him back as soon as you heard his message?' There was a long silence while Harriet listened. I tried to disengage my fingers from the goo by using a wooden spoon, gave up, and finally just wiped them clean with a paper towel and sat down opposite to Harriet. 'He didn't know you were upset though, right? Good.' She shook her head at me, pursing her lips.

I drank a sip of wine. 'And he hasn't said anything about you visiting again? No? No, you can't suggest it. You *can't*. It's got to be his idea, okay? Good. Good. Here's what I would say, and then I have to get off the phone: Do not call him, do not e-mail him. When he does call, you be happy. You're on your way somewhere, and you be vague. You don't say who you're going out with, or when you're going home. No, you

COURTNEY WEAVER

don't make a plan to call him back later. The thing you're doing is that you're very busy, not trying to make him jealous though. Always be busy and friendly and happy. Don't offer too much information.' I gulped some more wine. Love Lori was ten years older than Harriet, and had never been married. 'And she wants *desperately* to be married!' Harriet had said to me. Well, certainly the Rules couldn't hurt, then.

'Yes, I think it's still reparable,' she was saying, but to me she was shaking her head, mouthing, *She blew it.* 'Yes, I know his brother lives near Chicago, but don't you go suggesting it. He's a man, he knows maps. He'll figure it out if he's so inclined. Uh huh, mmm hmm. Mmm hmm. Okay, and one more thing. You have to make yourself more busy. Because otherwise you'll be sitting around waiting for the phone to ring. And you *can't* do that. I did that for *years* with Clark. I can't tell you how many times he'd call me at eleven o'clock at night and say, "I'm at the bar at the corner — come meet me for a drink." And I would. I'd slap on some make-up and go and meet him. All the Rules does —' Here she paused, and I could tell this was for my benefit, ' — is make you value yourself and recognize a bad man earlier and avoid hurt. You know Lori, maybe you should even *screen* your calls. Pull *way* back. Well, he does sound like a great guy. My Jerry is a great guy — I didn't want to marry a *bad* guy. Okay, now I have to go. I really do. Do not call him. Uh huh. Talk to you soon. Good bye.'

She beeped off and looked at me. 'He's never going to call her again.'

'What did she do?' I asked, mildly curious, feeling like I was about to hear a description of a gruesome head-on collision. 'Incidently — and I've been thinking about where this Rules stuff goes awry — there are some men who just wouldn't respond to the Rules. If I never called Sean, he would have assumed I wasn't interested and never would have called me. We never would have gone out at all.'

'And don't you think that might have been a better thing?' Harriet asked pointedly.

'Okay, well. Maybe you have something there.' I stood up, and began chopping scallions on my tiny wooden chopping block, scattering them around the kitchen with every tap. 'But what happened with Love Lori?'

Harriet shuddered. She glanced in the cheese bowl and stuck her finger around the edge, licking it. 'Yum. This is good. Are you *sure* I can't contribute to this party tomorrow night?'

'No,' I said for the hundredth time. 'Thank you anyway. Tell me about Lori.'

Harriet stretched out her legs and settled back in the chair. 'Now here is a textbook example of what not to do with a man. She invites herself out to New York, after having met him at a tax consultancy conference in Chicago. She has to stay with him the whole weekend because I told her my mother was staying with me and I didn't have room. I told her not to have sex with him, but of course she did. He was pretty nice to her up until that point, paying for everything, and took her out to dinner to meet his friends but then he didn't really talk to her at the dinner. He sat and talked to this little kid the whole time, who was sitting on his mom's lap, on the other side of the table.'

'Not a good sign,' I commented. 'Even I know that.'

'No. Anyway, after they had sex, which sounds like she sort of initiated, he said to her, "Well, that was very friendly." And she said, "Friendly? Don't you mean something sort of *like* friendly, but not – friendly?" And he said, "Well, what synonym would you use?" She didn't really tell me, which leads me to believe she said something that scared him to death. Soon after that, he said that his head was spinning, because all of this was happening so fast.'

'Also not a good sign,' I said. 'See Harriet? I have better instincts than you give me credit for.'

'Wait. You haven't heard the worst. At one point, he says to her, "Lori, you're like a good stiff drink." And—'

'What is that supposed to mean?' I interrupted. 'A drink? Like, a belt of whiskey?'

'Yes. Or something like that. Meaning that she's intense and hits you in the gut. Let's just put it this way: he wasn't calling her a nice elegant glass of Bordeaux.'

'I guess not,' I said, 'although I wouldn't want to be compared to a glass of wine either, elegant or no. Is that the worst? This already has disaster written all over it.'

'See? You're learning. No, when she got back to Chicago, he called her at home and left a message. She was checking her machine from work every fifteen minutes, of course, and she called him right back, within minutes. Then he didn't call her for a day or so, and she called him and told him she was feeling "needy." And that's when she initiated phone sex with him!'

'Oh, God,' I groaned. 'Phone sex! Didn't Monica Lewinsky scare all of us off that forever?'

'And he got incredibly embarrassed and said he wasn't into that. And he got off the phone really quickly. He called her the next day to apologize, saying he just didn't feel comfortable. And he hasn't called her since! I think she really blew it. He's not going to call her after that.'

I stuck my finger in the bowl and licked it off. 'But Harriet,' I said, 'if she's that kind of intense, needy person, isn't it better that he knows that from the outset? So they can move on and find other people that are better suited?'

'No,' Harriet said. 'Nobody wants a needy, desperate person! Don't you think if Aidan had been playing a little harder to get with you, and was a little more aloof, you'd want to be his girlfriend? You may say that has nothing to do with it, but I'm telling you that it does.'

'Aidan,' I said stiffly, as if she'd just said 'Ross Perot.' Still, I added, 'You know, he says he isn't going out with anyone, but I'm sure he is. I'm *sure* of it. I would bet my grandmother's life on it.'

Harriet looked at me sympathetically. 'I'm sure he still really cares for you.'

'Besides,' I said, 'I wouldn't have called Aidan exactly needy or desperate—'

'Yes, but he told you on his first date about his fiancée dumping him for her old boyfriend. He shouldn't have told you that so soon! It was too much information. And ever since then you've implied that he's been looking for someone to fill that hole, that it isn't really *you* that he's into – just that he's into having a committed relationship.'

I licked my finger. 'Isn't it funny how all this stuff starts to sound familiar after a while?'

'Anyway,' Harriet said, backing off, 'all I'm pointing out is that if Lori practiced the Rules, she wouldn't feel so needy all the time. She'd be bargaining from a position of strength, instead of feeling humiliated. If he's coming to her, all interested and willing to do anything to be with her, she won't feel desperate.'

'Does it really work like that?' I asked. 'It sounds a little . . . simple.'

'It *is* simple. Humans are simple. Look how Aidan became much more attractive to you the less available he was. When you didn't know where he was all the time, when he was busy and had lots of other things or women to interest him? You started to think about him in a whole different way.' Harriet finished her wine and held a hand to her forehead. 'I'm drunk.'

I threw the scallions in and gave the dip a thoughtful whirl with the wooden spoon. I stood there looking at it, thinking about Harriet's words, fishing out a tiny circle of green onion that was clinging to the side like a barnacle. Oh God, no wonder I didn't like the Rules. I was the type of person they worked on.

That night we sat in my kitchen and drank two bottles of

wine, finished the blue cheese dip, ate the rest of the green onions and made up Harriet's bed on the brown sofa at 2:30 in the morning. 'Good night,' she slurred from the living room. 'I'm glad I'm here.'

Harriet was the only person I knew who made a point of saying 'good night' before falling asleep – it was one of those touching little qualities that couldn't be experienced by our normal phone relationship. 'So'm I,' I called, equally drunk. 'And congratulations . . .' Then I was going to add that we had an appointment with Marie the next morning at 10 a.m., but I fell asleep and dreamed about flying to Azerbaijan to rescue a herd of sheep that were being led to the kebab machine.

'Just so you know,' Marie shouted when I walked in, 'I'm going through a slut phase.'

'Oh, goody,' I said, and Harriet and I slumped down in the nearest two chairs. It was a bright, fresh, cold Saturday morning as Harriet and I plunged down the hills toward Hayes Valley, still feeling drunk. I'd brought Harriet a cup of coffee and set it next to the phone only thirty minutes ago. She had been lying on her back, a lock of hair thrown across her face, snoring with abandon. Harriet slept the deep, heavy sleep of the dead, or of small children, and I looked at her with envy. She snuffled and mumbled, 'what time is it?' and when I told her our hair appointment was in half an hour, she moaned and heaved herself off the sofa, grabbing the coffee cup and holding it to her forehead.

Still, here we were, ready to be cut and bleached and colored. The salon was dark and warm, and a beehive of activity. Marie had hired a manicurist, and two women were sitting on one of the lime green sofas, leafing through *Details* and *Cosmopolitan*, waiting to be worked on. A new stylist with orange and black striped hair, reminiscent of a tiger, was clipping away at a woman who resembled Annie Lennox on the far side of the salon. In the middle chair, Eve was standing over a timid woman with gray hair, pulling strands of wispy hair on either side of her face, saying something about volume. Marie was covered in the same black rubber smock from two months ago, teetering on the same black rubber platform sandals, dabbing bleach into the hair of an ebony-haired teenager, who looked like she was about to fall asleep. The CD was roaring with some crashing techno sounds – actually, the same soundtrack I'd heard at the Power Exchange.

I pointed at her feet. 'You know, if you break your ankle in those, they're going to have to shoot you.'

'I can't hear you,' Marie shouted. 'We're running a little off schedule. Hi there!' she directed to Harriet. 'What do you need done again? Your roots, right?'

'Hello,' Harriet said, smiling and putting out her hand, which Marie waved her elbow at. 'No, just a cut, actually. Are my roots that bad?'

'No, Marie, I'm the one who needs the roots work,' I yelled. 'This is my friend from New York. The one I was telling you about—'

'Oh, *you're* the Rules chick!' Marie interrupted, as Harriet smiled shyly and smoothed her trousers, starting to say, 'Why, yes, I suppose I am,' while stealing a glance at me which read *Just exactly what have you told her, Courtney?* Marie continued, 'Hel-*lo*. No, you don't need to have your roots done today. You could leave it a week or so,' and Harriet looked relieved. 'Do you guys want some coffee? Courtney, go get some coffee, will you sweetheart? Just so we can get this all going. You know where the coffee is. Unless you want a glass of wine, that is.'

I turned to Harriet, who shook her head and shuddered. 'I'll be right back,' I told her. As I started to walk back to the kitchen, I heard Marie shouting to Harriet, 'I hope you're not still cutting your hair with manicure scissors! My husband used to do that – oh, this is the husband who had an affair on me eight months ago,' and Harriet pretended to look shocked.

'Didn't Courtney tell you? Oh, well, anyway, Carrie and I here were just talking about boyfriends after big significant relationships, and I was just telling her about Brian, my boyfriend now whose last girlfriend died in a car crash last year —'

I came back and handed Harriet a large ceramic orange cup. Marie was inspecting the bleach brush, and saying to Harriet, 'Well, now I love Brian, I really do, but he can't give me 100 per cent, and I am not going through another thing like that again. Meanwhile, I met another guy – Eve, what are all these blue dots in this brush? Do you know?'

'Maybe the brush wasn't clean?' Eve yelled from her chair. She smiled at me faintly.

I said, 'What is going on here Marie? This is a little hair factory you've got going.'

'Hired more people,' Marie said, dabbing again at Carrie's head, before taking up her shears and snipping a single strand of hair that was falling across Carrie's nose. 'I had to. I was here every night until ten. I never got to see my daughter.'

I settled back into the chair and looked at Harriet, who said, 'Marie was telling me that she's feeling very fickle toward Gavin and Brian. And that she'd get back together with Gavin in ten years.' Marie nodded.

'Is that true?' I demanded.

'Yup,' she said, covered a burp with her hand. 'He's gotta grow up. He's just an idiot right now.'

'He'll still be the same idiot who had an affair on you in ten years,' Harriet said.

'The same *dog*,' I added, then shouted at Marie, 'Harriet's just gotten engaged!'

'Really? Wow, that is *so* great.' Marie actually put the brush and the bowl down on the trolley and came over to give Harriet an enormous bear hug. 'That is so cool!'

'Well, thanks,' Harriet said, a little startled but turning red with pleasure. 'I'm pretty happy about it, as I'm sure you could guess.'

'Absolutely! Right on! Long Live the Rules!' Marie shouted, smiling away. But then she picked up the brush and bowl, back to business as usual. 'Carrie, you doing okay down there?'

'Uh huh,' the girl said, who looked ready to drop off, asleep.

'And Gavin is a dog,' Eve shouted. Her client, the timid woman, was paging through *People* and didn't even look up.

'We've moved beyond that topic, now, Eve,' Marie said. 'Are you still having sex with that Irish guy?' she directed at me. 'Do you *never* listen to me? What is the matter with you? Either shit or get off the pot.' Harriet shrugged.

'How come his friends never tell *him* to shit or get off the pot?' I asked. 'Anyway, no – we're not. He's dating someone else and doesn't want to talk to me as much anymore.'

'It's all she thinks about,' Harriet put in.

'That is not true,' I said. 'He doesn't want to be a couple just as much as I don't. He says I drive him completely insane.' I examined the ends of my hair. Marie rolled her eyes in the mirror to Harriet. 'I saw that,' I said.

'Until you both are going out with other people, you are not "just friends." At least while you're still sleeping together. And believe me, his friends are telling him things. And not anything you'd want to hear, because it's not very nice about you.'

'And just how do you know that?'

'Because I know how men's minds work.' I refrained from pointing out the irony of this statement coming from the woman who told her husband to go have an affair. Harriet picked up a copy of *Glamour* and pretended to look at the index. The CD switched over and suddenly nonsensical chanting filled the room. 'Did I tell you my new boyfriend is a Buddhist?' Marie yelled over the moaning. 'Hang on, I'm going to turn this down.' She disappeared behind a tangerine-colored velvet curtain, as Eve called over to me, 'You won't believe the stuff she's been doing.'

'What is going on with *you* Marie?' I said when she returned. 'You have a high color to your cheeks, as Jane Austen would say.'

'I fucked a fireman last weekend,' Marie said, her hands on her hips, as Harriet and I looked at her, our eyes wide. 'I haven't done something like that in, um, *years*. It was wild. But now I feel guilty.' She scratched her wine-colored mane and looked closely under her nails. 'This color is *still* coming out.'

'Is this your boyfriend?' I asked. 'I thought you said he was a snowboarder. He fights fires too?'

'No, this is someone else. I'm still going out with Brian, though. The fireman and I have been doing the checking out thing at the gym lately, and then I went to this bar with my friend Theresa, and *there* he was. I had three bottles of champagne in me, so bold person that I am, I just went up to him—'

'You just walked up to him? What did you say?' I interrupted. Harriet tossed *Glamour* back on the pile and sat back in her chair. We both arranged ourselves in a comfy position for the long haul. 'Boy, it didn't take long for you to get back on the horse.'

'It *has* been almost a year since my husband screwed around me behind my back,' Marie said, rather primly. Leaning over, she pulled a drawer open from the top of her trolley. 'What do you think of this dress?' she said, handing us a card from a wedding boutique. 'I was thinking if I ever got married again, I'd wear something like this. What do you think of it?' she asked Harriet.

'It's really pretty,' said Harriet, staring at the photo of a sultry model with bee-stung lips, all sheathed in white and seed pearls, looking like a cross between a hooker and a vestal virgin, which was obviously the point.

'Would you wear something like that?' I asked her.

'I don't think so,' she said, thoughtfully, and handed the

card back to Marie. 'And I'm having a really hard time imagining myself in one of those big, poofy ball gown type things too. I think I'd look like such a fool.'

'What will you wear?' Marie asked.

'I have no idea. I'm hoping Courtney will help me figure it out. Maybe a pant suit.'

'With a veil?' I asked 'And a long train?'

Harriet laughed, hearing a verging-on-mocking tone she thought I was taking on. I didn't *feel* mocking, though – just a little left out. 'I doubt it.'

'So you really trust this fiancé, huh?' Marie was brushing in the last of the bleach into Carrie's hair. 'Yeah, I trust Brian too. He wouldn't do the kind of stuff I'm doing right now.' I caught her eye and said, 'Well?'

'First of all, this sex stuff? It's like riding a bike. Comes right back,' she said confidently.

'What bar did you see him in?' I interrupted, wanting to picture it. I couldn't classify Marie anymore as a member of the dirty life, nor as alternative mom, nor really as anything else. I thought about her walking into the bar at the Ritz Carlton and ordering a glass of champagne, but that didn't seem very likely either.

'Paradise Lounge,' Marie said, naming a dirty life bar. Old habits apparently died hard. 'I haven't been there in a long time. Way before the baby was born. So we walk in, and I see this fireman there—'

'Was he wearing his helmet?' I asked.

Marie ignored that. 'I went right up to him and told him to come over and talk to us.' I turned to Harriet and was about to say something, but she was listening with intent interest to Marie, leaning her head onto her hand, coffee forgotten. Marie snapped a plastic cap around Carrie's head, who awoke with a jump, as Marie dragged a hair dryer on wheels across the salon. 'Tilt your head,' she commanded to Carrie, and carefully flipped the hood over, switching it on. 'After half an hour of talking to him,' she yelled over the noise, 'we started making out at the bar. And five minutes after that, he says, "Wanna come to my house?" I said "Great." Is that too hot, Carrie?'

'No, it's fine,' Carrie said loudly.

'Only ten minutes,' Marie shouted. 'I'm sorry the streaks didn't work out.'

'Oh, it's okay,' replied Carrie.

'Where was the snowboarder that night?' I asked.

Marie put her hand on her hip, her myriad silver bracelets falling down around her hand. 'He screwed up and was supposed to meet me but didn't. He just never showed up, so Theresa and I—'

'He stood you up?' Harriet asked.

'Well, yeah. It was at the Folsom Street Fair, so I just assumed he got lost in the shuffle and didn't see me.' Marie seemed nonplussed. Harriet rearranged her hands and took a measured sip of coffee, looking at Marie, I could tell, in such a way as to assess the degree of Marie's outrage about this obvious Rules transgression.

'Were you angry?' I asked, more for Harriet.

'Well, kind of. It kind of prompted me to do what I did. But this boy was hot. Like I said, we've been checking each other out for months—'

'How old is this boy?' I felt like Marie's mother.

'Twenty-nine,' Marie shouted, and paused. 'He's kinda small though.'

'How small?' Harriet and I asked in unison.

'Like this?' Marie spread her fingers.

Both Harriet and I appraised her measurement. 'Well, according to the statistics, that's average,' I shouted.

'*Average?*' Marie squealed. 'Four or five inches? And he fucked like a rabbit. You know, like uh-uh-uh-uh-uh.'

'Oooh, I hate that,' I said, and Harriet wrinkled her nose.

'Do they think women like that?' Marie shouted. 'The whole time I'm having sex with him, my head is banging into the wall. And I'm like, *Karl, c-c-can we back up a little bit?'*

'Oh, my God.' Carrie shook her head under the dryer.

'Did you use condoms?' I demanded.

'Of course,' Marie said immediately. 'What do you take me for?'

'Marie, do you want to go under the dryer?' Eve interrupted loudly. Now I noticed that Marie had tiny aluminum foil squares tucked here and there in her burgundy mane. I'd thought it was some kind of new fad, like hair jewelry.

'Yeah, I guess I should.' She looked at both of us and said, 'Do you mind? You do know that your appointment isn't for another hour, right?'

'Whoops,' I said, and grimaced toward Harriet. 'Are you sure?'

'Eleven o'clock,' said Marie. 'It's in the book. You did make it a while ago.'

'Oh, well,' I said. 'Sorry about that. I guess I got a little mixed up.'

'That's fine,' Harriet said cheerfully 'You know who should come and talk to Marie? Love Lori, that's who.' I got up and sat next to the pile of magazines on the ledge by the mirror, while Marie, wearing an amused expression, disappeared again behind the tangerine curtain, and came back wheeling out another dryer. She got down on her hands and knees to plug it in, and plopped down on the other side of Carrie. 'I used condoms but I didn't vote in November.' She twisted around in her chair, fiddling with the dials until the dryer finally came on with a roar. She set it atop her head and looked at me expectantly.

'So the sex was eeehhhhh,' I said, raising my voice above the din.

'Yeah, it wasn't great,' Marie said cheerfully and loudly. Now that there were two dryers going, we were all yelling again. 'But I kind of think you should give people three chances. The first time the sex is always awkward. The second time you're still sniffing around. The third time you know. You can really tell if it'll work out.' Harriet and I sat silently, pondering that little Marie-ism.

'Did you just get up and leave after?' I asked.

'What?' Marie screamed.

'DID YOU JUST LEAVE AFTER HAVING SEX WITH HIM?' I yelled.

'Oh,' Marie said. 'I didn't finish. Neither one of us had orgasms. Because Theresa was knocking on the door —'

Harriet squawked, 'You mean she was in the apartment with you two the whole time?'

I covered my eyes with a hand. 'No.'

Marie laughed. 'Yep. She was hanging out in the living room with this other guy.'

Now Eve was laughing too, saying, 'Marie, Marie. You *are* a slut.' Harriet started to laugh then, and so did Carrie and the timid woman.

I sat up. 'In the same apartment? What are you, in high school?'

Marie chortled again. 'I know. I felt like I was in high school that night. Then we get walked in on by this other chick, Megan, who used to work at the bar with Gavin and Veronica. She lives with the fireman, see? So I'm on top of him, and I've got my tiny dress on with my g-string, and she walks right in. Remember what I said about San Francisco being just a small town with big buildings? Ouch, this is way too hot.' Marie twisted around and adjusted a dial. 'She hated Gavin. She said to me later, "Your husband is a big fucking bastard." I said, "Yeah, well I could have told you that."'

'She told you this while you were having sex?' Eve screamed.

'No, this was leading up to it. Eve, could you turn Carrie's dryer off or check her color? It's been ten minutes. I'm going to stay under a minute more.'

'Then what?' I asked.

280

'Okay, well, so after we were having sex for a while, I thought *Oh my God, I shouldn't be here, it's 4.15 in the morning*, Theresa's banging on the door, so I got my clothes on and said, "Karl, I gotta go, I gotta go." I was just trying to end it there – "We'll figure out when," I'm saying – I wrote my number down and was like, "Here's my number, call me." So he's like, "I'll come with you!" To take Theresa home. And I'm like, "No, no, you don't have to come with me." And he's like, "Oh, I'll come with you." So I tried to get rid of him, and couldn't get rid of him. We got dressed, dropped Theresa off, and then I drove him home and he's like "Come in, come in," and I just said, "I can't, I've got to get home to my daughter." Davia of course was with Gavin, but I just wanted to go home at that point. I didn't want my head bashed in the wall anymore.'

She turned around and switched the dryer off. 'The next day he called me twice. I was totally sick the next day, completely hung over.' Leaning over, she grabbed a banana off the black linoleum counter. 'Were you the one who told me that bananas fight depression?'

'Yeah, that's Harriet here,' I said, and Harriet looked proud. It would be interesting to be a fly on the wall inside Harriet's head right now. While she was hardly a prude, she didn't think sex on the first night was a good thing, simply because the woman no longer had any bait to dangle in front of the suitor. 'He called twice, huh? That's sounds like he's pretty darn interested,' I said – again, more for Harriet's benefit.

'Yeah, I guess. I felt guilty, though. I felt like . . . Gavin – a cheating, fucking asshole.' Marie inspected her bracelets and then flipped the dryer hood up. 'But now I'm thinking of seeing the fireman again.'

Eve and I groaned, and Marie laughed at us. Harriet shook her head, but I could tell even she was impressed. Eve walked over and unfolded a little square of tin foil from Carrie's head, inspecting the bit of hair inside. 'I don't think she should go any lighter,' she warned Marie.

'Okay. Let's get this crap out of all our hair.' The five of us walked to the back of the room and Marie stood behind the sink and motioned for Carrie to sit. There was a minor back-and-forth about who would get rinsed first, until finally Carrie sat in the chair and bent her head back into the slot. Marie tucked a lime colored towel around her neck and turned on the faucet. Eve said, 'Call me when you need me to rinse you out,' and said, 'excuse me,' as she brushed past Harriet and me, who were leaning against the wall of the narrow sink room.

'So that's my crazy teenage life,' Marie said loudly.

'What about your snowboarder?' I asked. 'Your boyfriend?'

'Oh, well.' Marie scrubbed extra-hard on Carrie's scalp, and a waft of pineapples floated over to Harriet and me. 'I told Brian I was in love with him two days after the fireman fucking thing. I do love him. But he says he can't give me 100 per cent – but of course I went and did this, so maybe I can't either. Oh, I don't *know*,' she said. 'It was fun though. I wouldn't do it every day, but it definitely was worth it.'

'Did you tell Brian about the fireman?' Harriet asked.

'Are you nuts?' Marie stared at Harriet. 'Is this a New York woman thing?' she asked me. 'Total honesty with boyfriends?'

'Ha!' I said. 'Why don't you answer that, Harriet?'

'Oh, gosh, I'm not saying you should—' Harriet hastily added.

'Good. No, no, no, no, no. Of course not. Brian got drunk that night with his friends, and ended up skateboarding down Columbus Avenue in a dress at 2.30 in the morning.' She giggled. 'And you think I'm juvenile.'

'Where did he get the dress?' I asked suspiciously.

'He was at some chick's party. And in answer to your next question, yeah, I do believe him, because Brian may be many things but he's not, you know, a skirt-chaser.' Carrie suddenly squirmed, and Marie hastily said, 'Oops. Sorry about that. A little hot.' She readjusted the taps.

'When was the last time you did something like this?' I asked.

'A one-night stand? Oh, a long time ago, way before Gavin.'

'Well, I could have figured that out,' I said.

'Actually, the last time is sort of funny, now that I think about it. This is right before I met Gavin. It was with this French boy, Michel – he rode a BSA, I remember that – and he was at this birthday party at this bar on Haight Street. We started talking and he's saying "You're very attractive," in his little French accent. And I'm like, "Well, thanks." So then he said to me straight out that he was married and that he and his wife had an open relationship. I'm like, "What do you mean – open?" He says, "We can have sex with whomever we want—"' Marie paused as she wrung Carrie's hair hard into a towel. 'Wait a minute. I should put some of that stuff that's in the black bottle into your hair. Harriet, can you hand it to me? It should be to the left of the conditioner up there.' Harriet looked above at a shelf and plucked a bottle off as Marie said, 'That's it. I'll just squirt it all in. And we'll sit here for a minute.'

'Don't tell me you believed him,' I said.

'What does this "Prisms" do?' Harriet asked, cocking her head to read the bottle.

'It's a sealant. And yeah, I did believe him. I'm getting to that. So I said to him, "So you want to fuck me, huh?" And he's like "Mais oui!" So we went to my friend Danielle's apartment – she lived in a studio right around the corner from the bar—'

Harriet and I started laughing. 'Where was she?' I demanded.

'In the closet. It was a huge, walk-in closet. She was just like, eating a pizza, smoking cigarettes. This is about five in the morning, mind you.' Marie kept squeezing, shaking the container like it was a bottle of ketchup, working the goo in, and we all exchanged looks.

'That is one ... good ... friend,' observed Harriet, emphasizing the words with wonder.

'Isn't she?' Marie agreed cheerfully. 'One time she walks out and Michel and I are going at it and she says, "You guys want some pizza?" And I said, "Go away, I can't concentrate." She says, "Oh, right, sorry. But I need to get some water." Michel says to me, "Let's go in the bathroom" so we went in the bathroom and did it over the tub.'

'Was it fun?' I asked.

'Yeah, it was a lot of fun,' Marie said, sounding dazed, squeezing and squirting. 'It seems like a really long time ago, though.'

'Did you see him again?' Harriet asked.

'Nope. Oh, the funny thing was, he called his wife on his cell phone. He says to her, "Sophie, I met this girl tonight. I'm going to have sex with her right now."'

'You heard this?' Eve asked, reappearing.

'Oh yeah,' Marie said. 'Okay, that should be enough of the sealant. Now I'll rinse you out.' She turned on the taps again, and continued, 'He says to her, "Do you want to talk to her? I think you'd find her very attractive."'

'Oh, God,' Harriet and I groaned at once. Eve looked at all of us, and said, 'I'll be in the other room when you need me.'

'Yep,' Marie said, spraying away at Carrie's head, working her hands through. 'I thought to myself, God – I guess they really do have an open relationship. Kind of funny, given all the stuff that's happened with Gavin.' Marie turned off the faucet and pumped some lavender cream into her palm, massaging it in. 'But I do feel guilty about the fireman. I'd be pissed if Brain fucked some girl that he met. He's leaving for three weeks on Friday. Snowboarding thing in Canada.'

'Bad time for him to leave,' Harriet said, and I nodded.

I said, 'So you feel guilty but you're in love with this Brian anyway? You sound like a guy. I mean, a dumb guy – the kind that we get angry about.' You sound like Gavin, is what I really wanted to say. 'Is Gavin still calling you and saying he loves you?'

'Yeah.' Marie frowned as she massaged Carrie's scalp, and turned off the faucet. 'Not so much as before. He's not seeing that Veronica chick anymore, I hear.'

'How do you know this?'

'Friends,' Marie said, turning the water on again. 'Ones that work with her at the bar. The same ones that told me her schedule so I could go threaten her—'

'Acck!' Carrie said. 'The water's too cold!'

'You threatened her in person?' I said. 'When was this? You never told me this.'

'Oh, I didn't exactly threaten her – I just glared at her. I was sitting at the bar, having a drink with one of the bartenders, and she'd pass me. "Hey Veronica!" I'd say. "Looking good!" She wouldn't look me in the face – just said "Oh, hi Marie." ' Marie sighed loudly, and wrapped Carrie's hair hard in a towel. 'All this frickin' pride.' The CD clicked again, and what sounded like a brass marching band filled the salon. 'I should be alone,' she said loudly. 'But I don't want to break up with Brian – I really care about him. He's really grown on me, and he loves the baby. Maybe he'll come back from Canada totally missing me.'

Harriet and I were silent. I examined the ends of my hair again. 'You don't think he's going to, do you?' said Marie.

'I don't know,' I said truthfully.

'I don't know either,' said Harriet. 'I'm not sure what I would advise you.'

I said, 'I can understand about not wanting to be alone. I just – I don't know anymore. You thought you knew Gavin really well, and look what he did.'

'I thought I knew Gavin better than anyone,' said Marie. 'In some ways I feel like I still do. And there's a part of me that feels like I don't know him at all. I just really did not see that coming. I sometimes wonder if I'd had sex with him when I was pregnant, maybe this wouldn't have happened – but fuck that.' Marie suddenly looked explosive. Her face turned red and she touched her sticky mop that was piled on top of her head with a finger and stared at it. 'I shouldn't have to spread my legs to keep my family. But I can't seem to file for divorce either, because somewhere in the back of my mind I hope I'm going to get my family back.'

'And now you're entering this slut phase,' said Harriet.

'Yep,' agreed Marie. 'All I want to do is fuck guys and go out and carouse. But still be a good mom.' She looked at her finger again. 'I should rinse this stuff out.'

Ten minutes later, after Marie was rinsed out, she was back working on Carrie's hair with a pair of scissors. Harriet and I returned to our original places, me on the ledge and her in the chair next to Carrie. By this point we'd moved on to wine, and the three of us were holding paper cups, sipping and talking as if we were at a cocktail party.

Marie was telling us how she and Gavin had an argument soon after he'd moved out, and he was yanking on her ponytail, pulling her to the floor, screaming. Davia was in her arms, crying and she was screaming at him to let go of her hair. 'So I held Davia as tight as I could with one arm, and I swung around and *punched* him. He let go of my hair after that.'

'Oh, my,' Harriet said. 'Were you scared? Were you crying?'

'No,' said Marie. 'I've never been scared of Gavin. I was laughing at him actually. I'm going to make this more jagged in the front, okay Carrie? No, that was our worst fight. He apologized after that, all over himself. Still apologizes about it.'

'Doesn't this bother you to talk about it?' asked Harriet.

'No, it's good for me to talk about it,' she said. 'It reminds me of all the things about why we can't get back together. It fills me with rage. Rage is good. Better than self-pity. I'm going to call Teentsy-Dick again —'

'Marie!' Eve scolded from her chair on the other side of the salon.

'I am,' she said. 'That's terrible, isn't it? Does size matter? Yeah.' Marie put down the scissors and Carrie jumped up, brushing the bits of hair off the smock. 'Now you don't look like one of those mall chicks with the orange streaks hair.' Carrie smiled and went in the other room to get dressed. Marie put her hands on her hips.

'Is that all?' I asked.

'Isn't that enough?' Marie asked.

'Are we next?' Harriet said.

'Yup. Get in,' she directed toward Harriet. 'The other thing is, I'm going to have my tits done. Did I tell you?'

'No,' I said.

'It's going to cost $3,000, and I'm going to put it on the credit card. I have no money, but I'm going to get this done because I can't take it anymore. My tits used to be my favorite part of my body. Now, since breast feeding, they're down at my waist.'

'Are you doing this because of Gavin?' I asked.

'What?' she squawked. 'No. Besides, I'm not enlarging them, silly, just getting them pulled up.'

'Does Brian want you to do it?' Harriet asked.

'What is *with* you two?' Marie said, hands on her hips again, looking at us back and forth. 'No. This has nothing to do with any guy. This is for *me*. No, Brian loves my tits. He doesn't want me to do anything to them.'

'Won't it hurt?' I asked incredulously.

'Sure,' Marie said, offhand. She tightened an ice-cream pink towel around Harriet's neck and looked at us in the mirror. 'But I have a very high threshold for pain.'

In the street outside, Harriet and I passed a woman who was wearing a bridal veil with jeans and a button-down shirt, getting into a cab. She was holding a leather backpack and I realized she had just come out of Marie's salon, where she'd obviously had her hair and make-up done before her wedding ceremony. She looked completely calm and was now consulting a leather address book, giving directions to the driver. As she pulled away from the curb, she glanced over at us and smiled. We smiled back and waved, as if we'd just seen the Queen.

I wondered if I just was becoming more sensitive to the issue, or was marriage – in one form or another – making its presence known in virtually every circumstance? 'Look, that'll be you soon,' I said to Harriet, after a moment.

In fact, Harriet said, 'She looked like a ghost.'

'She did seem a little heavy in the foundation department, that's true,' I agreed.

'A visitation, I mean. But in a good way.' Harriet smiled cheerfully, and we continued to walk down the street in the direction of a restaurant that I remembered had wonderful hamburgers some years back. 'Now, if I'd seen her a week ago at this time, it probably would have sent me into a depression.' She looked over at me. 'How did it make *you* feel?'

'Oh.' I stopped and looked in my knapsack for a band to pull my hair up in its daily ponytail. Again, I was socked by that mix of emotions that had been intermittently washing over me ever since Harriet had announced her engagement. It was like somebody ringing a doorbell, leaning on it every few minutes or so. 'I guess it makes me feel . . . *tired*. That I have to get back on the dating horse soon, and go through all that rigmarole, the passion, the ups, the downs, the arguments, the reconciliations, the drama, blah, blah, blah, to get anywhere *near* that point.'

'Not everyone wants to be married,' she said, in a soothing tone that if I didn't know her better could come across as verging-on-pity.

'That's not really what I meant.' We stepped apart to allow a father drive his stroller bearing two gurgling babies down the sidewalk. 'Maybe it's part of my heritage to be alone. My mom's alone. My grandmothers, both of them, are alone. My sister has a boyfriend but has never lived with anyone. It all fits.' We turned the corner and threaded our way down the crowded street to the restaurant.

Harriet hesitated, slowing as we walked. She was glancing over, watching as I fussed with my hair, nearly elbowing a passerby in the face as I tried to twist the hairband around my newly colored locks. Finally she said, 'Honestly, I just don't think you've met the right person yet. Aidan sounds very nice, but he's not right for you.'

'Really?' I stopped walking. Of course I knew this all along, but finally having the stamp of approval from Harriet to let him go and not feel guilty or panicked about it brought a surprising sense of relief. We continued our stroll, while I, dazed, nearly walked into a fire hydrant. 'Marie says the same thing – which is pretty funny since neither one of you have met him.'

Harriet stopped to look at a window display of pointy-toed boots. 'You'll meet someone else that's right for you. Men are like a bus – if you miss one, there's always another rounding the corner.'

'Not if you live in San Francisco,' I said. 'I mean that about the men *and* the buses.' Harriet humphed and I asked, unable to wait any longer, 'What did you think of Marie's story?'

'Great!' Harriet said, and we meandered down to the next window. 'No, I'm serious. Look what a sense of humor she has! Laughing at herself driving around looking for her husband at 3 a.m., paging him 72 times or whatever it was, peering into the back of every Honda Civic trying to see if she can catch him screwing that woman!' We started to laugh, and Harriet said, 'Isn't it a beautiful day?'

'It is,' I said, noticing it fully for the first time. 'But what do you think about her going out and being such a . . . a . . . *guy*?'

'Oh, good for her,' Harriet said carelessly. 'She deserves it. She's just going out and having fun. She doesn't really want to marry any of those men. So there's no reason for her to be playing the Rules.'

'Oh, okay,' I said, a little disappointed. I was looking forward to debating this instance of outrageous, aggressive sexuality.

'The fireman knew Marie wasn't really interested,' Harriet continued. 'She was trying to get away from him, and he was all into her. Now if she'd been needy or desperate like Love Lori, you can guarantee that he wouldn't have called her twice the next day.'

'I'm sure that's true,' I said, trying to nip this in the bud. Despite myself, I couldn't help but add, 'You know, I tell Aidan about the Rules and he says if he knew a woman who was doing that, he'd never want to see her again.'

'Oh, really?' Harriet chortled. 'That's pretty funny, coming from him – someone who couldn't be more interested in you, a woman who's just playing the Rules naturally.'

'Yeah, and look where it got me,' I said. I stopped and looked around. 'Where is this damn restaurant? I thought it was on this block.'

Harriet rubbed my arm affectionately. 'I am very optimistic for you,' she said. 'You're too fascinated by the ways and means of love to not be right in the thick of it.'

'Whatever,' I said. 'But there is such a thing as too much information. Oh, for God's sake, here it is.' We were standing right in front of it. I held the heavy brass door open for her as Harriet stepped into the restaurant's foyer, looking like a little girl arriving at her best friend's birthday party.

CHAPTER 11

The doorbell buzzed, loudly. I was standing in Aidan's bathroom, rooting around in his medicine cabinet for something to put in my hair to make it less frizzy. I picked up a blue bottle of 'Hair Fixative,' sprayed some on my hand, and sniffed. It smelled like mint and rosemary – something my mother would smear on her Christmas leg of lamb, and seemed awfully girlie for Aidan. Then I remembered Little Missy, so I sprayed the majority of it in my hair before dumping the rest of the contents down the sink and replacing it with water. Jealousy knew not the difference between the Mr Rights and the Mr Right Nows.

The door buzzed again, this time extra loud. 'Do you want me to get that?' I screamed. I leaned from the mirror where I could see Aidan and Harriet calmly drinking a glass of wine, standing by the mantel in his living room. Aidan was wearing the orange shirt I'd given him for Christmas the previous year, a white apron around his waist, and he and my friend were talking as if they'd known each other all their lives. Aidan was saying something about proposals and then, 'No man could be that stupid just to give you a cheese grater —' as they both started laughing.

He looked over at me, as if he'd forgotten I was there. 'No, I'll get it.' He put his glass down on the table which we'd moved out from the kitchen, laden with Christmas-type food that he'd made over the past two days – homemade gravlax, Irish soda bread, oysters with mignonette, tortilla chips and a huge vat of salsa. My puny bowl of newly made blue cheese dip looked sad and forgotten, sitting on the edge.

'He's very sweet!' Harriet hissed in my ear as I joined her standing next to the table. Aidan was escorting his friend Thomas in – I could hear them exchanging comments on the latest *Deep Space Nine* episode. 'I can see now why you were struggling. And he cooks! Look at this food! This is so sweet of him.'

'Well, it's his party too. But, yes, Aidan is sweet.' Good Lord. 'Sweet.' 'Decent.' 'Kind.' If one didn't know better, one would think we were all in search of good stuffed animals, not suitable life partners. I patted my hair, and Harriet suddenly looked at it, frowning. 'I know, I used a little too much spray gel. It's okay, it'll dry.'

'It certainly smells good,' she said. 'I thought it was the gravlax for a minute.'

I whispered to her, 'I think it's Aidan's new girlfriend's product – he didn't say anything to you about her, did he?' I paused, mid-bite of a tortilla chip.

'No, of course not.' Harriet put on her social, Texas-style smile as she reached out and shook Thomas's hand, who was shuffling in, holding a bottle of designer beer.

'Hi Thomas,' I said. Thomas was one of Aidan's better friends – a shy, highly intelligent guy who worked in Silicon Valley, whom we all suspected of being a secret billionaire. Thomas raised his eyebrows in greeting in my direction, and I said, 'This is Harriet – she just got engaged!'

'Great,' Thomas said, and looked in his beer bottle. I excused myself, knowing that Harriet would find something in common with him, and within five minutes they'd be talking and laughing as if they were old college buddies.

'How's it going?' I said to Aidan, who was fussing around the gravlax, trying to spread the dill out evenly in between the slices of soda bread.

'Good,' he said. He smiled at me shortly, and reached

around. I thought it was the start of a celebratory embrace, and I started to put my arms around his neck but he was only trying to retrieve his wine glass, as I found out when he just slightly backed away from me.

I felt foolish. We hadn't seen each other for over a month, planning this party over the telephone, and I'd been worried how we were going to respond to one another. At one point, earlier in the evening while we were trying to decide whether to keep the double doors to his bedroom open, I tried to steal a glance into the nightstand drawer, which was slightly ajar. The condoms were kept there, and what I thought I would figure out by rooting around wasn't exactly clear to me. But Aidan firmly shut the drawer with a significant look, and I backed away. Neither of us said anything.

Now Harriet was saying, 'He's getting married, did you know that, Courtney?'

I returned to Harriet's side. 'No, I didn't. Congratulations!' Thomas looked at his shoes and mumbled some thanks, while I looked around him, as if he were hiding his fiancée behind his back.

'She couldn't come,' Harriet said, in explanation. 'She's working tonight. So, what made you decide to get engaged?'

I felt a prick of irritation. Of course Harriet automatically assumed that the girlfriend had been wheedling and cajoling for a ring, while Thomas had been dragging his feet, reluctantly succumbing only when he'd been drunk or tricked into it. It would never occur to her that maybe the man had been desperate for a commitment – but in fact, Thomas said noncommittedly, 'It just seemed like it was time.'

Harriet had her hair pulled off her face in a girlish, messy ponytail, and the wine had given a touch of pink to her cheeks and forehead. She looked positively like a teenager. 'Yes, it tends to happen that way,' she said, and we all nodded knowingly. 'I asked Jerry the other day, "So, when did you start to think about proposing to me?" He said, "Oh, pretty much right when we started dating." And then he went on to say that he would have liked to – and I quote – "stretch it out a little longer, maybe a year or two," but he knew that I wouldn't wait.'

' "Stretch it out"!' I cried.

'Sort of like a bucket of popcorn at the movies,' observed Thomas.

Now Aidan was leading a gaggle of my friends that I hadn't seen in a while, making introductions all around. 'Harriet,' I said, 'over there is Marco, and the woman he's with must be his new girlfriend, another Ms Trouble, and then there's Lizzie and her boyfriend, and that couple over there with the kid is Adam and Marta, my married friends, and—'

'This is a big party,' Thomas observed.

'Where will you be getting married?' Harriet asked politely.

'Excuse me,' I said, as more people started to crush in the door.

After an hour, the small living room was packed – a mixture of Aidan's track friends, restaurant colleagues, my high school friends and passing acquaintances. Some of them were sitting on the futon sofa, others were gathered around the chip bowl, still others had piled into the kitchen and were discussing the pros and cons of beer in a bottle versus the good ole keg. I'd been worried how such a motley group was going to inter-mingle, but they all seemed to be chatting away, eating and pontificating. Aidan was dashing about, refilling glasses and the salsa bowl, while I drifted, making sure everyone was talking to somebody. That wasn't a problem, since just about everybody was half of a couple, and when in need they could turn to their partner and point out the homemade bread or Aidan's track medals hanging on one side of the living room wall. The noise had reached that crescendo where snatches of phrases sang above the crowd – 'No, it's all reruns now,' '—haven't been back home since last Easter, but why would we?', '—miss the burritos and that was it—', 'anyone would jog instead of watching TV?' and the like. I looked around for a woman that might be Aidan's new sex partner but couldn't pick anyone out. Aidan liked women who were short and had short hair – the exact opposite to me, as it happened – and there were a few of those here, but they were all attached to boyfriends.

'Your friends don't drink very much,' Harriet said to me, when I refilled her glass. 'Not half as much as you and me.'

'I know,' I said. 'Isn't that depressing?'

'If I lived here, yes,' she said cheerfully.

'Have you tried the blue cheese dip—' I began, when Aidan caught my eye and leaned his head in the direction of the door. There, coming in, with the highly decorated gloss of those fresh to a party were Jemma and Sir. Swathed in black coats, they looked dramatic and expectant, like the main characters of a play that was already in progress.

'Well, hi!' I said, making my way toward them. We kissed cheeks all around, as Jemma said 'Hullo, darling!' and Sir grunted in a friendly way. I wondered if Ellen were going to pop up, but Sir shut the door behind him firmly. I took their coats and threw them on top of the stack on Aidan's bed, and ran back. 'Can I get you two something to drink?' I asked. They were squeezed between the wall and the track gaggle who were standing in the foyer shouting out their personal best times for the 5,000 meters.

'I'll have a glass of wine,' Jemma managed to shout over the din, 'and he'll have a Coke.'

'Okay,' I said, wondering who I would have them talk to. It was too bad my mother couldn't come, now that I thought about it, because I could prop her in front of just about anybody and away she'd go on a charming little prattle, like the Energizer Bunny. I could just hear her chattering away to Sir, 'And *where* is it that you get these custom-made leather waistcoats? They look for all the world like the Gaultier vests I saw at Neiman's!'

On the way to the drinks table, I hissed to Aidan, 'Go talk to them,' who nodded and made his way through the crowd. I poured Jemma some white wine in a cup, looked around for the liter bottle of Coke, found it empty, and started to make my way back to the kitchen.

On the way, I ran into Harriet, who was telling Marco the cheese grater story. 'Yeah, my father gave my mother an electric can opener for her birthday one year,' Marco was saying. 'She filed for divorce soon after that.'

'Yes, but now Harriet's engaged!' I shouted.

'Really?' Marco said. 'Wow. That's great, I guess.'

Harriet turned to me. 'Marco was asking me about Christine, that friend of mine that I'd set him up with a long time ago,' she said.

'Oh, yeah, how is she anyway?' I asked. 'Marco! How are you! Hang on a second, I've got to go—'

'Go ahead,' he said, and kissed me perfunctorily on the cheek, and whispered, 'I have a new Ms Trouble for you to meet. But she's not a Ms Trouble, this time—'

'Hold that thought,' I said. 'I just have to deliver this—'

But when I returned to Jemma and Sir they had moved toward the living room, and Sir had even managed to find an empty chair which he dropped into. 'Here you go,' I said brightly, handing a cup to Jemma, who was now sitting on the floor, wedged between Sir's feet and the TV/VCR stand. 'And I'm just on the way to get – oh.' Sir was holding a plastic cup of Coke and looked up at me cheerfully.

'I got it,' Jemma said hastily. 'We just happened to be standing by an available bottle.'

'Well, good,' I said. I stood there for a moment. 'So – how are you doing?'

'Wonderful,' said Jemma. 'We went Christmas shopping today, downtown. They have all the decorations up, and it was so pretty on Union Square. I bought this.' She pulled on a low-cut black mohair sweater that emphasized her bosom.

'That's really pretty,' I told her. 'Is it scratchy?'

'Oh, no, it's lovely,' she said. 'It only looks scratchy, but it's made of cotton and angora, not —' Harriet was drifting toward us, and I grabbed her arm.

'Harriet!' I said. 'This is – *Jemma*.' I hadn't meant to put any special emphasis on it, but all three of them glanced at me simultaneously. Sir chuckled and I felt foolish for the second time that evening. 'And this is Harriet. She just got engaged!' I shouted.

'Hello!' Harriet said, and glanced at me with a *what-is-up-with-you-and-this-shouting?* look. But I could tell she was secretly pleased. I moved away to pick up some empty glasses, wondering what the consummate Texas hostess would come up with in conversation with this pair. I should have invited Marie, I thought, but then again, she said she had dinner with the snowboarder and his family every Sunday night.

I'd fully intended to go back and check on them, but an hour later, I was still caught in the throng around the food table, refilling and re-plating, trying to keep things in control as I talked to those who came in my direction. 'Everything going well?' I asked Lizzie under my breath, when Evan had gone off to find another beer.

'Oh, yes,' she said. I stood back with my arms folded, amused. Every man in the room, including Aidan, had given Lizzie the once-over and a few brave souls were now cautiously circling her, making a big show of getting more tortilla chips which she was standing in front of.

She leaned toward me, 'He's such a great guy, Evan,' she said whispering, 'even though we *still* haven't had sex, and we've been going out for two months —'

Aidan suddenly appeared at my elbow and said to me, 'Everything going okay?'

'Aidan, this is Lizzie,' I said automatically. They shook hands and Evan magically appeared again, handing Lizzie a beer which she glugged down with enthusiasm.

'I know what that was,' I told Aidan a minute later, as we shouted goodbyes to some of the track gaggle who were making their way out the door. The room was hot and I felt dizzy.

'What was what?' he asked innocently.

'You thought she was alone,' I said. 'Were you really going to hit on one of my friends – right in front of me?'

'Her?' Aidan glanced at Lizzie, and shaking his head, laughed and then suddenly got annoyed. 'Good God, Courtney.' He untied his apron and threw it on the floor. 'What do you want from me? I came over to tell you that Jemma and Sir and Harriet are all deep in conversation. I thought you might think that's funny.' He turned on his heel and began talking to one of the marrieds, ignoring me.

I stood there and looked at his back. '*Men are like buses . . . if you miss one there's always another rounding the corner . . .*' It would be nice if this were true, but even nicer if it made any difference at all when one was in the throes of feeling rejected. I caught Harriet's eye and she smiled at me sympathetically, before she made her way across the room, bringing me another plastic cup of wine.

The three of us were sitting on the futon couch. It was 12.30 at night, fairly early for a party to break up but it was Sunday night, after all, and as Harriet pointed out, 'You Californians are just as healthy as you've been made fun of to be.' New Yorkers, she said, not only would have eaten all the chips, they would certainly have downed all the wine and would still be hanging around, hoping some late-night arrivals would straggle in, armed with more alcohol and snacks.

Harriet was sitting between Aidan and me. We looked around the room, assessing all the empty bottles and cups. I started to get up but Aidan, one hand over his eyes and the other holding a bottle of Coors, said, 'Leave it. I'll deal with it tomorrow.'

'Okay,' I said, and plopped back down. 'Why are you drinking that terrible beer?'

'It's the only beer left.'

'So drink wine.' Harriet and I triumphantly held up our cups, still full of jug burgundy. I asked her, 'Did you have a good time?'

'Oh, yes!' she said. For someone who had been drinking steadily for six hours, she looked remarkably lucid. Her brown eyes were still clear and perky, and she'd even lost that redness that had tinged the tip of her nose and ears earlier in the evening. Aidan had some Texan track friends and he'd always said they could drink him under the table, no matter what the circumstances.

'Your friend Marco is very nice,' she said, volleying the opening shot in the party post-mortem. 'I see what you mean about him being a flake, but he's pretty smart. He's really into that girlfriend of his. Did you talk to her at all?'

'Uh uh,' I said. 'My extent of interaction was bringing her a Diet Coke. She had nice teeth though, I noticed.'

'And nice, shaped eyebrows,' Harriet said. 'I wonder if she gets them waxed.'

'Probably,' I said. 'Then tweezes them like a maniac. Did you notice her eyebrows, Aidan?'

'Nope,' he mumbled, from under his hand.

'Men *say* they don't notice these things,' I half-whispered to Harriet, 'but then watch when we let it lapse. Then out comes all the squeamishness about mustaches, and gorilla legs and dishwater hair.' I patted Aidan's hand sympathetically and he ignored me, saying 'Huh,' under his breath. I wondered if Little Missy waxed or shaved her legs.

'What did you and Jemma and her boyfriend talk about?' I asked Harriet. Earlier in the evening I'd told Harriet about the Power Exchange and Jemma's proclivity, but I hadn't gone into too much detail. During the party, I'd been surprised that the master/servant relationship was in effect at all times, which I'd been reminded of when Jemma had fetched Sir's cup of Coke.

'Well, I liked her very much,' Harriet said. 'She's very funny and likeable, a much stronger personality than I would have thought. She talked the whole time, almost. And around me, that's quite a feat.'

'Wow,' I said. 'What did you think of um, her boyfriend? Aidan? Did you talk to him?'

'Not really,' Aidan said sleepily. 'Did you notice that Jemma sat at his feet the whole party?'

'Yeah, that was interesting,' Harriet said. 'At first I thought it was normal, since there weren't any other chairs, but then I realized it was a thing that they did, all night long.'

Aidan sat up. 'And then did you see them in line at the food table?'

'Oh, yes,' Harriet said.

'What?' I asked.

'Well, he was standing off to the side, watching everyone get in line,' Aidan said, and drank some more beer. 'I said to him, "Can I get you a plate?" He said, "No thanks, she's doing it for me," pointing to Jemma. And there Jemma was filling up a plate for him. And seeming perfectly happy to do it.'

'She *is* happy to do it,' I said. 'That's their arrangement.'

'Ugh,' Aidan said. 'I do not get that.'

'What did you guys talk about?' I asked Harriet.

Harriet considered, looking into her cup. 'Let's see . . . we talked about shopping,' she said. 'She's really opinionated. She was saying how much she loves living in the United States because of all the customer service here – and how she goes into stores when she's back in England and says 'Hi!' to the clerks, and they just stare at her like she's insane. She said her mother bought a jacket from the Gap when she was here last time that had a button falling off and Jemma made her take it back. Her mother couldn't believe you could return clothes like that.'

I nodded. 'That sounds like the Jemma I know.' Harriet was proffering a wine bottle again and I accepted another refill. 'What did you think of him?' I asked her.

Harriet drank some more and said, 'To tell you the truth, I was a little disappointed. I wanted to see what it was that had Jemma under his spell. I guess I thought he would be more . . . sinister-looking. Or that he would be swaggering, or powerful, or . . . but really, he just seemed like a normal guy with a belly and maybe he should have washed his hair.'

'That's what I thought,' said Aidan. 'Although he was perfectly pleasant.'

'He *was* perfectly pleasant,' Harriet assented. 'And aloof. He just seemed like – well, the King. The King doesn't say very much. It wasn't that he was above it all, it's just that the King doesn't engage with the court jesters or the staff. He sits back and watches them patter around him.'

'The King,' I repeated. 'Huh. Jemma will like that.'

Aidan said lazily, 'It was a good party. All the salmon and soda bread got eaten. And the oysters. Next time I want to do nachos. People love nachos at a party.'

'Nachos are way too messy for a big party,' I said.

'If it's my party, I can serve whatever I want, messy or not.'

'Well, fine,' I said. 'Serve nachos, then.'

'When you have a party at your house, you can serve what *you* like.'

I could see this new arrangement of ours – the arrangement of normality – was going to be even more difficult than I'd thought. Aidan seemed to be adjusting much easier than I; in fact, if anyone was aloof and perfectly pleasant that night, it was him. I slumped down into the sofa, rearranging my head, thinking at some point in the future I would laugh about it, feeling strong in my 'alone-ness.' But for now I just felt defensive and jealous. 'Maybe you could borrow Harriet's cheese grater,' I said, moving the topic away from this shifty ground. Harriet giggled, and I continued, 'Also, most importantly everyone talked to one another. I always worry about that.'

'That's so like you to worry about stuff like that,' Aidan said, sounding irritated. Once upon a time he would have thought it was charming. He got up and I heard him rustling around in his refrigerator. A minute later, he reappeared with three coffee cups, brandishing a bottle of champagne.

'Champagne!' Harriet exclaimed. He uncorked it and it fizzed all over the carpet and down his trousers.

'That's really sweet, Aidan,' I said, and a wave of friendliness washed over me. Between my reaction to Harriet's engagement and Aidan's and my platonic arrangement, it would be a miracle if I wasn't hospitalized for acute schizophrenia. I turned to Harriet as I handed him some cocktail napkins that were lying on the sofa. 'What will you do if you have people at your wedding who have no one to talk to?'

'Everyone will be fine,' Harriet said. 'You and my mother – the two of you are such worriers. I'm just worried about my hair.'

'Maybe I'll fly Marie out for your wedding present. I'm a little concerned about what I'm going to do about my hair, too.' I touched it – it was rock hard, like the head of a statue. Aidan said, dabbing at his pants with the paper napkins, 'You should be, because what you're doing to it right now isn't going to work.'

Sixteen-personality Sybil reared her head up again. 'Thank you, Aidan,' I said, thinking with evil pleasure about the next time he or his little filly used the 'Hair Fixative' to combat frizziness before going out on the town.

'Maybe *you'll* be getting married soon,' Harriet said. 'You just never know.'

'*Harriet*,' I said, and Aidan and I looked at each other, rolling our eyes. But the moment of tension passed, and Aidan and Harriet at least laughed.

'Oh, I think I can pretty much guarantee we won't be having

this conversation about me anytime soon,' I said.

'So can I,' said Aidan.

'Eat me,' I said, smiling.

'You're young,' Harriet said perkily. 'You've got a lot of time.'

'That's true,' I said, thinking the exact opposite.

As we sipped our champagne – after Aidan had rattled off a traditional wedding toast in Irish and we clinked our coffee cups, resulting in Harriet chipping the edge of hers so that she and I had to drop to our knees to search for the little white ceramic chip in the shag carpet – I thought, *Who would I go to the wedding with?* Maybe I *would* bring Marie. Or Jayne, who in an e-mail I'd received just that evening before the party, had said she wanted to come to New York next year. Or Jemma? It was a thought anyway.

'Maybe you'll want to come,' I said to Aidan. I'd found the coffee cup chip and dropped it into his hand. He stared at it with a baffled expression and tossed it over his shoulder – a knee-jerk response, probably some Celtic act of superstition. I scrambled back up to my feet. But I'll probably come on my own, I thought . . . and right now, that was exactly how it should be.

I thought again about Jayne's e-mail. *Unsurprisingly, Nigel and Kath broke up again,* she'd written. *Anna has returned to America, and she apparently hasn't given him a second thought – she's got a new boyfriend over there. And Kath – well she's alone for now but it will only be a matter of time before she finds someone to fit her ideal of perfect husband. Meanwhile, we're all supposed to head off to Wales together, twenty of us, in a trip that was planned months ago. Despite the fact that they're not speaking, neither Kath nor Nigel will back down – both insist on coming, saying the other should graciously not go, all of which I'm sure is going to put the rest of us in a lovely position . . .*

I thought about Jayne's last line: *Why can't Kath or Nigel find strength in solitude?*

❊   ❊   ❊

We were approaching the first hill of the Pacific Heights run, shuffling along Jackson Street, and the sun was cresting on the far edge below the blanket of grayness. I pulled my baseball cap down tighter, and Harriet and I started to slow as we saw the hill looming across Van Ness Avenue. 'What else did Jayne write?' Harriet prodded, 'Please try to keep talking. It'll keep my mind off of this.'

It was two days later, and we were embarking on the inaugural walk/run that Harriet said she needed if she were to fit into any kind of wedding dress at all by next year. She'd wanted me to take her on the run I used to do regularly after Sean and I broke up, where I would count the sports utility vehicles. It was time to exorcize this route, Harriet said. Aidan had been on the phone that morning with all sorts of running tips. 'Now girls,' he'd said, 'remember to *attack* the hills. Don't slow down! Otherwise you'll *die*. And use your arms!'

We crossed against the light at Van Ness, and started up. 'So then she confronted Kath at Jayne's party, saying she needed more girlfriends,' I puffed, hearing Aidan's voice in my head: *Get your knees up! For God's sake, why do women shuffle when they run?* Harriet and I slowed even more, and I gasped, 'Okay, isn't this a long enough run for you?'

'I don't think so,' Harriet said, breathing heavily as we inched our way up. 'It flattens out at the top, doesn't it? Look, there's a Sean-mobile.' She pointed as a black Jeep Cherokee roared past us.

'Fifteen points,' I said, and I realized that something was missing. For the first time, I suddenly felt . . . *nothing* about Sean. Now how did that happen? I was about to tell Harriet, but she was pulling on the waist of her sweatpants and looking distressed. 'Harriet, why did you get so tongue-tied with those bridal salespeople yesterday? All she asked you was your dress size, and you looked at her as if she'd launched into Mandarin Chinese.'

Harriet huffed, 'I don't know – all these wedding trappings – seems so ridiculous. I got overwhelmed, I guess.' At one point the saleswoman tried to put a tiara on her head, and Harriet shrank away from her. 'Harriet!' I'd whispered. 'What's the matter with you? We're all trying to help you. Tell the woman what you want – it's her job.'

'How about . . . a wedding band?' I said, between heavy inhales and exhales. 'You two going to do that?'

'Not important,' she gasped. 'Almost at the top,' she said. 'Just seems like those wedding stores are trying to whip my emotions up – I'd read about this, you know, but I had no idea—'

'Yeah but . . .' I answered. Funny – I would have thought Harriet would be beaming throughout this wedding dress hunt, chatting away to the salespeople about veils and flowers and how many tiers the cake should be – but it turned out that I was more interested in discussing these details with the eager staff than she had been. In the first store, she was stunned when she glanced at the price tag on one of the 100% polyester ball gowns, and after that, yielded all control to me, letting me be her mouthpiece as well as her fashion consultant. Of course, for me it was not unlike when I would dress up my Barbie for her date with Ken.

'Uh huh . . . it just seemed so silly – all this. So much money – and we're paying for it ourselves—' We took our little baby steps across the top, at Franklin, and a rush of cold evening air almost blew us back. 'Whew!' she breathed. 'So Anna never went out for coffee with Kath?'

'I don't think so,' I said. 'Jayne said that Nigel was just a plaything for Anna. That he seemed – desperate to her. She went back to New York without even so much as a goodbye to him.' A man in bright blue shorts and singlet zoomed by us, breathing, 'Hi.'

'Hi,' we said weakly, in unison.

'See,' Harriet prodded. 'Lots of buses coming around the

corner. Weddings are good places to meet people too.'

'Your wedding is a long way away.'

'Not so long. Did Kath ever find out about Anna?'

'Never,' I said, and Harriet looked disappointed. 'So after she left for New York, Nigel and Kath moved in together. Jayne said he didn't want to, but Kath told him if they didn't have a future then where was it going?' I stopped talking so I could breathe a bit more.

'Then what,' Harriet prodded.

'So she gave him an ultimatum and he succumbed – grumbling all the way.' I heard Aidan intone, *Relax – open your stride!*

'Never issue an ultimatum unless you're prepared to lose,' Harriet said brightly. 'Ouch. I think I'm starting to get a blister. Okay, then what?'

'She moved in on the Tuesday,' I puffed, 'and she was gone by the following Tuesday. Nigel told Jayne soon after she'd moved in that it was the worst mistake he'd made of his life, letting her move in. And that she moved all her little Scottish girlie things in and pictures of all of her cousins and didn't even consult him . . .' We shuffled by the bus stop where I stood waiting for the 3 Jackson bus after school, every Monday through Friday afternoon, from age eight to thirteen. It never occurred to me then to simply walk the mile home. 'And he said to Jayne, "I think the Pope has got a lot to answer for." And . . . he came home later and later that week, until finally he came home at two in the morning, offering no explanation, and Kath punched him when he got into bed. She sobbed and cried and moved out the next day.'

'God,' Harriet said. Now that we were on the flat blocks, we were starting to feel better. 'Was she serious? She played this all wrong. What then?'

'She said to him, as she was leaving, "you can stop me if you want." And he lay there on the sofa, crying his eyes out, but did nothing. And so she moved back in with her girlfriends, all the while thinking he'd come to his senses and want her back. See, it was just like a soap opera for her.' I stopped to readjust the tongue of my battered shoes. 'But you know, as I'm telling it, I feel kind of bad for all of them. I think Nigel and Kath might of actually been really in love with each other. But the timing was all wrong.'

'Timing is everything,' Harriet said. 'Maybe they'll get back together.'

'Nope,' I said. 'As far as I know, they're still broken up. Meanwhile, Kath's father says to her —' We were approaching the corner market where I used to buy all my afternoon candy, and I considered ducking in now, but it had turned into a flower and juice bar, so I continued. 'Where was I?'

'Kath's father,' Harriet said.

'Oh, get this: he said to her when she told him that she was moving in, "Don't do it Kath – Marriage is the exchange you get for giving men sex and if you move in with him he'll get it for free and you'll never have any bargaining power to get him to go up the altar." ' I smiled brightly at Harriet through my sweat. 'Sound familiar?'

'Absolutely not,' Harriet said, laughing. 'What did her mother say?'

'She said, "I won't say I told you so." ' I slowed a little as another black sports utility vehicle drove by in the opposite direction, and Harriet said, 'Okay?'

'Yup,' I said. 'I thought you said this would be a walk/run. I'm still waiting for this walk part.'

'Coming,' she said. 'Soon as we pass your Mom's house. It's coming up, isn't it? All this is starting to look familiar.'

'Oh, another twenty minutes or so,' I said. Now we were on the flat section going past the green expanse of Alta Plaza Park. Fingers of fog drifted through the pine trees, and the moan of fog horns to the north was suddenly audible. 'What do you think of that story?' I asked her.

'I think . . .' Harriet unzipped her windbreaker and

struggled to tie it around her waist, '. . . they sound like they're selfish and uncommunicative. And probably well-matched. And she shouldn't have moved in with him, and she certainly shouldn't have put all her pictures and tchochkes around the house. I still don't even keep a toothbrush at Jerry's house. Rule Number 22.'

'Gosh,' I said, impressed. We started on a descent. 'Harriet, will you please move to San Francisco? Running with you would be a breeze if you could keep coming up with lines like those.' We passed the boys' school and headed toward the big brown shingled house on the corner where my best friend from eighth grade lived.

'I know,' Harriet giggled. 'Isn't it funny?'

I put my baseball cap on backwards in honor of my mother as we cruised by her house. I wondered if Harriet was just reciting these rules for my benefit, and she'd really stopped believing them a long time ago. 'I stopped having my recurring dream,' she said suddenly. 'I was having it every night – something about opening a door in my apartment and realizing I had a whole other room to use that I'd forgotten about.'

'I've had that dream too.' I stopped and looked at her. 'What does that mean?'

'I have no idea,' Harriet said, and we were silent. Then we began walking again.

We turned and crossed Arguello, where I pointed out the apartment building where my family lived when I was born. Then, still breathing heavily, we walked up through the twilight and the fog on Washington – past Cherry, Maple, Spruce, Locust and Laurel Streets – looping back around past my mother's house again, where I looked up at my old bedroom window, on toward the hills, and to home.

EPILOGUE

It's two months before Harriet's wedding.

When I get home, I put the key in the lock and turn. I hear the cat leap down from the kitchen table and approach the door. I flip on the hall light, pat her head, and drop my keys and the mail on the bookshelf next to the door. Then I head into the living room where I see the Caller ID blinking – four calls, all 'Anonymous' or 'Unavailable.' Amazingly, there are four messages, one from Aidan, and one from my mother, and from Harriet, who begins by saying, 'Listen, about this wedding tiara thing, do you think this is just a fad or is it a necessity, like all these bridal people are telling me?'

And a message from the son of a friend of my mother's, who is in town on business, whom I've never met. 'Hi Courtney,' he says, hesitating. 'You don't know me, but your mother gave me your phone number, and I was wondering if I could talk to you about writing . . .' I knew this was coming – it had been the number two topic of last week's telephone volley with my mother. 'And he's, he's a writer as well!' she said, after reciting a laundry list of suitable partner plusses. I'd groaned at that and said, 'Mom. *Everyone* is a writer!' but finally crumbled, giving her the clearance to pass my number along. (The number one topic was Zippy, who had been found cold and

309

stiff on the floor of his cage by one of the contractors, which my mother and I both took as a sign, although of what I'm not certain.) I listen to my messages as I'm walking around the apartment, turning on lights and peering into the refrigerator.

I scribble this guy's number down and stare at it. Then I look in the refrigerator again. There's some canned tuna, half a head of romaine lettuce, half a red onion and a little Sauvignon Blanc. Also lots of dried pasta, cans of black beans, half a pound of rice and a box of instant mashed potatoes that I'd been meaning to throw out. I take my lettuce dryer off the shelf and meticulously wash all the lettuce, and put some water on to boil for the pasta. I glance again at the newspaper that I'd left next to my cereal bowl that morning, feed the cat who's driving me to distraction with her continuous meow-meow-meow, wash the cereal bowl and put it on the dish rack. Then I turn on the TV that's on top of my refrigerator to watch *Entertainment Tonight* or the news on PBS, depending on my mood, as I chop and stir and poke and then eat.

I call Aidan somewhere during all this, get his machine and leave a message. I call my mother and get her machine, thinking sadly about Zippy who is no longer doing his anxiety dance, nor listening to all the dozens of incoming messages that my mother receives everyday. Harriet too is not home – probably being talked into a must-have garter belt that no bride should be without. I replace the phone and now surf through the channels, seeing if there is anything worth watching that won't be too guilt-inducing or moronic. I decide I can stomach the rerun of *Mad About You*, if it isn't one of the particularly gooey episodes, and I clear a place for my salad among the newspapers, mail, magazines, and fruit bowl that's covering my kitchen table. I throw a black banana away.

This is my life, I sometimes think as I eat my pasta salad – I am here, alone, in my life that I created, with my table and my TV and my cat and my newspaper and my telephone and my computer and my bike. My double bed with my favorite white sheets and comforter that I bought on sale at Esprit before heading off to graduate school five years ago is waiting for me to slide into, which I look forward to doing in about six hours' time. I wonder if this is how men feel when they enter their apartments, put down their mail, say hello to their dog and flip on the TV. I stare again at the phone number that I'd written on the edge of 'The Living Arts' section of the *Times*.

I think about if there were someone else here, someone who lived in this apartment with me, who was not a cat or a bird but my partner – and how that would feel. Would he become like the computer and the bike and cat – another fixture of the life that I created? Or would it be a continual interaction, a dialogue, internal and external that picks up where it had left off the last time we'd seen each other? Would we talk about what we did that day, or would we fall silent, concentrating on the tasks of the evening homecoming – would we flip on the TV or listen to messages together, would one of us be in a good mood and the other a bad, would we decide what to eat together or would we go out?

And mostly, I wonder if it would be *better* than what I have right now, or would it just be . . . *different*? How did my mom adjust to her solo lifestyle after being indoctrinated for so many decades that the partner route was the way to go? It must have been a relief, and frightening, and elating and despairing . . . probably all of those things. A vision of my grandmother pops into high relief, living on her own in the Midwest, a few hundred miles away from her favorite brother and his wife and their nine children – I wonder if she felt her entire life was a sociological failure because she was divorced from her first husband, and abandoned by her second. And she has the pressures of Catholicism to contend with, too.

Maybe this is my lot in life. When I sometimes cry to my mother – as I am wont to do at least once a year – that I feel lonely and not just alone, she is surprisingly harsh. 'We all feel alone,' she says coldly. 'We enter life by ourselves and we exit by ourselves, and I think most people feel that way.' Her words are not a comfort, needless to say. I point out that I know many people who don't feel that existential or realistic loneliness: Marie, Harriet, Aidan. (Jemma probably does, admittedly.) Finding partners and maintaining the relationship is one of their main preoccupations. I wonder where I went off the trail, or is it something that has been passed down to me from this legacy of partner-less women?

Somehow I came to a decision that to feel alone and not lonely was the strongest place a woman could be. There are days that I am weak and weepy; nights that I wish not to face by myself; whole months in which I could honestly be described as a lonely, pathetic, Internet-using loser – and the fact that these times are a result of choices that I have made only makes them tolerably better.

The phone rings. It's Harriet. After a ten-minute discussion on whether anyone will actually notice the corn pad making its impression through her specially dyed wedding shoes, I tell her about my telephone message from the 'writer.'

'Why haven't you called him back yet?' she squawks. 'Call him back right now. Then call me back.' She starts to hang up.

'Wait! Right now? He just called an hour ago. Shouldn't I wait?'

'Good God no. You can do the Rules later if you need to. Call him back.'

'Oh, Harriet, I don't know. I guess I just think – Why?'

'Why?' she shouts. 'Because what else have we been talking about the entire time we've known each other?'

'Now what kind of reason is that?' I demand.

'As good a reason as any,' she points out.